T0331654

Large–Scale Fuzzy Interconnected Control Systems Design and Analysis

Zhixiong Zhong
Xiamen University of Technology, China

Chih–Min Lin
Yuan Ze University, Taiwan

A volume in the Advances in Systems Analysis, Software Engineering, and High Performance Computing (ASASEHPC) Book Series

www.igi-global.com

Published in the United States of America by
   IGI Global
   Information Science Reference (an imprint of IGI Global)
   701 E. Chocolate Avenue
   Hershey PA, USA 17033
   Tel: 717-533-8845
   Fax: 717-533-8661
   E-mail: cust@igi-global.com
   Web site: http://www.igi-global.com

Library of Congress Cataloging-in-Publication Data

Names: Zhong, Zhixiong, 1979- author. | Lin, Chih-Min, 1959- author.
Title: Large-scale fuzzy interconnected control systems design and analysis /
   by Zhixiong Zhong and Chih-Min Lin.
Description: Hershey, PA : Information Science Reference, [2017] | Includes
   bibliographical references.
Identifiers: LCCN 2017000833| ISBN 9781522523857 (hardcover) | ISBN
   9781522523864 (ebook)
Subjects: LCSH: Automatic control. | Fuzzy systems. | Fuzzy automata. | Large
   scale systems.
Classification: LCC TJ213 .Z525 2017 | DDC 629.8--dc23 LC record available at https://lccn.loc.
gov/2017000833

This book is published in the IGI Global book series Advances in Systems Analysis, Software Engineering, and High Performance Computing (ASASEHPC) (ISSN: 2327-3453; eISSN: 2327-3461)

British Cataloguing in Publication Data
A Cataloguing in Publication record for this book is available from the British Library.

For electronic access to this publication, please contact: eresources@igi-global.com.

Advances in Systems Analysis, Software Engineering, and High Performance Computing (ASASEHPC) Book Series

ISSN:2327-3453
EISSN:2327-3461

Editor-in-Chief: Vijayan Sugumaran, Oakland University, USA

MISSION

The theory and practice of computing applications and distributed systems has emerged as one of the key areas of research driving innovations in business, engineering, and science. The fields of software engineering, systems analysis, and high performance computing offer a wide range of applications and solutions in solving computational problems for any modern organization.

The **Advances in Systems Analysis, Software Engineering, and High Performance Computing (ASASEHPC) Book Series** brings together research in the areas of distributed computing, systems and software engineering, high performance computing, and service science. This collection of publications is useful for academics, researchers, and practitioners seeking the latest practices and knowledge in this field.

COVERAGE

- Distributed Cloud Computing
- Virtual Data Systems
- Computer System Analysis
- Network Management
- Parallel Architectures
- Human-Computer Interaction
- Storage Systems
- Computer graphics
- Software Engineering
- Performance Modelling

IGI Global is currently accepting manuscripts for publication within this series. To submit a proposal for a volume in this series, please contact our Acquisition Editors at Acquisitions@igi-global.com or visit: http://www.igi-global.com/publish/.

Titles in this Series

www.igi-global.com

701 East Chocolate Avenue, Hershey, PA 17033, USA
Tel: 717-533-8845 x100 • Fax: 717-533-8661
E-Mail: cust@igi-global.com • www.igi-global.com

Table of Contents

Chapter 8

Foreword

Present-day the demand for rapid and sustained development has pushed control scholars and engineers to focus on increasingly higher dimensional and more complex interconnected systems. Such kind of systems exists widely in the real world, including power networks, transportation systems, ecological systems, and river pollution systems, and is referred to as large-scale interconnected systems, which rely on the cooperation of several subsystems. A distinguish property of such kind of systems is that a perturbation of one subsystem can affect the other subsystems as well as the overall stability and performance. Moreover, its tasks cannot be solved simply by using faster computers with larger memories due to excessive information processing and heavy computational burdens. They necessitate new ideas for decomposing and dividing the problems of stability analysis and controller design from the large-scale system to each local subsystem.

In practice, it is generally difficult to obtain complete model available for large-scale nonlinear interconnected systems, but each local model describes only a part of the whole system. With the development of modern high-speed computers, microelectronics, and communication networks, increasing research efforts have been devoted to networked control systems. Unfortunately, the network-induced imperfections, such as quantization errors, packet dropouts, and time delays, can degrade significantly the performance of the closed-loop control system and may even lead to instability. It is noted that the design of a networked control systems often requires tradeoffs among the network-induced imperfections. More specifically, these features of sending larger control-packets and requiring time stamping of messages will reduce quantization errors and packet dropouts but typically result in transmitting larger or more packets and inducing larger transmission delays. In that case, an important issue arises in the implementation of networked control systems as to how to identify methods such that the limited network bandwidth can be more effectively utilized.

This book presents the systematic methods showing how T-S fuzzy control theory is used to solve analytical and design tasks for large-scale nonlinear interconnected systems. Emphasis is placed on the derivation of methods which include the decentralized and distributed control frameworks. It devotes to develop not only stability analysis, but also sampled-data control, event-triggered control, sliding mode control, practical applications, and future research, and various approaches, which have led to the large number of available stability analysis and controller design results, are presented together with their interrelationships and distinctions. The proposed methodologies provide effective techniques to overcome specific difficulties in the considered systems, such as high dimensionality, interconnections, and coupling nonlinearities. The book is primarily intended for students, researchers and engineers. It can also serve as complementary reading for fuzzy control system theory at the post-graduate level.

Two different kinds of examples are used. Simple numerical examples give an intuitive understanding of the methodology proposed in Chapters 2-6, illustrate the significance of the results or algorithms, and make trends obvious. Practical application in Chapter 7 studies how real-world control problems for large-scale nonlinear interconnected systems are solved by means of the proposed methods. They show that some of the concepts presented here can be applied to microgrid and multi-motors driven from practical perspective. The challenges in control problems of large-scale nonlinear interconnected systems are both difficult and interesting. People are working on them with enthusiasm, tenacity, and dedication to develop new methods of analysis and provide new solutions to this scheme. In this new age of rapid development, real-world systems become more and more complex, thus it is necessary to provide simple and effective solutions. This book makes a good step in that direction.

Preface

With the development of modern industries, more and more attention has been paid to develop control theories for large-scale interconnected systems, and various approaches have been reported for the control of large-scale interconnected systems: the centralized approach, the decentralized approach, and the distributed approach. In practice, uncertainties, incomplete plant information, and nonlinear dynamics are frequently encountered, inevitably turn large-scale interconnected systems to large-scale interconnected complex systems. The biggest challenge, nowadays, is the lack of formal mathematical tools for stability analysis and controller design of large-scale nonlinear interconnected systems. This book will give a foundational and comprehensive treatment of large scale nonlinear interconnected systems using T-S fuzzy model approach. The central subject of this book is a systematic framework for the stability analysis and controller design of large-scale fuzzy interconnected control systems. Building on the so-called T-S fuzzy model, a number of important issues in fuzzy interconnected control systems are addressed. These include stability analysis, stabilization design procedures, incorporation of sampled-data, event-triggered control, sliding mode control, and numerical implementations.

The book is primarily intended for researchers and engineers in the system and control communities. It can also serve as complementary reading for large-scale system theories at the post-graduate level. Throughout this book and seeking computational convenience, all the developed results are cast in the form of LMIs, which can be easily solved using the solver of LMI Toolbox in Matlab. The book is divided into eight chapters.

Chapter 1 provides an overview of the concepts and techniques of large-scale nonlinear interconnected systems, and introduces model description for large-scale T-S fuzzy interconnected systems and motivation of the study.

Chapter 2 derives some results on stability analysis of large-scale fuzzy interconnected systems. In order to avoid the well-known "rule-explosion" problem, by using some bounding techniques, the fuzzy rules in interconnections to other subsystems are eliminated. A comparison of the general and reduced LMI-based conditions is given by the simulation.

Chapter 3 deals with the stabilization problem for large scale fuzzy interconnected systems. Firstly, the general and reduced LMI-based results on state-feedback controller design are presented respectively for both the continuous-time and discrete-time cases in the decentralized control structure. Then, based on transformation matrix and descriptor system approaches, the LMI-based results on decentralized SOF controller design are also derived. Furthermore, the obtained results on decentralized control are developed for distributed control scheme.

Chapter 4 focuses on the sampled-data control for large-scale T-S fuzzy interconnected systems. First, by using input delay approach, the closed-loop sampled-data fuzzy control system is formulated into a continuous-time system with time-varying delay. Then, based on the new model, we use two approaches to design the decentralized fuzzy sampled-data controller: Wirtinger's inequality and scaled small gain (SSG) theorem. We further introduce a novel Lyapunov-Krasovskii functional (LKF), where not all of the Lyapunov matrices are required to be positive definite. The co-design problem consisting of the controller gains and sampled period can be solved in terms of a set of LMIs. Also, the obtained results on decentralized control are developed for distributed control scheme.

Chapter 5 studies the event-triggered control problem for large-scale networked T-S fuzzy systems with transmission delays and nonlinear interconnections, where they exchange their information through a digital channel. Our considered scheme is decentralized event-triggered control in the sense that each subsystem is able to make broadcast decisions by using its locally sampled data when a prescribed event is triggered. We propose two different approaches to solve the co-design problem consisting of the controller gains, sampled period, network delay, and event-triggered parameter in terms of a set of LMIs. Also, we consider a self-triggered control scheme in which the next triggered time is precomputed.

Chapter 6 studies the decentralized adaptive control strategies of large-scale fuzzy interconnected systems. It addresses both cases of discrete-time and continuous-time systems.

Chapter 7 considers the practical application to microgrids and multi-motors driven.

Chapter 8 remarks conclusions and recommendations for further research.

The material contained in this book not only organized to focus on the new developments in the analysis and control methods for large-scale nonlinear interconnected systems, but it also integrates the impact of the network like delay-factor, sampled-data, and communication constraints. After an introductory chapter is presented, it is intended to divide the book into several independent chapters that equipped with introduction, problem formulation, main results, and illustrative examples. Each chapter of the book will be supplemented by an extended bibliography, and some appropriate appendices are summarized in the end of this book.

The main features of the book are summarized as below:

1. It provides a foundational and comprehensive treatment of large-scale nonlinear interconnected systems using T-S fuzzy model approach;
2. It establishes a theoretical framework of decentralized control and distributed control schemes with their proof;
3. It gives some typical applications.

Zhixiong Zhong
Xiamen University of Technology, China

Chih-Min Lin
Yuan Ze University, Taiwan
5 January 2017

Acknowledgment

I thank Courtney Tychinski, Assistant Managing Editor in IGI Global, and Kelsey Weitzel-Leishman, Editorial Assistant in CyberTech Publishing, and IGI Global Production Team for their assistance. Many researchers have made significant contribution to large-scale system theory. Owing to the structural arrangement and length limitation of the book, many of their published results are not included or even not cited. I would extend my apologies to these researchers.

I would also like to thank my parents, and my wife Yanyu Hong, and my sons Hongli Zhong and Ceyi Zhong for their continuous support in every aspect. I am grateful to my supervisors Prof. Huijun Gao, Prof. Lixian Zhang, and Prof. Jianbin Qiu from Harbin Institute of Technology; Prof. Li-An Chen and Min Xu from Xiamen University of Technology; Prof. Rong-Jong Wai for National Taiwan University of Science and Technology; and Prof. Hai-Bo Pan from Fujian Key Lab of Medical and Pharmaceutical Technology for their help, suggestions, and support. The reviewers of the book have given some real valuable and helpful comments and suggestions, which are indeed very much appreciated.

The author would like to gratefully acknowledge the financial support kindly provided by the many sponsors, including High-Voltage Key Laboratory of Fujian Province, Xiamen University of Technology, and the Natural Science Foundation of Fujian Province (2017J01781, 2016J01222), and also the Advanced Research Project of XMUT (YKJ16008R).

At the last, I would indeed appreciate if readers could possibly provide any comments, questions, criticisms, or corrections about this book via email: zhixiongzhong@xmut.edu.cn or zhixiongzhong2012@126.com. Your help will certainly make any future editions of the book much better.

Zhixiong Zhong
Xiamen University of Technology, China

Chapter 1
Introduction

ABSTRACT

The book presents a foundational and comprehensive treatment of the analysis and design tasks for large-scale nonlinear interconnected systems based on the Takagi-Sugeno (T-S) model. Expect stability analysis, an emphasis is laid on the derivation of methods which have a decentralized or a distributed control structure. These include sampled-data control, event-triggered control, sliding mode control, practical applications, and last but not the least, conclusions and future research. The proposed methodologies provide effective techniques to overcome specific difficulties in the considered systems, such as high dimensionality, interconnections, and coupling nonlinearities.

1.1 LARGE-SCALE INTERCONNECTED SYSTEMS

The demand for rapid and sustained development has pushed control scholars and engineers to focus on increasingly higher dimensional and more complex systems. Such kind of systems is referred to as large-scale systems, which relies on the cooperation of several subsystems (Šiljak, 1978; Šiljak & Zečević, 2005). In large-scale systems, two kinds of analytical models are developed with respect to interconnections and non-interconnections among subsystems, respectively. Such general models for large-scale systems with non-interconnections are multi-agent systems. Control community has studied extensively coordination control of multi-agent systems, including unmanned aerial vehicles, unmanned underwater vehicles, and unmanned ground vehicles. Some important results and progress in coordination control of multi-agent

DOI: 10.4018/978-1-5225-2385-7.ch001

have been published in major control systems and robotics journals (Ren, Beard & Atkins, 2005; Oh, Park & Ahn, 2015). Large-scale interconnected systems exist widely in the real world, such as power networks, transportation systems, ecological systems, and river pollution systems (Lunze, 1992; Mahmoud, 2011). A distinguish property of such large-scale interconnected systems is that a perturbation of one subsystem can affect the other subsystems as well as the overall stability and performance, its structure is shown in Figure 1.

Large-scale interconnected systems invoke control theory with the following challenges:

- The large size of the plants leads to the high dimension of its mathematical model. This condition requires a control restriction on hardware and software costs;
- Every subsystem has several interconnections connecting to other subsystems, which have to be considered explicitly in the stability analysis and controller design;
- The dynamics among all subsystems can be different each other. The design aims at including not only stability or optimality for systems with simple dynamics, but also a variety of hybrid dynamics in interconnections, such as continuous-discrete time, coupling nonlinearity, and network-induced uncertainties.

Figure 1. Structure of large-scale interconnected systems

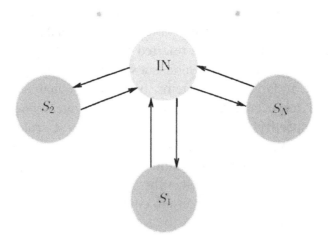

On the other hand, computer systems undergo several revolutions. From 1945, when the modern computer began to emerge, until 1985, computers became large and expensive. Since 1980, however, two technologies began to change the situation. One was the development of powerful microprocessors, and the other was the invention of high-speed computer networks (Tanenbaum & Steen, 2007). A network allows that hundreds of machines within different areas could be connected. Put together the systems with a large numbers of computers over a network, they are usually called computer networks or distributed systems. Recently, complex networks have been developed for large-scale systems, such as communication protocols (Simon, Volgyesi, Maróti, & Ákos, 2003), synchronization and consensus of nodes (Tang, Qian, Gao, & Jürgen, 2014).

1.2 GENERAL METHODOLOGIES

The control of large-scale systems is one of the foremost challenges facing control engineers today. There exist three approaches adopted for the control of large-scale interconnected systems: the centralized approach, the decentralized approach, and the distributed approach.

The centralized approach is shown in Figure 2, which is based on the assumption that a central station is available and sufficiently powerful to control a whole group of subsystems. In fact, the assumption fails to hold due to the issues, such as the economic cost and reliability of communication links particularly when systems are characterized by geographical separation, which limits the implementation for centralized control (Mahmoud & Singh, 1981).

Figure 2. Centralized control

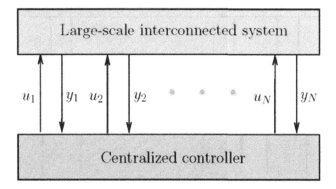

These limitations have motivated the development of an extensive literature in the area of decentralized control as shown in Figure 3. Its idea is to decompose the overall system into several subsystems with lower dimensionality. Given such a decomposition structure, the control design is performed locally with a subsequent inclusion of the interconnection effect (Sandell et al., 1978). However, the decentralized control strategy appears weaker performance and stability margins, especially when the interconnections among subsystems are strong.

Figure 4 shows the distributed control in which a central station for control is not required at the cost of becoming far more complex in structure and organization, and the interconnections connecting other subsystems provide

Figure 3. Decentralized control

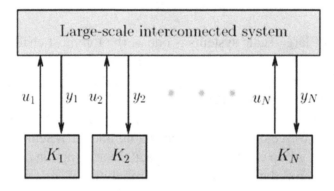

Figure 4. Distributed control

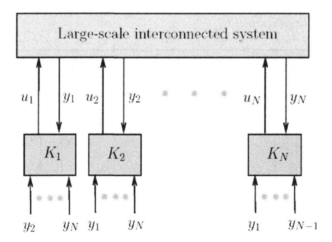

supplemental feedbacks for the local controllers to enhance the stability and performance requirements. Although the centralized and decentralized approaches are considered to be practical depending on the situations and conditions of the real-world applications, the distributed control is believed more promising due to many inevitable physical constraints such as limited resources and energy, short wireless communication ranges, narrow bandwidths, and large sizes of devices to manage and control. Therefore, the decentralized control may be suitable for large-scale systems with weak interconnections, but the distributed control is considered for large-scale systems with strong ones (Kazempour & Ghaisari, 2013).

1.3 LARGE-SCALE FUZZY INTERCONNECTED SYSTEMS

In 1973, Lofti A. Zadeh first introduced the concept of linguistic variables, and used IF-THEN rules to formulate human knowledge. This work establishes the foundation for fuzzy control method (Zadeh, 1973). Afterwards, many efforts have led to numerous important issues on fuzzy control systems, and the first journal *Fuzzy Sets and Systems*, which has been devoted to the international advancement in the theory and application of fuzzy sets and systems, is launched in 1978. In 1980s, Sugeno first proposed fuzzy control to water purification plants (Sugeno, 1985). In 1990s, the rapid development of the fuzzy control in Japan invoked increasing interest of research and engineering societies. IEEE International Conference on Fuzzy Systems and IEEE Transactions on Fuzzy Systems, has been set up to study fuzzy-based control. The fruitful results are not only in theories but also in practical applications (Babuka, 1998; Zimmermann, 2001). Among various model-based fuzzy control methods, the widely used are rule-based fuzzy systems, in which the relationship between variables is represented by means of fuzzy IF-THEN rules. Rule-based fuzzy systems include Mamdani models, fuzzy relation models, and Takagi–Sugeno (T–S) fuzzy models. In particular, the approach based on T–S model is well suited to controller design for model-based nonlinear systems (Feng, 2006; Lin et al., 2007; Qiu, Gao, & Ding, 2016).

Recently, attention has been focused on large-scale nonlinear interconnection systems in order to take the complexity and dynamic behavior of such systems. Modeling of such systems often result in very high-order models imposing great difficulties to the stability analysis and controller design. The so-called Takagi-Sugeno (T-S) model-based method is introduced to overcome the

5

difficulties induced by nonlinearities (Feng, 2010). Once a smooth nonlinear system is represented by the T-S fuzzy model, its advantages are twofold: 1) The T-S fuzzy model is capable of approximating the nonlinear system at any preciseness; 2) Based on the T-S fuzzy model, powerful linear control methods can be developed for its control problems.

Consider a continuous-time large-scale nonlinear interconnected system contains N subsystems as follows:

$$\dot{x}_i\left(t\right) = A_i\left(t\right)x_i\left(t\right) + \sum_{j=1,j\neq i}^{N} \overline{A}_{ij}\left(t\right)x_j\left(t\right) + B_i\left(t\right)u_i\left(t\right), \tag{1}$$

where $i \in \mathcal{N} := \left\{1,2,\cdots,N\right\}$, N is the number of the subsystems; $x_i\left(t\right) \in \mathfrak{R}^{n_{xi}}, u_i\left(t\right) \in \mathfrak{R}^{n_{ui}}$ denote the system state and the control input, respectively; $\left\{A_i\left(t\right), B_i\left(t\right)\right\}$ is partially unknown smooth nonlinear function; $\overline{A}_{ij}\left(t\right)$ denotes the nonlinear interconnection of the i-th and j-th subsystems.

Takagi and Sugeno proposed the fuzzy dynamic model, which is described by the number of IF–THEN rules representing local linear input–output relations of a given nonlinear system (Takagi & Sugeno, 1985). Thus, the i-th nonlinear subsystem in (1) is represented by the following T-S fuzzy model:

Plant Rule R_i^l: **IF** $\varsigma_{i1}\left(t\right)$ is F_{i1}^l and $\varsigma_{i2}\left(t\right)$ is F_{i2}^l and $\cdots$ and $\varsigma_{ig}\left(t\right)$ is F_{ig}^l,

   THEN

$$\dot{x}_i\left(t\right) = A_i^l x_i\left(t\right) + \sum_{j=1,j\neq i}^{N} \overline{A}_{ij}^l x_j\left(t\right) + B_i^l u_i\left(t\right), l \in \mathcal{L}_i := \left\{1,2,\cdots,r_i\right\} \tag{2}$$

where for the i-th subsystem, R_i^l is the l-th fuzzy inference rule; r_i is the number of inference rules; $F_{i\varnothing}^l\left(\varnothing = 1,2,\cdots,g\right)$ are fuzzy sets; $\varsigma_i\left(t\right) := \left[\varsigma_{i1}\left(t\right), \varsigma_{i2}\left(t\right), \cdots, \varsigma_{ig}\left(t\right)\right]$ are the measurable variables; $\left\{A_i^l, B_i^l\right\}$ is the l-th local model; $\overline{A}_{ij}^l$ denotes the nonlinear interconnection of the i-th and j-th subsystems for the l-th local model.

Define the inferred fuzzy set $F_i^l := \Pi_{\varnothing=1}^{g} F_{i\varnothing}^l$ and normalized membership function $\mu_i^l\left[\varsigma\left(t\right)\right]$, it yields

$$\mu_i^l\left[\varsigma_i\left(t\right)\right] := \frac{\Pi_{\varnothing=1}^g \mu_{i\varnothing}^l\left[\varsigma_{i\varnothing}\left(t\right)\right]}{\sum_{\varsigma=1}^{r_i}\Pi_{\varnothing=1}^g \mu_{i\varnothing}^\varsigma\left[\varsigma_{i\varnothing}\left(t\right)\right]} \geq 0, \sum_{l=1}^{r_i}\mu_i^l\left[\varsigma_i\left(t\right)\right] := 1, \tag{3}$$

where $\mu_{i\varnothing}^l\left[\varsigma_{i\varnothing}\left(t\right)\right]$ is the grade of membership of $\varsigma_{i\varnothing}\left(t\right)$ in $F_{i\varnothing}^l$. Here we will denote $\mu_i^l := \mu_i^l\left[\varsigma_i\left(t\right)\right]$ for brevity.

By fuzzy blending, the i-th global T-S fuzzy dynamic model is obtained by

$$\dot{x}_i\left(t\right) = A_i\left(\mu_i\right)x_i\left(t\right) + \sum_{j=1,j\neq i}^{N}\overline{A}_{ij}\left(\mu_i\right)x_j\left(t\right) + B_i\left(\mu_i\right)u_i\left(t\right), \tag{4}$$

where

$$A_i\left(\mu_i\right) := \sum_{l=1}^{r_i}\mu_i^l A_i^l, \overline{A}_{ij}\left(\mu_i\right) := \sum_{l=1}^{r_i}\mu_i^l A_{ij}^l, B_i\left(\mu_i\right) := \sum_{l=1}^{r_i}\mu_i^l B_i^l. \tag{5}$$

We are aware of no systematic work formally analyzing and designing for large-scale fuzzy interconnected systems as shown in (4), which motivates us to write this book.

1.4 OUTLINE OF THE BOOK

The biggest challenge, nowadays, is the lack of formal mathematical tools for the analysis and design of large-scale nonlinear systems consisting of several subsystems with interconnections. This book will give a foundational and comprehensive treatment of large-scale nonlinear interconnected systems using T-S fuzzy model approach. The central subject of this book is a systematic framework for the stability analysis and controller design of large-scale fuzzy interconnected control systems. Building on the so-called T-S fuzzy model, a number of important issues in fuzzy interconnected control systems are addressed. These include stability analysis, stabilization design procedures, incorporation of sampled-data, event-triggered control, sliding mode control, and numerical implementations.

The book is primarily intended for researchers and engineers in the system and control communities. It can also serve as complementary reading for large-scale system theories at the post-graduate level. Throughout this book and seeking computational convenience, all the developed results are cast in the form of LMIs, which can be easily solved using the solver of LMI Toolbox in Matlab (Gahinet, 1995). The book is divided into eight chapters.

- Chapter 1 provides an overview of the concepts and techniques of large-scale fuzzy interconnected systems and introduces the system description and motivation of the study.
- Chapter 2 derives some results on stability analysis of large-scale fuzzy interconnected systems, and general and reduced LMI-based conditions are considered, respectively.
- Chapter 3 deals with the stabilization problem for large-scale fuzzy interconnected systems, and various design results on state-feedback and static-output feedback controls are presented.
- Chapter 4 focuses on the sampled-data controller design. The appropriate models are formulated by using input-delay approach, and various design results on decentralized and distributed sampled-data controls are presented.
- Chapter 5 examines data reduction for large-scale networked systems, where event-triggered and self-triggered controls are considered respectively, and the corresponding results on controller design are derived.
- Chapter 6 studies the decentralized adaptive control strategies of large-scale fuzzy interconnected systems. It addresses both cases of discrete-time and continuous-time systems.
- Chapter 7 considers the practical application to microgrids and multi-motors driven.
- Chapter 8 remarks conclusions and recommendations for further research.

The material contained in this book not only organized to focus on the new developments in the analysis and control methods for large-scale fuzzy interconnected systems, but it also integrates the impact of the network like delay-factor, sampled-data, and communication constraints. After an introductory chapter is presented, it is intended to divide the book into several independent chapters that equipped with introduction, problem formulation, main results, and illustrative examples. Each chapter of the book will be supplemented by an extended bibliography, and some appropriate appendices are summarized in the end of this book.

REFERENCES

Babuka, R. (1998). *Fuzzy Modeling for Control* (1st ed.). USA: Kluwer Academic Publishers. doi:10.1007/978-94-011-4868-9

Feng, G. (2006). A survey on analysis and design of model-based fuzzy control systems. *IEEE Transactions on Fuzzy Systems, 14*(5), 676–697. doi:10.1109/TFUZZ.2006.883415

Feng, G. (2010). *Analysis and Synthesis of Fuzzy Control Systems—A Model Based Approach* (1st ed.). USA: CRC. doi:10.1201/EBK1420092646

Gahinet, P., Nemirovski, A., Laub, J., & Chilali, M. (1995). LMI Control Toolbox for Use with Matlab (1st ed.). Natick: Math Works.

Kazempour, F., & Ghaisari, J. (2013). Stability analysis of model-based networked distributed control systems. *Journal of Process Control, 23*(3), 444–452. doi:10.1016/j.jprocont.2012.12.010

Lin, C., Wang, G., & Lee, T. et al.. (2007). *LMI Approach to Analysis and Control of Takagi-Sugeno Fuzzy Systems With Time Delay* (1st ed.). New York: Springer.

Lunze, J. (1992). *Feedback control of large-scale systems* (1st ed.). London: Prentice-Hall.

Mahmoud, M. (2011). *Decentralized systems with design constraints* (1st ed.). New York: Springer Science & Business Media. doi:10.1007/978-0-85729-290-2

Mahmoud, M., & Singh, M. (1981). *Large-Scale Systems Modelling* (1st ed.). London: Pergamon Press.

Oh, K., Park, M., & Ahn, H. (2015). A survey of multi-agent formation control. *Automatica, 53*, 424–440. doi:10.1016/j.automatica.2014.10.022

Qiu, J., Gao, H., & Ding, S. (2016). Recent advances on fuzzy-model-based nonlinear networked control systems: A survey. *IEEE Transactions on Industrial Electronics, 63*(2), 1207–1217. doi:10.1109/TIE.2015.2504351

Ren, W., Beard, R., & Atkins, E. (2005). A survey of consensus problems in multi-agent coordination systems. *Proceedings of the American Control Conference* (pp. 1859–1864).

Sandell, N., Varaiya, P., Athans, M., & Safonov, M. (1978). Survey of decentralized control methods for large scale systems. *IEEE Transactions on Automatic Control, 23*(2), 108–128. doi:10.1109/TAC.1978.1101704

Šiljak, D. (1978). *Large-Scale Dynamic Systems: Stability and Structure* (1st ed.). New York: North Holland.

Šiljak, D., & Zečević, A. (2005). Control of large-scale systems: Beyond decentralized feedback. *Annual Reviews in Control, 29*(2), 169–179. doi:10.1016/j.arcontrol.2005.08.003

Simon, G & Volgyesi, P & Maróti, M & Ákos, L (2003). Simulation-based optimization of communication protocols for large-scale wireless sensor networks. *Proceedings of the IEEE aerospace conference* (Vol. 2003, pp. 1339-1346).

Sugeno, M. (1985). *Industrial Applications of Fuzzy Control* (1st ed.). USA: North-Holland.

Takagi, T., & Sugeno, M. (1985). Fuzzy identification of systems and its applications to modeling and control. *IEEE Transactions on Systems, Man, and Cybernetics, 15*(1), 116–132. doi:10.1109/TSMC.1985.6313399

Tanenbaum, A., & Steen, M. (2007). *Distributed Systems* (2nd ed.). USA: Prentice-Hall.

Tang, Y., Qian, F., Gao, H., & Jürgen, K. (2014). Synchronization in complex networks and its application–a survey of recent advances and challenges. *Annual Reviews in Control, 38*(2), 184–198. doi:10.1016/j.arcontrol.2014.09.003

Zadeh, L. (1973). Outline of a new approach to the analysis of complex systems and decision processes. *IEEE Transactions on Systems, Man, and Cybernetics, 3*(1), 28–44. doi:10.1109/TSMC.1973.5408575

Zimmermann, H. (2001). *Fuzzy Set Theory and Its Applications* (1st ed.). USA: Kluwer Academic Publishers. doi:10.1007/978-94-010-0646-0

`

Chapter 2
Stability of Large-Scale Fuzzy Interconnected System

ABSTRACT

This chapter studies the asymptotic stability of large-scale fuzzy interconnected systems. It firstly focused on the general stability analysis. Then, by using some bounding techniques, the fuzzy rules in interconnections to other subsystems are eliminated. Such condition leads to a reduced number of LMIs. Also, we will present the stability result for the discrete-time case. Finally, we give several examples to illustrate the use of corresponding results.

2.1 INTRODUCTION

It is well known that one of the most important and difficult part of analysis and synthesize for large-scale nonlinear interconnected systems is to handle their interconnections. Due to the fact that each subsystem has several interconnections to the other subsystems, an overall large-scale nonlinear system contains a lot of interconnections. In general, if a nonlinear subsystem in large-scale system is represented by a T–S fuzzy system, its interconnections maybe include the nonlinear dynamics of the other nonlinear subsystems. In that case, such condition leads to the well-known "rule-explosion" problem in (Liu & Li, 2004), when increasing the number of subsystems. The work in (Wang & Luoh, 2004) derived the stability results on the large-scale fuzzy interconnected systems, where it required the matrix-equality constraints that were not easy to solve by using LMI toolbox. A special class of large-scale

DOI: 10.4018/978-1-5225-2385-7.ch002

nonlinear systems with linear interconnection matrix $\bar{A}_{ij}$ was investigated in (Hsiao & Hwang, 2002; Zhang, Li, & Liao, 2005; Zhang & Feng, 2008; Lin, Wang, & Lee, 2006). The restrictive condition with linear interconnection is not always suitable for practical implementations.

The chapter firstly derives the stability results for continuous-time systems and for discrete-time systems, respectively. Then, by using some bounding techniques, the fuzzy rules generated by the interconnections to other subsystems are eliminated. In that case, the corresponding stability results with reduction number of LMIs are obtained.

2.2 GENERAL STABILITY ANALYSIS

This section will derive the general stability conditions for large-scale T-S fuzzy interconnected systems.

2.2.1 Problem Formulation

Consider a continuous-time large-scale nonlinear system containing N subsystems with interconnections, where the i-th nonlinear subsystem is represented by the following T-S fuzzy model:

Plant Rule R_i^l: IF $\varsigma_{i1}\left(t\right)$ is F_{i1}^l and $\varsigma_{i2}\left(t\right)$ is F_{i2}^l and $\cdots$ and $\varsigma_{ig}\left(t\right)$ is F_{ig}^l, THEN

$$\dot{x}_i\left(t\right) = A_i^l x_i\left(t\right) + \sum\nolimits_{j=1,j\neq i}^{N} A_{ij}^{-1} x_j\left(t\right), l \in L_i := \left\{1,2,\cdots,r_i\right\} \tag{1}$$

where $i \in \mathcal{N} := \left\{1,2,\cdots,N\right\}$, N is the number of the subsystems. For the i-th subsystem, R_i^l is the l-th fuzzy inference rule; r_i is the number of inference rules; $\mathrm{F}_{i\varnothing}^l \left(\varnothing = 1,2,\cdots,g\right)$ are fuzzy sets; $x_i\left(t\right) \in \mathfrak{R}^{n_{xi}}$ denotes the system state; $\varsigma_i\left(t\right) := \left[\varsigma_{i1}\left(t\right),\varsigma_{i2}\left(t\right),\cdots,\varsigma_{ig}\left(t\right)\right]$ are the measurable variables; A_i^l is the l-th local model; $\bar{A}_{ij}^l$ denotes the nonlinear interconnection of the i-th and j-th subsystems for the l-th local model.

Define the inferred fuzzy set $\mathrm{F}_i^l := \Pi_{\varnothing=1}^g \mathrm{F}_{i\varnothing}^l$ and normalized membership function $\mu_i^l\left[\varsigma_i\left(t\right)\right]$, it yields

$$\mu_i^l\left[\varsigma_i\left(t\right)\right] := \frac{\Pi_{\varnothing=1}^g \mu_{i\varnothing}^l\left[\varsigma_{i\varnothing}\left(t\right)\right]}{\sum_{\varsigma=1}^{r_i} \Pi_{\varnothing=1}^g \mu_{i\varnothing}^\varsigma\left[\varsigma_{i\varnothing}\left(t\right)\right]} \geq 0, \sum_{l=1}^{r_i} \mu_i^l\left[\varsigma_i\left(t\right)\right] := 1, \tag{2}$$

where $\mu_{i\varnothing}^l\left[\varsigma_{i\varnothing}\left(t\right)\right]$ is the grade of membership of $\varsigma_{i\varnothing}\left(t\right)$ in $\mathrm{F}_{i\varnothing}^l$. Here we will denote $\mu_i^l := \mu_i^l\left[\varsigma_i\left(t\right)\right]$ for brevity.

By fuzzy blending, the i-th global T-S fuzzy dynamic model is obtained by

$$\dot{x}_i\left(t\right) = A_i\left(\mu_i\right)x_i\left(t\right) + \sum_{j=1, j\neq i}^N \bar{A}_{ij}\left(\mu_i\right)x_j\left(t\right), \tag{3}$$

where

$$A_i\left(\mu_i\right) := \sum_{l=1}^{r_i}\mu_i^l A_i^l, \bar{A}_{ij}\left(\mu_i\right) := \sum_{l=1}^{r_i}\mu_i^l A_{ij}^l. \tag{4}$$

Before moving on, we give the following lemma which will be used to derive the main results.

Lemma 2.2.1 Given the interconnected matrix $\bar{A}_{ij}^l$ in the system (1), and symmetric positive definite matrix $M_{ij} \in \mathfrak{R}^{n_{xi}\times n_{xi}}$, the following inequality holds:

$$\sum_{i=1}^N \sum_{j=1, j\neq i}^N \bar{A}_{ij}\left(\mu_i\right)M_{ij}\bar{A}_{ij}^T\left(\mu_i\right) \leq \sum_{i=1}^N \sum_{j=1, j\neq i}^N \mu_i^l\left[\bar{A}_{ij}^l\right]M_{ij}\left[\bar{A}_{ij}^l\right]^T. \tag{5}$$

Proof. Note that

$$\left[\bar{A}_{ij}^l - \bar{A}_{ij}^f\right]^T M_{ij}\left[\bar{A}_{ij}^l - \bar{A}_{ij}^f\right] \geq 0, \quad \{l,f\} \in \mathcal{L}_i, \{i,j\} \in \mathcal{N}, j \neq i \tag{6}$$

which implies that

$$\left[\bar{A}_{ij}^{l}\right]M_{ij}\left[\bar{A}_{ij}^{l}\right]^{T}+\left[\bar{A}_{ij}^{f}\right]M_{ij}\left[\bar{A}_{ij}^{f}\right]^{T}\geq\left[\bar{A}_{ij}^{l}\right]M_{ij}\left[\bar{A}_{ij}^{f}\right]^{T}+\left[\bar{A}_{ij}^{f}\right]M_{ij}\left[\bar{A}_{ij}^{l}\right]^{T}. \tag{7}$$

By taking the relations in (6) and (7), we have

$$
\begin{aligned}
\sum_{i=1}^{N}\sum_{j=1,j\neq i}^{N}&\bar{A}_{ij}\left(\mu_{i}\right)M_{ij}\bar{A}_{ij}^{T}\left(\mu_{i}\right)\\
&=\sum_{i=1}^{N}\sum_{j=1,j\neq i}^{N}\sum_{l=1}^{r_{i}}\sum_{f=1}^{r_{i}}\mu_{i}^{l}\mu_{i}^{f}\left[\bar{A}_{ij}^{l}\right]M_{ij}\left[\bar{A}_{ij}^{f}\right]^{T}\\
&=\frac{1}{2}\sum_{i=1}^{N}\sum_{j=1,j\neq i}^{N}\sum_{l=1}^{r_{i}}\sum_{f=1}^{r_{i}}\mu_{i}^{l}\mu_{i}^{f}\left\{\left[\bar{A}_{ij}^{l}\right]M_{ij}\left[\bar{A}_{ij}^{f}\right]^{T}+\left[\bar{A}_{ij}^{f}\right]M_{ij}\left[\bar{A}_{ij}^{l}\right]^{T}\right\}\\
&\leq\frac{1}{2}\sum_{i=1}^{N}\sum_{j=1,j\neq i}^{N}\sum_{l=1}^{r_{i}}\sum_{f=1}^{r_{i}}\mu_{i}^{l}\mu_{i}^{f}\left\{\left[\bar{A}_{ij}^{l}\right]M_{ij}\left[\bar{A}_{ij}^{l}\right]^{T}+\left[\bar{A}_{ij}^{f}\right]M_{ij}\left[\bar{A}_{ij}^{f}\right]^{T}\right\}\\
&=\frac{1}{2}\sum_{i=1}^{N}\sum_{j=1,j\neq i}^{N}\sum_{l=1}^{r_{i}}\mu_{i}^{l}\left[\bar{A}_{ij}^{l}\right]M_{ij}\left[\bar{A}_{ij}^{l}\right]^{T}\\
&\quad+\frac{1}{2}\sum_{i=1}^{N}\sum_{j=1,j\neq i}^{N}\sum_{f=1}^{r_{i}}\mu_{i}^{f}\left[\bar{A}_{ij}^{f}\right]M_{ij}\left[\bar{A}_{ij}^{f}\right]^{T}\\
&=\sum_{i=1}^{N}\sum_{j=1,j\neq i}^{N}\sum_{l=1}^{r_{i}}\mu_{i}^{l}\left[\bar{A}_{ij}^{l}\right]M_{ij}\left[\bar{A}_{ij}^{l}\right]^{T}
\end{aligned} \tag{8}
$$

Thus, this proof is completed.

2.2.2 Main Results for Continuous-Time Systems

Based on the continuous-time large-scale fuzzy interconnected system in (3), the stability condition is presented as follows.

Theorem 2.2.1 The large-scale fuzzy interconnected system in (3) is asymptotically stable, if there exist symmetric positive definite matrices $\left\{Q_{i},M_{ij}\right\}\in\mathfrak{R}^{n_{zi}\times n_{zi}}$, such that for all $l\in\mathcal{L}_{i},j\neq i,\{i,j\}\in\mathcal{N}$, the following LMIs hold:

$$\left[\begin{array}{cc} \mathrm{Sym}\left\{A_i^l Q_i\right\} + \displaystyle\sum_{j=1,j\neq i}^{N} \left[\overline{A}_{ij}^l\right] M_{ij} \left[\overline{A}_{ij}^l\right]^T & Q_i \mathbb{I} \\ \star & -\mathbb{M}_i \end{array} \right] < 0, \qquad (9)$$

where $\mathbb{I} = \underbrace{\left[\mathrm{I}\cdots\mathrm{I}\cdots\mathrm{I}\right]}_{N-1}, \mathbb{M}_i = \mathrm{diag}\underbrace{\left\{M_{1i} \cdots M_{ji,j\neq i} \cdots M_{Ni}\right\}}_{N-1}.$

Proof. Choose the Lyapunov functional as

$$\begin{aligned} V\left(x(t)\right) &= \sum_{i=1}^{N} V_i\left(x_i(t)\right) \\ &= \sum_{i=1}^{N} x_i^T(t) P_i x_i(t), i \in \mathcal{N} \end{aligned} \qquad (10)$$

where $P_i \in \mathfrak{R}^{n_{zi} \times n_{zi}}$ is symmetric positive definite matrix.

By taking the time derivative of $V\left(x(t)\right)$, and along the trajectories of (3), one has

$$\begin{aligned} \dot{V}\left(x(t)\right) &= \sum_{i=1}^{N}\left\{\dot{x}_i^T(t) P_i x_i(t) + x_i^T(t) P_i \dot{x}_i(t)\right\} \\ &= \sum_{i=1}^{N} 2x_i^T(t) P_i A_i\left(\mu_i\right) x_i(t) + 2x_i^T(t) P_i \sum_{j=1,j\neq i}^{N} \overline{A}_{ij}\left(\mu_i\right) x_j(t) \end{aligned} \qquad (11)$$

Note that the Young's inequality

$$2\overline{x}^T \overline{y} \leq \overline{x}^T M^{-1} \overline{x} + \overline{y}^T M \overline{y}, \qquad (12)$$

where $\left\{\overline{x}, \overline{y}\right\} \in \mathfrak{R}^n$, and $M \in \mathfrak{R}^{n \times n}$ is a positive definite symmetric matrix.

Define symmetric positive definite matrix $M_{ij} \in \mathfrak{R}^{n_{zi} \times n_{zi}}$, and it follows from (11) that

$$\sum_{i=1}^{N} 2x_i^T\left(t\right) P_i \sum_{j=1,j\neq i}^{N} \bar{A}_{ij}\left(\mu_i\right) x_j\left(t\right)$$

$$= \sum_{i=1}^{N} 2x_i^T\left(t\right) P_i \sum_{j=1,j\neq i}^{N} \sum_{l=1}^{r_i} \mu_i^l \bar{A}_{ij}^l x_j\left(t\right)$$

$$\leq \sum_{i=1}^{N} \sum_{j=1,j\neq i}^{N} x_i^T\left(t\right) P_i \left[\sum_{l=1}^{r_i} \mu_i^l \bar{A}_{ij}^l\right] M_{ij} \left[\sum_{l=1}^{r_i} \mu_i^l \bar{A}_{ij}^l\right]^T P_i x_i\left(t\right)$$

$$+ \sum_{i=1}^{N} \sum_{j=1,j\neq i}^{N} \left\{ x_j^T\left(t\right) M_{ij}^{-1} x_j\left(t\right) \right\} \tag{13}$$

$$\leq \sum_{i=1}^{N} \sum_{j=1,j\neq i}^{N} x_i^T\left(t\right) P_i \sum_{l=1}^{r_i} \mu_i^l \left[\bar{A}_{ij}^l\right] M_{ij} \left[\bar{A}_{ij}^l\right]^T P_i x_i\left(t\right)$$

$$+ \sum_{i=1}^{N} \sum_{j=1,j\neq i}^{N} \left\{ x_i^T\left(t\right) M_{ji}^{-1} x_i\left(t\right) \right\}$$

By extracting the fuzzy premise variables, it is easy to see that $\dot{V}\left(x\left(t\right)\right) < 0$ if the following inequality holds,

$$\text{Sym}\left\{P_i A_i^l\right\} + \sum_{j=1,j\neq i}^{N} \left\{ \left[\bar{A}_{ij}^l\right] M_{ij} \left[\bar{A}_{ij}^l\right]^T P_i + M_{ji}^{-1} \right\} < 0, \ l \in \mathcal{L}_i, \{i,j\} \in \mathcal{N}. \tag{14}$$

By using Schur complement to (14), it yields

$$\begin{bmatrix} \text{Sym}\left\{P_i A_i^l\right\} + \displaystyle\sum_{j=1,j\neq i}^{N} P_i \left[\bar{A}_{ij}^l\right] M_{ij} \left[\bar{A}_{ij}^l\right]^T P_i & \mathbb{I} \\ \star & -\mathbb{M}_i \end{bmatrix} < 0, \tag{15}$$

where $\mathbb{I} = \underbrace{\left[I \cdots I \cdots I\right]}_{N-1}, \mathbb{M}_i = \text{diag}\underbrace{\left\{M_{1i} \cdots M_{ji,j\neq i} \cdots M_{Ni}\right\}}_{N-1}.$

Define

$$\Gamma_i := \text{diag}\left\{Q_i \quad \underbrace{I \cdots I \cdots I}_{N-1}\right\}, \tag{16}$$

where $Q_i = P_i^{-1}$.

Now, by performing a congruence transformation to (15) by Γ_i given in (16), it is easy to see that the inequality in (9) implies $\dot{V}\big(x(t)\big) < 0$. Thus, completing this proof.

NOTE: It is noted that the matrix dimensions in the derived result (9) maybe large when increasing the number of subsystems. It is well known that larger matrix dimensions lead a high computational cost. Here, we define $M_0 \le M_{ij}$, then the following inequality implies (15),

$$\left[\begin{matrix} \mathrm{Sym}\big\{ P_i A_i^l \big\} + \displaystyle\sum_{j=1, j \ne i}^{N} P_i \big[\bar{A}_{ij}^l \big] M_{ij} \big[\bar{A}_{ij}^l \big]^T P_i & I \\ \star & -M_0 \end{matrix} \right] < 0.$$

In that case, the computational complexity can be reduced, but increases the design conservatism to some extent.

2.2.3 Extension to Discrete-Time Systems

This subsection considers a discrete-time large-scale fuzzy interconnected system as below:

$$x_i(t+1) = A_i(\mu_i) x_i(t) + \sum_{j=1, j \ne i}^{N} \bar{A}_{ij}(\mu_i) x_j(t), \tag{17}$$

where

$$A_i(\mu_i) := \sum_{l=1}^{r_i} \mu_i^l A_i^l, \bar{A}_{ij}(\mu_i) := \sum_{l=1}^{r_i} \mu_i^l A_{ij}^l. \tag{18}$$

Based on the model in (17), we extend the stability condition of continuous-time large-scale fuzzy models into discrete-time case, and the corresponding result is given as below.

Theorem 2.2.2 The large-scale fuzzy interconnected system in (17) is asymptotically stable, if there exist symmetric positive definite matrices $\left\{\bar{P}_i, M_{ij}\right\} \in \mathfrak{R}^{n_{zi} \times n_{zi}}$, and the matrix G_i, such that for all $l \in \mathcal{L}_i, j \neq i, \{i,j\} \in \mathcal{N}$, the following LMIs hold:

$$
\begin{bmatrix}
\bar{P}_i - G_i - G_i^T + \displaystyle\sum_{j=1, j\neq i}^{N} \left\{ \left[\bar{A}_{ij}^l\right] M_{ij} \left[\bar{A}_{ij}^l\right]^T \right\} & A_i^l G_i^T & 0 \\
\star & -\bar{P}_i & G_i \mathbb{I} \\
\star & \star & -\mathbb{M}_i
\end{bmatrix} < 0,
\tag{19}
$$

where $\mathbb{I} = \underbrace{\left[I \cdots I \cdots I \right]}_{N-1}, \mathbb{M}_i = \text{diag} \underbrace{\left\{ M_{1i} \cdots M_{ji, j\neq i} \cdots M_{Ni} \right\}}_{N-1}$.

Proof. Choose the Lyapunov functional as

$$
\begin{aligned}
V\big(x(t)\big) &= \sum_{i=1}^{N} V_i\big(x_i(t)\big) \\
&= \sum_{i=1}^{N} x_i^T(t) P_i x_i(t), i \in \mathcal{N}
\end{aligned}
\tag{20}
$$

where $P_i \in \mathfrak{R}^{n_{zi} \times n_{zi}}$ is symmetric positive definite matrix.

Define $\Delta V\big(x(t)\big) = V\big(x(t+1)\big) - V\big(x(t)\big)$, one has

$$
\Delta V\big(x(t)\big) = \sum_{i=1}^{N} \left\{ x_i^T(t+1) P_i x_i(t+1) - x_i^T(t) P_i x_i(t) \right\}.
\tag{21}
$$

Similar to (13), define the matrix $G_i^{-1} \in \mathfrak{R}^{n_{zi} \times n_{zi}}$ and symmetric positive definite matrix $M_{ij} \in \mathfrak{R}^{n_{zi} \times n_{zi}}$, and take the relation in Lemma 2.2.1, it yields

$$
\begin{aligned}
0 &= \sum_{i=1}^{N} 2x_i^T(t+1)G_i^{-1}\left[-x_i(t+1) + A_i(\mu_i)x_i(t) + \sum_{j=1,j\neq i}^{N} \bar{A}_{ij}(\mu_i)x_j(t)\right] \\
&\leq \sum_{i=1}^{N} 2x_i^T(t+1)G_i^{-1}\left[-x_i(t+1) + A_i(\mu_i)x_i(t)\right] \\
&\quad + \sum_{i=1}^{N}\sum_{j=1,j\neq i}^{N} x_i^T(t+1)G_i^{-1}\left[\bar{A}_{ij}(\mu_i)\right]M_{ij}\left[\bar{A}_{ij}(\mu_i)\right]^T G_i^{-T}x_i(t+1) \\
&\quad + \sum_{i=1}^{N}\sum_{j=1,j\neq i}^{N}\left\{x_j^T(t)M_{ij}^{-1}x_j(t)\right\} \\
&\leq \sum_{i=1}^{N} 2x_i^T(t+1)G_i^{-1}\left[-x_i(t+1) + A_i(\mu_i)x_i(t)\right] \\
&\quad + \sum_{i=1}^{N}\sum_{j=1,j\neq i}^{N} x_i^T(t+1)G_i^{-1}\left\{\sum_{l=1}^{r_i}\mu_i^l\left[\bar{A}_{ij}^l\right]M_{ij}\left[\bar{A}_{ij}^l\right]^T\right\}G_i^{-T}x_i(t+1) \\
&\quad + \sum_{i=1}^{N}\sum_{j=1,j\neq i}^{N}\left\{x_i^T(t)M_{ji}^{-1}x_i(t)\right\}
\end{aligned}
\tag{22}
$$

It is easy to see from (22) that $\Delta V\left(x(t)\right) < 0$ if the following inequality holds,

$$
\begin{bmatrix}
P_i - G_i^{-1} - G_i^{-T} + \sum_{j=1,j\neq i}^{N}\left\{G_i^{-1}\left[\bar{A}_{ij}^l\right]M_{ij}\left[\bar{A}_{ij}^l\right]^T G_i^{-T}\right\} & G_i^{-1}A_i^l \\
\star & -P_i + \sum_{j=1,j\neq i}^{N} M_{ji}^{-1}
\end{bmatrix} < 0
\tag{23}
$$

with $l \in \mathcal{L}_i, i \in \mathcal{N}$.

By using Schur complement to (23), it yields

$$
\begin{bmatrix}
P_i - G_i^{-1} - G_i^{-T} + \sum_{j=1,j\neq i}^{N}\left\{G_i^{-1}\left[\bar{A}_{ij}^l\right]M_{ij}\left[\bar{A}_{ij}^l\right]^T G_i^{-T}\right\} & G_i^{-1}A_i^l & 0 \\
\star & -P_i & \mathbb{I} \\
\star & \star & -\mathbb{M}_i
\end{bmatrix} < 0, l \in \mathcal{L}_i, i \in \mathcal{N},
\tag{24}
$$

where $\mathbb{I} = \underbrace{\left[I \cdots I \cdots I\right]}_{N-1}, \mathbb{M}_i = \text{diag} \underbrace{\left\{M_{1i} \cdots M_{ji,j\neq i} \cdots M_{Ni}\right\}}_{N-1}$.

Define

$$\Gamma_i 6 = \text{diag} \left\{G_i G_i \underbrace{I \cdots I \cdots I}_{N-1}\right\}, \bar{P}_i = G_i P_i G_i^T. \tag{25}$$

Now, by performing a congruence transformation to (24) by Γ_i, and considering the relation in (25), it is easy to see that the inequality in (19) implies $\dot{V}\left(x(t)\right) < 0$. Thus, this proof is completed.

NOTE: It is noted that the premise variables of the j-th subsystem maybe involve in the nonlinear interconnection $\bar{A}_{ij}^l$, which leads to the well-known "rule-explosion" problem (Liu & Li 2004) when increasing the number of subsystems. In the following, by using some bounding techniques, the premise variables in the j-th subsystem will be eliminated.

2.3 STABILITY ANALYSIS WITH REDUCED NUMBER OF LMI'S

In this section, by using some bounding techniques, the fuzzy rules generated by the interconnections to the j-th fuzzy subsystem will be eliminated. In that case, the derived results lead to a significant reduction in the number of LMIs.

2.3.1 Problem Formulation

First, the large-scale fuzzy interconnected system in (1) can be rewritten as

Plant Rule R_i^{ls} : IF

$$\varsigma_{i1}\left(t\right) \text{ is } F_{i1}^{l} \text{ and } \varsigma_{i2}\left(t\right) \text{ is } F_{i2}^{l} \text{ and } \cdots \text{ and } \varsigma_{ig}\left(t\right) \text{ is } F_{ig}^{l};$$

$$\varsigma_{11}\left(t\right) \text{ is } F_{11}^{s_1} \text{ and } \varsigma_{12}\left(t\right) \text{ is } F_{12}^{s_1} \text{ and } \cdots \text{ and } \varsigma_{1g}\left(t\right) \text{ is } F_{1g}^{s_1};$$

$$\vdots$$

$$\varsigma_{j1,j\neq i}\left(t\right) \text{ is } F_{j1,j\neq i}^{s_j} \text{ and } \varsigma_{j2,j\neq i}\left(t\right) \text{ is } F_{j2,j\neq i}^{s_j} \text{ and } \cdots \text{ and } \varsigma_{jg,j\neq i}\left(t\right) \text{ is } F_{jg,j\neq i}^{s_j}$$

$$\vdots$$

$$\varsigma_{N1}\left(t\right) \text{ is } F_{N1}^{s_N} \text{ and } \varsigma_{N2}\left(t\right) \text{ is } F_{N2}^{s_N} \text{ and } \cdots \text{ and } \varsigma_{Ng}\left(t\right) \text{ is } F_{Ng}^{s_N};$$

THEN

$$\dot{x}_i\left(t\right) = A_i^l x_i\left(t\right) + \sum_{j=1,j\neq i}^{N} \bar{A}_{ij}^{ls} x_j\left(t\right), \tag{26}$$

where $l \in \mathcal{L}_i := \left\{1,2,\cdots,r_i\right\}$,

$$s \in \left\{s_1 \cup s_2 \cdots \cup s_{j,j\neq i} \cdots \cup s_N\right\},$$

$$s_{j,j\neq i} \in \mathcal{L}_j := \left\{1,2,\cdots,r_j\right\},$$

$$i \in \mathcal{N} := \left\{1,2,\cdots,N\right\},$$

N is the number of the subsystems; R_i^{ls} is the fuzzy inference rule; $\left\{r_1,r_2,\cdots,r_j\right\}$ is the number of inference rules;

$$\left\{F_{1\varnothing}^l, F_{2\varnothing}^l, \cdots, F_{N\varnothing}^l, \varnothing = 1,2,\cdots,g\right\}$$

are fuzzy sets; $x_i\left(t\right) \in \mathfrak{R}^{n_{xi}}$ denotes the system state;

$$\varsigma_i\left(t\right) := \left[\varsigma_{i1}\left(t\right), \varsigma_{i2}\left(t\right), \cdots, \varsigma_{ig}\left(t\right)\right]$$

are the measurable variables; A_i^l is the l-th local model; $\bar{A}_{ij}^{ls}$ denotes the nonlinear interconnection of the i-th and j-th subsystems.

Define the inferred fuzzy set $F_i^l := \Pi_{\varnothing=1}^g F_{i\varnothing}^l$ and normalized membership function $\mu_i^l \left[\varsigma_i \left(t \right) \right]$, it yields

$$\mu_i^l \left[\varsigma_i \left(t \right) \right] := \frac{\Pi_{\varnothing=1}^g \mu_{i\varnothing}^l \left[\varsigma_{i\varnothing} \left(t \right) \right]}{\sum_{\varsigma=1}^{r_i} \Pi_{\varnothing=1}^g \mu_{i\varnothing}^\varsigma \left[\varsigma_{i\varnothing} \left(t \right) \right]} \geq 0, \sum_{l=1}^{r_i} \mu_i^l \left[\varsigma_i \left(t \right) \right] := 1, \tag{27}$$

where $\mu_{i\varnothing}^l \left[\varsigma_{i\varnothing} \left(t \right) \right]$ is the grade of membership of $\varsigma_{i\varnothing} \left(t \right)$ in $F_{i\varnothing}^l$. Here we will denote $\mu_i^l := \mu_i^l \left[\varsigma_i \left(t \right) \right]$ for brevity.

By fuzzy blending, the i-th global T-S fuzzy dynamic model is obtained by

$$\dot{x}_i \left(t \right) = A_i \left(\mu_i \right) x_i \left(t \right) + \sum_{j=1, j \neq i}^N \overline{A}_{ij} \left(\mu_i, \mu_j \right) x_j \left(t \right), \tag{28}$$

where

$$A_i \left(\mu_i \right) := \sum_{l=1}^{r_i} \mu_i^l A_i^l, \overline{A}_{ij} \left(\mu_i, \mu_j \right) := \sum_{l=1}^{r_i} \sum_{s=1}^{r_j} \mu_i^l \mu_j^s \overline{A}_{ij}^{ls}. \tag{29}$$

NOTE: It is noted that the premise variables of the j-th subsystem are involved in the nonlinear interconnection $\overline{A}_{ij}^l \left(\mu_j \right)$, which may lead to the well-known "rule-explosion" problem (Liu & Li 2004) when increasing the number of subsystems. In the following, by using some bounding techniques, the premise variables with the index term **s** in interconnections will be eliminated, which leads to a significant reduction in the number of LMIs.

Before moving on, we give the following lemma, which will be used to obtain the main results.

Lemma 2.3.1 Given the interconnected matrix A_{ij}^{ls} in the fuzzy system (26), and symmetric positive definite matrix $M_{ij} \in \mathfrak{R}^{n_{zi} \times n_{zi}}$, the following inequality holds:

$$\sum_{i=1}^{N}\sum_{j=1,j\neq i}^{N} \bar{A}_{ij}\left(\mu_i,\mu_j\right) M_{ij} \bar{A}_{ij}^{T}\left(\mu_i,\mu_j\right) \leq \sum_{i=1}^{N}\sum_{j=1,j\neq i}^{N}\sum_{l=1}^{r_i}\mu_i^l\left\{\sum_{s=1}^{r_j}\left[\bar{A}_{ij}^{ls}\right]M_{ij}\left[\bar{A}_{ij}^{ls}\right]^{T}\right\}. \tag{30}$$

Proof. Note that

$$\left[\bar{A}_{ij}^{ls}-\bar{A}_{ij}^{fg}\right]^{T} M_{ij}\left[\bar{A}_{ij}^{ls}-\bar{A}_{ij}^{fg}\right]\geq 0,$$
$$\{l,f\}\in\mathcal{L}_i,\{s,g\}\in\mathcal{L}_j,\{i,j\}\in\mathcal{N},j\neq i \tag{31}$$

which implies that

$$\left[\bar{A}_{ij}^{ls}\right]M_{ij}\left[\bar{A}_{ij}^{ls}\right]^{T}+\left[\bar{A}_{ij}^{fg}\right]M_{ij}\left[\bar{A}_{ij}^{fg}\right]^{T}\geq$$
$$\left[\bar{A}_{ij}^{ls}\right]M_{ij}\left[\bar{A}_{ij}^{fg}\right]^{T}+\left[\bar{A}_{ij}^{fg}\right]M_{ij}\left[\bar{A}_{ij}^{ls}\right]^{T}. \tag{32}$$

By taking the relations in (31) and (32), we have

$$\sum_{i=1}^{N}\sum_{j=1,j\neq i}^{N}\bar{A}_{ij}\left(\mu_i,\mu_j\right)M_{ij}\bar{A}_{ij}^{T}\left(\mu_i,\mu_j\right)$$
$$=\sum_{i=1}^{N}\sum_{j=1,j\neq i}^{N}\sum_{l=1}^{r_i}\sum_{f=1}^{r_i}\sum_{s=1}^{r_j}\sum_{g=1}^{r_j}\mu_i^l\mu_i^f\mu_j^s\mu_j^g\left[\bar{A}_{ij}^{ls}\right]M_{ij}\left[\bar{A}_{ij}^{fg}\right]^{T}$$
$$=\frac{1}{2}\sum_{i=1}^{N}\sum_{j=1,j\neq i}^{N}\sum_{l=1}^{r_i}\sum_{f=1}^{r_i}\sum_{s=1}^{r_j}\sum_{g=1}^{r_j}\mu_i^l\mu_i^f\mu_j^s\mu_j^g\left\{\begin{array}{c}\left[\bar{A}_{ij}^{ls}\right]M_{ij}\left[\bar{A}_{ij}^{fg}\right]^{T}\\+\left[\bar{A}_{ij}^{fg}\right]M_{ij}\left[\bar{A}_{ij}^{ls}\right]^{T}\end{array}\right\}$$
$$\leq\frac{1}{2}\sum_{i=1}^{N}\sum_{j=1,j\neq i}^{N}\sum_{l=1}^{r_i}\sum_{f=1}^{r_i}\sum_{s=1}^{r_j}\sum_{g=1}^{r_j}\mu_i^l\mu_i^f\mu_j^s\mu_j^g\left\{\begin{array}{c}\left[\bar{A}_{ij}^{ls}\right]M_{ij}\left[\bar{A}_{ij}^{ls}\right]^{T}\\+\left[\bar{A}_{ij}^{fg}\right]M_{ij}\left[\bar{A}_{ij}^{fg}\right]^{T}\end{array}\right\} \tag{33}$$
$$=\sum_{i=1}^{N}\sum_{j=1,j\neq i}^{N}\sum_{l=1}^{r_i}\sum_{s=1}^{r_j}\mu_i^l\mu_j^s\left[\bar{A}_{ij}^{ls}\right]M_{ij}\left[\bar{A}_{ij}^{ls}\right]^{T}$$
$$\leq\sum_{i=1}^{N}\sum_{j=1,j\neq i}^{N}\sum_{l=1}^{r_i}\mu_i^l\left\{\sum_{s=1}^{r_j}\left[\bar{A}_{ij}^{ls}\right]M_{ij}\left[\bar{A}_{ij}^{ls}\right]^{T}\right\}$$

Thus, completing this proof.

2.3.2 Main Results for Continuous-Time Systems

Based on the system in (28), the stability condition is stated as follows.

Theorem 2.3.1 The large-scale fuzzy interconnected system in (28) is asymptotically stable, if there exist symmetric positive definite matrices $\{Q, M_{ij}\} \in \mathfrak{R}^{n_{xi} \times n_{xi}}$, such that for all $l \in \mathcal{L}_i, j \neq i, \{i, j\} \in \mathcal{N}$, the following LMIs hold:

$$\left(\begin{bmatrix} \mathrm{Sym}\{A_i^l Q_i\} + \sum_{j=1, j \neq i}^{N} \left[\sum_{s=1}^{r_j} \overline{A}_{ij}^{ls} M_{ij} \left[\overline{A}_{ij}^{ls}\right]^T \right] & Q_i \mathbb{I} \\ \star & -\mathbb{M}_i \end{bmatrix}\right) < 0, \tag{34}$$

where $\mathbb{I} = \underbrace{\left[I \cdots I \cdots I\right]}_{N-1}, \mathbb{M}_i = \mathrm{diag} \underbrace{\left\{M_{1i} \cdots M_{ji, j \neq i} \cdots M_{Ni}\right\}}_{N-1}$.

Proof. Define the symmetric positive definite matrix $M_{ij} \in \mathfrak{R}^{n_{xi} \times n_{xi}}$., and take the relation in Lemma 2.3.1, it yields

$$\sum_{i=1}^{N} 2x_i^T(t) P_i \sum_{j=1, j \neq i}^{N} \overline{A}_{ij}\left(\mu_i, \mu_j\right) x_j(t)$$

$$\leq \sum_{i=1}^{N} \sum_{j=1, j \neq i}^{N} x_i^T(t) P_i \left[\overline{A}_{ij}\left(\mu_i, \mu_j\right)\right]$$

$$M_{ij}\left[\overline{A}_{ij}\left(\mu_i, \mu_j\right)\right]^T P_i x_i(t) + \sum_{i=1}^{N} \sum_{j=1, j \neq i}^{N} \left\{x_j^T(t) M_{ij}^{-1} x_j(t)\right\}$$

$$\leq \sum_{i=1}^{N} \sum_{j=1, j \neq i}^{N} x_i^T(t) P_i \left[\sum_{l=1}^{r_i} \mu_i^l \begin{bmatrix} \sum_{s=1}^{r_j} \mu_j^s \left[\overline{A}_{ij}^{ls}\right] \\ M_{ij}\left[\overline{A}_{ij}^{ls}\right]^T \end{bmatrix}\right] P_i x_i(t) + \sum_{i=1}^{N} \sum_{j=1, j \neq i}^{N} \left\{x_j^T(t) M_{ij}^{-1} x_j(t)\right\}$$

$$< \sum_{i=1}^{N} \sum_{j=1, j \neq i}^{N} x_i^T(t) P_i \left[\sum_{l=1}^{r_i} \mu_i^l \begin{bmatrix} \sum_{s=1}^{r_j} \left[\overline{A}_{ij}^{ls}\right] \\ M_{ij}\left[\overline{A}_{ij}^{ls}\right]^T \end{bmatrix}\right] P_i x_i(t) + \sum_{i=1}^{N} \sum_{j=1, j \neq i}^{N} \left\{x_i^T(t) M_{ji}^{-1} x_i(t)\right\}$$

$$\tag{35}$$

In that case, it is easy to see from (35) that the premise variable μ_j^s is eliminated. Now, by taking the time derivative of $V(x(t))$ along the trajectory of the fuzzy system in (28), and the relation in (35), one has

$$
\begin{aligned}
\dot{V}(x(t)) &= \sum_{i=1}^{N} 2x_i^T(t) P_i \left[A_i(\mu_i) x_i(t) + \sum_{j=1,j\neq i}^{N} \bar{A}_{ij}(\mu_i,\mu_j) x_j(t) \right] \\
&\leq \sum_{i=1}^{N} \sum_{l=1}^{r_i} \mu_i^l \left\{ x_i^T(t) \left[\operatorname{Sym}(P_i A_i^l) \right] x_i(t) \right\} \\
&\quad + \sum_{i=1}^{N} \sum_{j=1,j\neq i}^{N} x_i^T(t) P_i \left[\sum_{l=1}^{r_i} \mu_i^l \sum_{s=1}^{r_j} \bar{A}_{ij}^{ls} M_{ij} \left[\bar{A}_{ij}^{ls} \right]^T \right] P_i x_i(t) \\
&\quad + \sum_{i=1}^{N} \sum_{j=1,j\neq i}^{N} \left\{ x_i^T(t) M_{ji}^{-1} x_i(t) \right\}
\end{aligned}
\tag{36}
$$

It is easy to see from (36) that $\dot{V}(x(t)) < 0$ if for all $l \in \mathcal{L}_i, s \in \mathcal{L}_j, \ j \neq i, \{i,j\} \in \mathcal{N}$ the following inequalities hold,

$$
\operatorname{Sym}\{P_i A_i^l\} + \sum_{j=1,j\neq i}^{N} P_i \left[\sum_{s=1}^{r_j} \bar{A}_{ij}^{ls} M_{ij} \left[\bar{A}_{ij}^{ls} \right]^T \right] P_i + \sum_{j=1,j\neq i}^{N} M_{ji}^{-1} < 0.
\tag{37}
$$

By using Schur complement to (37), it yields

$$
\begin{bmatrix} \operatorname{Sym}\{P_i A_i^l\} + \sum_{j=1,j\neq i}^{N} P_i \left[\sum_{s=1}^{r_j} \bar{A}_{ij}^{ls} M_{ij} \left[\bar{A}_{ij}^{ls} \right]^T \right] P_i & \mathbb{I} \\ \star & -\mathbb{M}_i \end{bmatrix} < 0, l \in \mathcal{L}_i,
\tag{38}
$$

where $\mathbb{I} = \underbrace{[I \cdots I \cdots I]}_{N-1}, \mathbb{M}_i = \operatorname{diag}\left\{ \underbrace{M_{1i} \cdots M_{ji,j\neq i} \cdots M_{Ni}}_{N-1} \right\}.$

Define

$$
\Gamma_i := \operatorname{diag}\left\{ P_i^{-1} \underbrace{I \cdots I \cdots I}_{N-1} \right\}, Q_i = P_i^{-1}.
\tag{39}
$$

By performing a congruence transformation to (38) by Γ_i given in (39), it is easy to see that the inequalities in (34) imply $\dot{V}\big(x(t)\big)<0$. Thus, completing this proof.

NOTE: It is noted that, by using Lemma 2.3.1 and the inequality in (35), the premise variables with the index term s in interconnections are eliminated, which leads to a significant reduction in the number of LMIs. However, it will induce the conservatism to some extent. This technique allows us to make tradeoffs between the number of LMIs and conservatism.

2.3.3 Main Results for Discrete-time Systems

Consider the following fuzzy system

$$x_i\big(t+1\big)=A_i\big(\mu_i\big)x_i\big(t\big)+\sum_{j=1,j\neq i}^{N}\overline{A}_{ij}\big(\mu_i,\mu_j\big)x_j\big(t\big), \tag{40}$$

where

$$A_i\big(\mu\big):=\sum_{l=1}^{r_i}\mu_i^l A_i^l,\ \overline{A}_{ij}\big(\mu_i,\mu_j\big):=\sum_{l=1}^{r_i}\sum_{s=1}^{r_j}\mu_i^l\mu_j^s\overline{A}_{ij}^{ls}. \tag{41}$$

Based on the model in (40), we extend the stability result of continuous-time large-scale fuzzy interconnected systems to discrete-time case as below.

Theorem 2.3.2 The large-scale fuzzy interconnected system in (40) is asymptotically stable, if there exist symmetric positive definite matrices $\big\{\overline{P}_i,M_{ij}\big\}\in\mathfrak{R}^{n_{zi}\times n_{zi}}$, and matrices $G_i\in\mathfrak{R}^{n_{zi}\times n_{zi}}$, such that for all $l\in\mathcal{L}_i,j\neq i,\{i,j\}\in\mathcal{N}$, the following LMIs hold:

$$\begin{bmatrix}\overline{P}_i-G_i-G_i^T+\displaystyle\sum_{j=1,j\neq i}^{N}\left[\displaystyle\sum_{s=1}^{r_j}\overline{A}_{ij}^{ls}M_{ij}\left[\overline{A}_{ij}^{ls}\right]^T\right] & A_i^l G_i^T & 0 \\ \star & -\overline{P}_i & G_i\mathbb{I} \\ \star & \star & -\mathbb{M}_i\end{bmatrix}<0,l\in\mathcal{L}_i,i\in\mathcal{N}, \tag{42}$$

where $\mathbb{I} = \underbrace{\left[I \cdots I \cdots I \right]}_{N-1}, \mathbb{M}_i = \text{diag} \underbrace{\left\{ M_{1i} \cdots M_{ji, j \neq i} \cdots M_{Ni} \right\}}_{N-1}$.

Proof. Choose the Lyapunov functional as

$$
\begin{aligned}
V\left(x\left(t \right) \right) &= \sum_{i=1}^{N} V_i \left(x_i \left(t \right) \right) \\
&= \sum_{i=1}^{N} x_i^T \left(t \right) P_i x_i \left(t \right), i \in \mathcal{N}
\end{aligned}
\tag{43}
$$

where $P_i \in \mathfrak{R}^{n_{zi} \times n_{zi}}$ is a positive definite symmetric matrix.

Define $\Delta V \left(x \left(t \right) \right) = V \left(x \left(t+1 \right) \right) - V \left(x \left(t \right) \right)$, one has

$$
\Delta V \left(x \left(t \right) \right) = \sum_{i=1}^{N} \left\{ x_i^T \left(t+1 \right) P_i x_i \left(t+1 \right) - x_i^T \left(t \right) P_i x_i \left(t \right) \right\}.
\tag{44}
$$

In addition, we define the matrix $G_i^{-1} \in \mathfrak{R}^{n_{zi} \times n_{zi}}$ and symmetric positive definite matrix $M_{ij} \in \mathfrak{R}^{n_{zi} \times n_{zi}}$, and take the relation in Lemma 2.3.1, one has

$$
\begin{aligned}
0 &= \sum_{i=1}^{N} \left\{ 2 x_i^T \left(t+1 \right) G_i^{-1} \left[-x_i \left(t+1 \right) + A_i \left(\mu_i \right) x_i \left(t \right) + \sum_{j=1, j \neq i}^{N} \bar{A}_{ij} \left(\mu_i, \mu_j \right) x_j \left(t \right) \right] \right\} \\
&\leq \sum_{i=1}^{N} \left\{ 2 x_i^T \left(t+1 \right) G_i^{-1} \left[-x_i \left(t+1 \right) + A_i \left(\mu_i \right) x_i \left(t \right) \right] \right\} \\
&\quad + \sum_{i=1}^{N} \left\{ x_i^T \left(t+1 \right) G_i^{-1} \left\{ \sum_{j=1, j \neq i}^{N} \sum_{l=1}^{r_i} \mu_i^l \sum_{s=1}^{r_j} \mu_j^s \left[\bar{A}_{ij}^{ls} \right] M_{ij} \left[\bar{A}_{ij}^{ls} \right]^T \right\} G_i^{-T} x_i \left(t+1 \right) \right\} \\
&\quad + \sum_{i=1}^{N} \sum_{j=1, j \neq i}^{N} x_j^T \left(t \right) M_{ij}^{-1} x_j \left(t \right) \\
&< \sum_{i=1}^{N} \left\{ 2 x_i^T \left(t+1 \right) G_i^{-1} \left[-x_i \left(t+1 \right) + A_i \left(\mu_i \right) x_i \left(t \right) \right] \right\} \\
&\quad + \sum_{i=1}^{N} \left\{ x_i^T \left(t+1 \right) G_i^{-1} \left\{ \sum_{j=1, j \neq i}^{N} \sum_{l=1}^{r_i} \mu_i^l \sum_{s=1}^{r_j} \left[\bar{A}_{ij}^{ls} \right] M_{ij} \left[\bar{A}_{ij}^{ls} \right]^T \right\} G_i^{-T} x_i \left(t+1 \right) \right\} \\
&\quad + \sum_{i=1}^{N} \sum_{j=1, j \neq i}^{N} x_i^T \left(t \right) M_{ji}^{-1} x_i \left(t \right)
\end{aligned}
\tag{45}
$$

By taking the relations in (44) and (45), and extracting the fuzzy premise variables, the following inequalities imply that $\Delta V\left(x\left(t\right)\right) < 0$ holds,

$$
\begin{bmatrix}
P_i - G_i^{-1} - G_i^{-T} + \displaystyle\sum_{j=1,j\neq i}^{N} G_i^{-1}\left[\sum_{s=1}^{r_j}\bar{A}_{ij}^{ls}M_{ij}\left[\bar{A}_{ij}^{ls}\right]^T\right]G_i^{-T} & G_i^{-1}A_i^l \\
\star & -P_i + \displaystyle\sum_{j=1,j\neq i}^{N} M_{ji}^{-1}
\end{bmatrix} < 0
$$
(46)

with $l \in \mathcal{L}_i, s \in \mathcal{L}_j, i \in \mathcal{N}$.

By using Schur complement to (46), it yields

$$
\begin{bmatrix}
P_i - G_i^{-1} - G_i^{-T} + \displaystyle\sum_{j=1,j\neq i}^{N} G_i^{-1}\left[\sum_{s=1}^{r_j}\bar{A}_{ij}^{ls}M_{ij}\left[\bar{A}_{ij}^{ls}\right]^T\right]G_i^{-T} & G_i^{-1}A_i^l & 0 \\
\star & -P_i & \mathbb{I} \\
\star & \star & -\mathbb{M}_i
\end{bmatrix} < 0
$$
(47)

with $l \in \mathcal{L}_i, i \in \mathcal{N}, \mathbb{I} = \underbrace{\left[I \cdots I \cdots I\right]}_{N-1}, \mathbb{M}_i = \mathrm{diag}\underbrace{\left\{M_{1i} \cdots M_{ji,j\neq i} \cdots M_{Ni}\right\}}_{N-1}$.

Define

$$
\Gamma_i 6 = \mathrm{diag}\left\{G_i\, G_i\, \underbrace{I \cdots I \cdots I}_{N-1}\right\}, \bar{P}_i = G_i P_i G_i^T.
$$
(48)

By performing a congruence transformation to (47) by Γ_i, and taking the relation in (48), it is easy to see that the inequalities in (42) imply $\Delta V\left(x\left(t\right)\right) < 0$. Thus, completing this proof.

2.4 ILLUSTRATIVE EXAMPLES

This chapter has shown theoretically some stability results on large-scale fuzzy interconnected systems, including both the continuous-time and discrete-time cases. In this section, we use several examples to further verify the derived results. The solver used in the section is the LMI Toolbox in Matlab.

Example 1

Consider a continuous-time large-scale fuzzy interconnected system with three subsystems as below:

Plant Rule R_i^{11}: IF $\varsigma_{i1}(t)$ is F_{i1}^1 and $\varsigma_{j2}(t)$ is F_{j2}^1 and $\varsigma_{k3}(t)$ is F_{k3}^1, THEN

$$\dot{x}_i(t) = A_i^1 x_i(t) + \bar{A}_{ij,j\neq i}^{11} x_j(t) + \bar{A}_{ik,k\neq i,k\neq j}^{11} x_k(t), i \in \{1,2,3\}$$

Plant Rule R_i^{12}: IF $\varsigma_{i1}(t)$ is F_{i1}^1 and $\varsigma_{j2}(t)$ is F_{j2}^2 and $\varsigma_{k3}(t)$ is F_{k3}^1, THEN

$$\dot{x}_i(t) = A_i^1 x_i(t) + \bar{A}_{ij,j\neq i}^{12} x_j(t) + \bar{A}_{ik,k\neq i,k\neq j}^{11} x_k(t), i \in \{1,2,3\}$$

Plant Rule R_i^{13}: IF $\varsigma_{i1}(t)$ is F_{i1}^1 and $\varsigma_{j2}(t)$ is F_{j2}^1 and $\varsigma_{k3}(t)$ is F_{k3}^2, THEN

$$\dot{x}_i(t) = A_i^1 x_i(t) + \bar{A}_{ij,j\neq i}^{11} x_j(t) + \bar{A}_{ik,k\neq i,k\neq j}^{12} x_k(t), i \in \{1,2,3\}$$

Plant Rule R_i^{14}: IF $\varsigma_{i1}(t)$ is F_{i1}^1 and $\varsigma_{j2}(t)$ is F_{j2}^2 and $\varsigma_{k3}(t)$ is F_{k3}^2, THEN

$$\dot{x}_i(t) = A_i^1 x_i(t) + \bar{A}_{ij,j\neq i}^{12} x_j(t) + \bar{A}_{ik,k\neq i,k\neq j}^{12} x_k(t), i \in \{1,2,3\}$$

Plant Rule R_i^{21}: IF $\varsigma_{i1}(t)$ is F_{i1}^2 and $\varsigma_{j2}(t)$ is F_{j2}^1 and $\varsigma_{k3}(t)$ is F_{k3}^1, THEN

$$\dot{x}_i(t) = A_i^2 x_i(t) + \bar{A}_{ij,j\neq i}^{11} x_j(t) + \bar{A}_{ik,k\neq i,k\neq j}^{11} x_k(t), i \in \{1,2,3\}$$

Plant Rule R_i^{22}: IF $\varsigma_{i1}(t)$ is F_{i1}^2 and $\varsigma_{j2}(t)$ is F_{j2}^2 and $\varsigma_{k3}(t)$ is F_{k3}^1, THEN

$$\dot{x}_i(t) = A_i^2 x_i(t) + \bar{A}_{ij,j\neq i}^{12} x_j(t) + \bar{A}_{ik,k\neq i,k\neq j}^{11} x_k(t), i \in \{1,2,3\}$$

Plant Rule R_i^{23}: IF $\varsigma_{i1}(t)$ is F_{i1}^2 and $\varsigma_{j2}(t)$ is F_{j2}^1 and $\varsigma_{k3}(t)$ is F_{k3}^2, THEN

$$\dot{x}_i(t) = A_i^2 x_i(t) + \bar{A}_{ij,j\neq i}^{11} x_j(t) + \bar{A}_{ik,k\neq i,k\neq j}^{12} x_k(t), i \in \{1,2,3\}$$

Plant Rule R_i^{24}: IF $\varsigma_{i1}(t)$ is F_{i1}^2 and $\varsigma_{j2}(t)$ is F_{j2}^2 and $\varsigma_{k3}(t)$ is F_{k3}^2, THEN

$$\dot{x}_i(t) = A_i^2 x_i(t) + \overline{A}_{ij,j\neq i}^{12} x_j(t) + \overline{A}_{ik,k\neq i,k\neq j}^{12} x_k(t), i \in \{1,2,3\}$$

where

$$A_1^1 = \begin{bmatrix} -2.1 & 0.4 \\ 0 & -3.3 \end{bmatrix}, A_1^2 = \begin{bmatrix} -2.5 & 0.2 \\ 0 & -2.8 \end{bmatrix}$$

$$A_{12}^{11} = \begin{bmatrix} 0.7 & 0 \\ 0 & 0.2 \end{bmatrix}, A_{12}^{12} = \begin{bmatrix} 0.6 & 0 \\ 0 & 0.2 \end{bmatrix}, A_{12}^{21} = \begin{bmatrix} 0.7 & 0 \\ 0 & 0.1 \end{bmatrix}, A_{12}^{22} = \begin{bmatrix} 0.6 & 0 \\ 0 & 0.3 \end{bmatrix}$$

$$A_{13}^{11} = \begin{bmatrix} 0.1 & 0 \\ 0 & 0.4 \end{bmatrix}, A_{13}^{12} = \begin{bmatrix} 0.2 & 0 \\ 0 & 0.4 \end{bmatrix}, A_{13}^{21} = \begin{bmatrix} 0.1 & 0 \\ 0 & 0.5 \end{bmatrix}, A_{13}^{22} = \begin{bmatrix} 0.2 & 0 \\ 0 & 0.5 \end{bmatrix}$$

for the subsystem 1, and

$$A_2^1 = \begin{bmatrix} -2.6 & 0.6 \\ 0 & -2.2 \end{bmatrix}, A_2^2 = \begin{bmatrix} -2.8 & 0.3 \\ 0 & -2.2 \end{bmatrix},$$

$$A_{21}^{11} = \begin{bmatrix} 0.4 & 0 \\ 0 & 0.1 \end{bmatrix}, A_{21}^{12} = \begin{bmatrix} 0.6 & 0 \\ 0 & 0.3 \end{bmatrix}, A_{21}^{21} = \begin{bmatrix} 0.5 & 0 \\ 0 & 0.2 \end{bmatrix}, A_{21}^{22} = \begin{bmatrix} 0.6 & 0 \\ 0 & 0.4 \end{bmatrix},$$

$$A_{23}^{11} = \begin{bmatrix} 0.1 & 0 \\ 0 & 0.3 \end{bmatrix}, A_{23}^{12} = \begin{bmatrix} 0.3 & 0 \\ 0 & 0.4 \end{bmatrix}, A_{23}^{21} = \begin{bmatrix} 0.2 & 0 \\ 0 & 0.5 \end{bmatrix}, A_{23}^{22} = \begin{bmatrix} 0.2 & 0 \\ 0 & 0.4 \end{bmatrix},$$

for the subsystem 2, and

$$A_3^1 = \begin{bmatrix} -1.9 & 0.5 \\ 0 & -2.6 \end{bmatrix}, A_3^2 = \begin{bmatrix} -2.1 & 0.1 \\ 0 & -2.3 \end{bmatrix},$$

$$A_{31}^{11} = \begin{bmatrix} 0.4 & 0 \\ 0 & 0.5 \end{bmatrix}, A_{31}^{12} = \begin{bmatrix} 0.2 & 0 \\ 0 & 0.6 \end{bmatrix}, A_{31}^{21} = \begin{bmatrix} 0.3 & 0 \\ 0 & 0.7 \end{bmatrix}, A_{31}^{22} = \begin{bmatrix} 0.2 & 0 \\ 0 & 0.8 \end{bmatrix},$$

$$A_{32}^{11} = \begin{bmatrix} 0.2 & 0 \\ 0 & 0.3 \end{bmatrix}, A_{32}^{12} = \begin{bmatrix} 0.4 & 0 \\ 0 & 0.2 \end{bmatrix}, A_{32}^{21} = \begin{bmatrix} 0.1 & 0 \\ 0 & 0.4 \end{bmatrix}, A_{32}^{22} = \begin{bmatrix} 0.3 & 0 \\ 0 & 0.5 \end{bmatrix},$$

for the subsystem 3.

Here, by using Theorem 2.2.1, we find a feasible solution to the stability problem for the considered system, and the number of LMIs is 60. However, by using Theorem 2.3.1, a feasible solution to the stability problem for the above system is also obtained, but the number of LMIs is 9.

Example 2

Consider a discrete-time large-scale fuzzy interconnected system with the parameters as below:

$$A_1^1 = \begin{bmatrix} 0.8 & 0 \\ 0.05 & 0.7 \end{bmatrix}, A_1^2 = \begin{bmatrix} 0.8 & 0 \\ 0.09 & 0.7 \end{bmatrix}$$

$$A_{12}^{11} = \begin{bmatrix} 0.04 & 0 \\ 0.02 & 0.07 \end{bmatrix}, A_{12}^{12} = \begin{bmatrix} 0.03 & 0 \\ 0.01 & 0.08 \end{bmatrix}, A_{12}^{21} = \begin{bmatrix} 0.05 & 0 \\ 0.01 & 0.06 \end{bmatrix}, A_{12}^{22} = \begin{bmatrix} 0.07 & 0 \\ 0.03 & 0.05 \end{bmatrix}$$

$$A_{13}^{11} = \begin{bmatrix} 0.04 & 0 \\ 0.04 & 0.03 \end{bmatrix}, A_{13}^{12} = \begin{bmatrix} 0.03 & 0 \\ 0.03 & 0.04 \end{bmatrix}, A_{13}^{21} = \begin{bmatrix} 0.04 & 0 \\ 0.02 & 0.05 \end{bmatrix}, A_{13}^{22} = \begin{bmatrix} 0.05 & 0 \\ 0.03 & 0.02 \end{bmatrix}$$

for the subsystem 1, and

$$A_2^1 = \begin{bmatrix} 0.8 & 0 \\ 0.05 & 0.7 \end{bmatrix}, A_2^2 = \begin{bmatrix} 0.6 & 0 \\ 0.09 & 0.7 \end{bmatrix}$$

$$A_{21}^{11} = \begin{bmatrix} 0.04 & 0 \\ 0.02 & 0.05 \end{bmatrix}, A_{21}^{12} = \begin{bmatrix} 0.05 & 0 \\ 0.01 & 0.06 \end{bmatrix}, A_{21}^{21} = \begin{bmatrix} 0.04 & 0 \\ 0.05 & 0.04 \end{bmatrix}, A_{21}^{22} = \begin{bmatrix} 0.05 & 0 \\ 0.06 & 0.02 \end{bmatrix}$$

$$A_{23}^{11} = \begin{bmatrix} 0.03 & 0 \\ 0.05 & 0.03 \end{bmatrix}, A_{23}^{12} = \begin{bmatrix} 0.05 & 0 \\ 0.04 & 0.05 \end{bmatrix}, A_{23}^{21} = \begin{bmatrix} 0.04 & 0 \\ 0.02 & 0.04 \end{bmatrix}, A_{23}^{22} = \begin{bmatrix} 0.06 & 0 \\ 0.03 & 0.03 \end{bmatrix}$$

for the subsystem 2, and

$$A_3^1 = \begin{bmatrix} 0.7 & 0 \\ 0.05 & 0.6 \end{bmatrix}, A_3^2 = \begin{bmatrix} 0.8 & 0 \\ 0.09 & 0.6 \end{bmatrix}$$

$$A_{31}^{11} = \begin{bmatrix} 0.02 & 0 \\ 0.02 & 0.04 \end{bmatrix}, A_{31}^{12} = \begin{bmatrix} 0.03 & 0 \\ 0.03 & 0.02 \end{bmatrix}, A_{31}^{21} = \begin{bmatrix} 0.04 & 0 \\ 0.01 & 0.02 \end{bmatrix}, A_{31}^{22} = \begin{bmatrix} 0.03 & 0 \\ 0.02 & 0.03 \end{bmatrix}$$

$$A_{32}^{11} = \begin{bmatrix} 0.03 & 0 \\ 0.02 & 0.04 \end{bmatrix}, A_{32}^{12} = \begin{bmatrix} 0.02 & 0 \\ 0.03 & 0.05 \end{bmatrix}, A_{32}^{21} = \begin{bmatrix} 0.01 & 0 \\ 0.04 & 0.04 \end{bmatrix}, A_{32}^{22} = \begin{bmatrix} 0.04 & 0 \\ 0.01 & 0.03 \end{bmatrix}$$

for the subsystem 3.

In this simulation, by using Theorem 2.3.1 we find a feasible solution to the stability problem for the above system, and the number of LMIs is 60. However, by using Theorem 2.3.2, a feasible solution to the stability problem for the considered system is also obtained, and the number of LMIs is 9.

2.5 CONCLUSION

The stability problem for large-scale T-S fuzzy interconnected systems has been studied in this chapter. Various LMI-based stability conditions have been established. Also, by using some bounding techniques, we further presented a reduction in the number of LMI-based stability conditions. Several examples have been given to illustrate the effectiveness of the proposed methods.

REFERENCES

Chang, W., & Wang, W. (2015). H∞ fuzzy control synthesis for a large-scale system with a reduced Number of LMIs. *IEEE Transactions on Fuzzy Systems*, *23*(4), 1197–1210. doi:10.1109/TFUZZ.2014.2347995

Hsiao, F., & Hwang, J. (2002). Stability analysis of fuzzy large-scale systems. *IEEE Transactions on Systems, Man, and Cybernetics. Part B, Cybernetics*, *32*(1), 122–126. doi:10.1109/3477.979967 PMID:18238111

Lin, C., Wang, Q., & Lee, T. (2006). Less conservative stability conditions for fuzzy large-scale systems with time delays. *Chaos, Solitons, and Fractals*, *29*(5), 1147–1154. doi:10.1016/j.chaos.2005.08.077

Liu, P., & Li, H. (2004). *Fuzzy Neural Network Theory and Application* (1st ed.). USA: World Scientific. doi:10.1142/5493

Wang, W., & Luoh, L. (2004). Stability and stabilization of fuzzy large-scale systems. *IEEE Transactions on Fuzzy Systems*, *12*(3), 309–315. doi:10.1109/TFUZZ.2004.825975

Zhang, H., & Feng, G. (2008). Stability analysis and controller design of discrete-time fuzzy large-scale systems based on piecewise Lyapunov functions. *IEEE Transactions on Systems, Man, and Cybernetics. Part B, Cybernetics*, *38*(5), 1390–1401. doi:10.1109/TSMCB.2008.927267 PMID:18784019

Zhang, H., Li, C., & Liao, X. (2005). Stability analysis and H_∞ controller design of fuzzy large-scale systems based on piecewise Lyapunov functions. *IEEE Transactions on Systems, Man, and Cybernetics. Part B, Cybernetics*, *36*(3), 685–698. doi:10.1109/TSMCB.2005.860133 PMID:16761821

Chapter 3

Stabilization of Large–Scale Fuzzy Interconnected System

ABSTRACT

The chapter addresses the stabilization problem for large-scale fuzzy interconnected systems. Our aim is to present the design results on both the state feedback and static-output feedback (SOF) stabilizing fuzzy controllers. Firstly, by using some bounding techniques, the reduced number of LMIs to the decentralized state feedback controller design will be derived. Then, by using some matrix transformation techniques and singular system approach, we will also derive some design results on decentralized SOF control in terms of LMIs. Moreover, the proposed design results on the decentralized control will be extended to address the distributed control problem. Finally, several examples are given to illustrate the use of corresponding results.

3.1 INTRODUCTION

It is well-known that usually only the measured output information, rather than the full state information, is available for feedback control of systems. Thus, in practical applications the SOF controller is more realistic and useful than the state feedback one. Moreover, dynamic-output-feedback (DOF) control problem can also be reformulated as the SOF control framework (He, Wu, & Liu, 2008). Since the most existing results on the SOF controller design are bilinear matrix inequalities (BMIs), for which the proposed methods are not convenient to facilitate the SOF controller design (Qiu et al., 2016). Recently, there has presented some valuable results on the SOF controller design for

DOI: 10.4018/978-1-5225-2385-7.ch003

T-S fuzzy dynamic systems in terms of LMIs. However, these results given in (Lo & Lin, 2003; Dong & Yang, 2007; Kau et al., 2007; Qiu, Feng, & Gao, 2010) are restrictive, and maybe lead to inefficient implementations in practice, due to the fact that they impose some constraints on the systematic input or output matrices. For example, in (Lo & Lin, 2003; Dong & Yang, 2007) it is assumed that output matrices of all local linear models are common. In (Kau, Lee, Yang et al., 2007), the restrictive assumption that the output matrices are common is relaxed, but the output matrices must satisfy some matrix-equality constraints. It seems that the problem of SOF controller design for T-S fuzzy dynamic systems can be solved efficiently via LMIs in (Qiu, Feng, & Gao, 2010). Nevertheless, the proposed approaches could not deal with the case when uncertainties emerge in the system input and output matrices.

In this chapter, we will present some design results on the state-feedback control for large-scale fuzzy interconnected systems. Moreover, by virtue of matrix transformations and singular system approaches, several design results on the SOF control will also be derived in terms of LMIs.

3.2 DECENTRALIZED STABILIZATION DESIGN

In this section, we will study decentralized stabilization for large-scale T-S fuzzy interconnected systems.

3.2.1 Problem Formulation

Consider a continuous-time large-scale nonlinear interconnected system containing N subsystems with interconnections, where the i-th nonlinear subsystem is represented by the following T-S fuzzy model:

Plant Rule R_i^{ls} : IF

$$\varsigma_{i1}\left(t\right) \text{ is } F_{i1}^l \text{ and } \varsigma_{i2}\left(t\right) \text{ is } F_{i2}^l \text{ and } \cdots \text{ and } \varsigma_{ig}\left(t\right) \text{ is } F_{ig}^l;$$
$$\varsigma_{11}\left(t\right) \text{ is } F_{11}^{s_1} \text{ and } \varsigma_{12}\left(t\right) \text{ is } F_{12}^{s_1} \text{ and } \cdots \text{ and } \varsigma_{1g}\left(t\right) \text{ is } F_{1g}^{s_1};$$
$$\vdots$$
$$\varsigma_{j1,j\neq i}\left(t\right) \text{ is } F_{j1,j\neq i}^{s_j} \text{ and } \varsigma_{j2,j\neq i}\left(t\right) \text{ is } F_{j2,j\neq i}^{s_j} \text{ and } \cdots \text{ and } \varsigma_{jg,j\neq i}\left(t\right) \text{ is } F_{jg,j\neq i}^{s_j}$$
$$\vdots$$
$$\varsigma_{N1}\left(t\right) \text{ is } F_{N1}^{s_N} \text{ and } \varsigma_{N2}\left(t\right) \text{ is } F_{N2}^{s_N} \text{ and } \cdots \text{ and } \varsigma_{Ng}\left(t\right) \text{ is } F_{Ng}^{s_N};$$

THEN

$$\dot{x}_i(t) = A_i^l x_i(t) + B_i^l u_i(t) + \sum_{j=1, j \neq i}^{N} \overline{A}_{ij}^{ls} x_j(t), \tag{1}$$

where
$l \in \mathcal{L}_i := \{1, 2, \cdots, r_i\}, s \in \{s_1 \cup s_2 \cdots \cup s_{j, j \neq i} \cdots \cup s_N\}, s_{j, j \neq i} \in \mathcal{L}_j := \{1, 2, \cdots, r_j\},$
$i \in \mathcal{N} := \{1, 2, \cdots, N\}$, N is the number of the subsystems; R_i^{ls} is the fuzzy inference rule; $\{r_1, r_2, \cdots, r_j\}$ is the number of inference rules; $\{F_{1\varnothing}^l, F_{2\varnothing}^l, \cdots, F_{N\varnothing}^l, \varnothing = 1, 2, \cdots, g\}$ are fuzzy sets; $x_i(t) \in \mathfrak{R}^{n_{xi}}$ and $u_i(t) \in \mathfrak{R}^{n_{ui}}$ denotes the system state and control input, respectively; $\varsigma_i(t) := [\varsigma_{i1}(t), \varsigma_{i2}(t), \cdots, \varsigma_{ig}(t)]$ are the measurable variables; A_i^l is the l-th local model; $\overline{A}_{ij}^{ls}$ denotes the nonlinear interconnection of the i-th and j-th subsystems.

Define the inferred fuzzy set $\mathrm{F}_i^l := \Pi_{\varnothing=1}^g \mathrm{F}_{i\varnothing}^l$ and normalized membership function $\mu_i^l[\varsigma_i(t)]$, it yields

$$\mu_i^l[\varsigma_i(t)] := \frac{\Pi_{\varnothing=1}^g \mu_{i\varnothing}^l[\varsigma_{i\varnothing}(t)]}{\sum_{\varsigma=1}^{r_i} \Pi_{\varnothing=1}^g \mu_{i\varnothing}^\varsigma[\varsigma_{i\varnothing}(t)]} \geq 0, \mu_i^l[\varsigma_i(t)] := 1, \tag{2}$$

where we will denote $\mu_{i1} := \mu_{i1}[\varsigma_i(t)]$ for brevity, and $\mu_{i\varnothing}^l[\varsigma_{i\varnothing}(t)]$ is the grade of membership of $\varsigma_{i\varnothing}(t)$ in $\mathrm{F}_{i\varnothing}^l$.

By fuzzy blending, the i-th global T-S fuzzy dynamic model is obtained by

$$x_i(t) = A_i(\mu_i) x_i(t) + B_i(\mu_i) u_i(t) + \sum_{j=1, j \neq i}^{N} \overline{A}_{ij}(\mu_i, \mu_j) x_j(t), \tag{3}$$

where

$$A_i(\mu_i) := \sum_{l=1}^{r_i} \mu_i^l A_i^l, B_i(\mu_i) := \sum_{l=1}^{r_i} \mu_i^l B_i^l, \overline{A}_{ij}(\mu_i, \mu_j) := \sum_{l=1}^{r_i} \sum_{s=1}^{r_i} \mu_i^l \mu_i^s \overline{A}_{ij}^{ls}. \tag{4}$$

A decentralized fuzzy controller is given by:

Plant Rule R_i^l: IF $\varsigma_{i1}(t)$ is F_{i1}^l and $\varsigma_{i2}(t)$ is F_{i2}^l and $\cdots$ and $\varsigma_{ig}(t)$ is F_{ig}^l,
   THEN

$$u_i(t) = K_i^l x_i(t), l \in \mathcal{L}_i \tag{5}$$

where $K_i^l \in \mathfrak{R}^{n_{ui} \times z_i}$ is controller gains to be determined.

Similarly, the overall controller can be given by

$$u_i(t) = K_i(\mu_i) x_i(t), i \in \mathcal{N} \tag{6}$$

where $K_i(\mu_i) := \sum_{l=1}^{r_i} \mu_i^l K_i^l$.

Combined with the fuzzy system in (3) and the fuzzy controller in (6), the closed-loop fuzzy control system can be given by

$$\dot{x}_i(t) = A_i(\mu_i) x_i(t) + B_i(\mu_i) K_i(\mu_i) x_i(t) + \sum_{j=1, j \neq i}^{N} \bar{A}_{ij}(\mu_i, \mu_j) x_j(t) \tag{7}$$

In this section, our aim is to design a decentralized fuzzy controller (6), such that the closed-loop fuzzy control system is asymptotically stable.

3.2.2 State Feedback Stabilizing for Continuous-Time Systems

Similar to the processing in Theorem 2.3.1, we can directly obtain the design result on decentralized state feedback fuzzy controller as blew.

Theorem 3.2.1 Given the large-scale T-S fuzzy interconnected system in (3) and a state-feedback fuzzy controller in the form of (6), then the closed-loop fuzzy control system in (7) is asymptotically stable, if there exist symmetric positive definite matrices $\{Q, M_{ij}\} \in \mathfrak{R}^{n_{zi} \times n_{zi}}$, and matrix $\bar{K}_i^f \in \mathfrak{R}^{n_{ui} \times n_{zi}}$, such that for all $\{l, f\} \in \mathcal{L}_i, j \neq i, \{i, j\} \in \mathcal{N}$, the following LMIs hold:

$$\Omega_i^{ll} < 0, l \in \mathcal{L}_i \tag{8}$$

$$\Omega_i^{lf} + \Omega_i^{fl} < 0, l \leq f \tag{9}$$

where

$$\left\{ \begin{array}{l} \Omega_i^{lf} = \begin{bmatrix} \mathrm{Sym}\left\{A_i^l Q_i + B_i^l \bar{K}_i^f\right\} + \displaystyle\sum_{j=1,j\neq i}^{N}\left[\sum_{s=1}^{r_j}\bar{A}_{ij}^{ls}M_{ij}\left[\bar{A}_{ij}^{ls}\right]^T\right] & Q_i \mathbb{I} \\ \star & -\mathbb{M}_i \end{bmatrix}, \\ \mathbb{I} = \underbrace{\left[\mathrm{I}\cdots\mathrm{I}\cdots\mathrm{I}\right]}_{N-1}, \mathbb{M}_i = \mathrm{diag}\underbrace{\left\{M_{1i}\cdots M_{ji,j\neq i}\cdots M_{Ni}\right\}}_{N-1} \end{array} \right. \tag{10}$$

In that case, the decentralized state feedback fuzzy controller gains can be obtained as

$$\bar{K}_i^f = \bar{K}_i^f Q_i^{-1}, f \in \mathcal{L}_i, i \in \mathcal{N}. \tag{11}$$

3.2.3 State Feedback Stabilizing for Discrete-time Systems

Consider a discrete-time closed-loop fuzzy control system

$$x_i\left(t+1\right) = A_i\left(\mu_i\right)x_i\left(t\right) + B_i\left(\mu_i\right)K_i\left(\mu_i\right)x_i\left(t\right) + \sum_{j=1,j\neq i}^{N}\bar{A}_{ij}\left(\mu_i,\mu_j\right)x_j\left(t\right). \tag{12}$$

Similar to a processing in Theorem 2.4.1, we can directly obtain the following design result.

Theorem 3.2.2 Given a discrete-time large-scale T-S fuzzy interconnected system and a state-feedback fuzzy controller, then the resulting closed-loop fuzzy control system in (12) is asymptotically stable, if there exist symmetric positive definite matrices $\left\{\bar{P}_i, M_{ij}\right\} \in \mathfrak{R}^{n_{xi}\times n_{xi}}$, and matrices $G_i \in \mathfrak{R}^{n_{xi}\times n_{xi}}$, $\bar{K}_i^f \in \mathfrak{R}^{n_{ui}\times n_{xi}}$, such that for all $\left\{l,f\right\} \in \mathcal{L}_i, j \neq i, \left\{i,j\right\} \in \mathcal{N}$, the following LMIs hold:

$$\Omega_i^{ll} < 0, l \in \mathcal{L}_i \tag{13}$$

$$\Omega_i^{lf} + \Omega_i^{fl} < 0, l \leq f \tag{14}$$

where

$$\begin{cases} \Omega_i^{ls} = \begin{bmatrix} \bar{P}_i - G_i - G_i^T + \sum\limits_{j=1, j\neq i}^{N} \left[\sum\limits_{s=1}^{r_j} \bar{A}_{ij}^{ls} M_{ij} \left[\bar{A}_{ij}^{ls}\right]^T \right] & A_i^l G_i^T + B_i^l \bar{K}_i^f & 0 \\ \star & -\bar{P}_i & G_i \mathbb{I} \\ \star & \star & -\mathbb{M}_i \end{bmatrix}, \\ \mathbb{I} = \underbrace{\left[\mathrm{I} \cdots \mathrm{I} \cdots \mathrm{I} \right]}_{N-1}, \mathbb{M}_i = \mathrm{diag} \underbrace{\left\{ M_{1i} \cdots M_{ji, j\neq i} \cdots M_{Ni} \right\}}_{N-1} \end{cases} \tag{15}$$

In that case, the state-feedback fuzzy controller gains can be obtained as

$$K_i^f = \bar{K}_i^f G_i^{-T}, f \in \mathcal{L}_i, i \in \mathcal{N}. \tag{16}$$

3.2.4 Output Feedback Stabilizing for Continuous-Time Systems

This subsection will give some design results on decentralized output-feedback controller for large-scale T-S fuzzy interconnected systems. First, consider a continuous-time large-scale T-S fuzzy system,

$$\begin{cases} x_i(t) = A_i(\mu_i) x_i(t) + B_i(\mu_i) u_i(t) + \sum\limits_{j=1, j\neq i}^{N} \bar{A}_{ij}(\mu_i, \mu_j) x_j(t), \\ y_i(t) = C_i(\mu_i) x_i(t), l \in \mathcal{L}_i := \{1, 2, \cdots, r_i\}. \end{cases} \tag{17}$$

Then, a decentralized SOF fuzzy controller can be given by

$$u_i(t) = K_i(\mu_i) y_i(t), i \in \mathcal{N} \tag{18}$$

where $K_i(\mu_i) := \sum\limits_{l=1}^{r_i} \mu_i^l K_i^l$

Combined with the fuzzy system in (17) and the controller in (18), the closed-loop fuzzy control system can be given by

$$\dot{x}_i(t) = A_i(\mu_i)x_i(t) + B_i(\mu_i)K_i(\mu_i)C_i(\mu_i)x_i(t) + \sum_{j=1,j\neq i}^{N} \bar{A}_{ij}(\mu_i,\mu_j)x_j(t)$$

(19)

Since the most existing results of the SOF controller design are bilinear matrix inequalities (BMIs), in order to facilitate the decentralized SOF controller design we assume that the output matrices $C_i(\mu_i) \equiv C_i$ and it is of full row rank.

Since the output matrix C_i is of full row rank. Then, there exist nonsingular transformation matrix $T_{Ci} \in \Re^{n_{zi} \times n_{zi}}, i \in \mathcal{N}$ satisfying (Qiu, Feng, & Gao, 2011),

$$C_i T_{Ci} \doteq \left[I_{n_{yi}} \quad 0_{n_{yi} \times (n_{zi} - n_{yi})} \right], i \in \mathcal{N}$$

(20)

Based on the above assumption, we can directly obtain the design result on decentralized SOF fuzzy controller as below.

Theorem 3.2.3 Given the large-scale T-S fuzzy interconnected system in (17) with the assumption in (20), and a SOF fuzzy controller in the form of (18), then the closed-loop fuzzy control system in (19) is asymptotically stable, if there exist symmetric positive definite matrices $M_{ij} \in \Re^{n_{zi} \times n_{zi}}, Q_{i(1)} \in \Re^{n_{yi} \times n_{yi}}, Q_{i(2)} \in \Re^{(n_{zi}-n_{yi}) \times (n_{zi}-n_{yi})}$, and matrices $G_i \in \Re^{n_{zi} \times n_{zi}}, \bar{K}_i^f \in \Re^{n_{ui} \times n_{zi}}$, such that for all $\{l,f\} \in \mathcal{L}_i, j \neq i, \{i,j\} \in \mathcal{N}$, the following LMIs hold:

$$\Omega_i^{ll} < 0, l \in \mathcal{L}_i$$

(21)

$$\Omega_i^{lf} + \Omega_i^{fl} < 0, l \leq f$$

(22)

where

$$\begin{cases} \Omega_i^{lf} = \begin{bmatrix} \mathrm{Sym}\left\{ A_i^l Q_i + B_i^l \begin{bmatrix} \bar{K}_i^f & 0 \end{bmatrix} T_{Ci}^T \right\} + \displaystyle\sum_{j=1,j\neq i}^{N} \sum_{s=1}^{r_j} \bar{A}_{ij}^{ls} M_{ij} \left[\bar{A}_{ij}^{ls} \right]^T & Q_i \mathbb{I} \\ \star & -\mathbb{M}_i \end{bmatrix} \\ Q_i = T_{Ci} \begin{bmatrix} Q_{i(1)} & 0 \\ 0 & Q_{i(3)} \end{bmatrix} T_{Ci}^T, \mathbb{I} = \underbrace{\begin{bmatrix} \mathrm{I}\cdots\mathrm{I}\cdots\mathrm{I} \end{bmatrix}}_{N-1}, \mathbb{M}_i = \mathrm{diag}\underbrace{\left\{ M_{1i} \cdots M_{ji,j\neq i} \cdots M_{Ni} \right\}}_{N-1} \end{cases}$$

$$\tag{23}$$

In that case, the decentralized SOF fuzzy controller gains can be obtained as

$$K_i^f = \bar{K}_i^f Q_{i(1)}^{-1}, f \in \mathcal{L}_i, i \in \mathcal{N}. \tag{24}$$

Proof. Similar to the processing in Theorem 2.3.1, it yields

$$\sum_{l=1}^{r_i} \sum_{f=1}^{r_i} \mu_i^l \mu_i^f \begin{bmatrix} \mathrm{Sym}\left\{ P_i A_i^l + P_i B_i^l K_i^f C_i \right\} + \displaystyle\sum_{j=1,j\neq i}^{N} P_i \left[\sum_{s=1}^{r_j} \bar{A}_{ij}^{ls} M_{ij} \left[\bar{A}_{ij}^{ls} \right]^T \right] P_i & \mathbb{I} \\ \star & -\mathbb{M}_i \end{bmatrix} < 0, \tag{25}$$

where $\mathbb{I} = \underbrace{\begin{bmatrix} \mathrm{I}\cdots\mathrm{I}\cdots\mathrm{I} \end{bmatrix}}_{N-1}$, $\mathbb{M}_i = \mathrm{diag}\underbrace{\left\{ M_{1i} \cdots M_{ji,j\neq i} \cdots M_{Ni} \right\}}_{N-1}$.

Now, define

$$P_i^{-1} = Q_i, \Gamma_i \doteq \mathrm{diag}\left\{ Q_i \underbrace{\mathrm{I}\cdots\mathrm{I}\cdots}_{N-1} \right\}, Q_i = T_{Ci} \begin{bmatrix} Q_{i(1)} & 0 \\ 0 & Q_{i(3)} \end{bmatrix} T_{Ci}^T, \bar{K}_i^f = K_i^f Q_{i(1)}. \tag{26}$$

By performing a congruence transformation by Γ_i and taking the relation in (26), the LMI-based result in (21) and (22) can be directly obtained. Thus, completing this proof.

NOTE: It is noted that the LMI-based result in Theorem 3.2.3 is obtained by using the assumption in (20). However, we can also assume that the input matrix satisfies $B_i\left(\mu_i\right) \equiv B_i$ and is of full row rank. Then, there exist nonsingular transformation matrices $T_{Bi} \in \mathfrak{R}^{n_{zi} \times n_{zi}}, i \in \mathcal{N}$ satisfying (Qiu, Feng, & Gao, 2011),

$$T_{Bi}B_i \doteq \begin{bmatrix} I_{n_{ui}} \\ 0_{(n_{xi}-n_{ui}) \times n_{ui}} \end{bmatrix}, i \in \mathcal{N}. \tag{27}$$

Based on the above assumption, the LMI-based result can also be obtained as below.

Theorem 3.2.4 Given the large-scale T-S fuzzy interconnected system in (17) with the assumption in (27), and a SOF fuzzy controller in the form of (18), then the closed-loop fuzzy control system in (19) is asymptotically stable, if there exist symmetric positive definite matrices $W_{ij} \in \Re^{n_{xi} \times n_{xi}}, P_{i(1)} \in \Re^{n_{ui} \times n_{ui}}, P_{i(2)} \in \Re^{(n_{xi}-n_{ui}) \times (n_{xi}-n_{ui})}$, and matrices $\bar{K}_i^f \in \Re^{n_{ui} \times n_{xi}}$, such that for all $\{l,f\} \in \mathcal{L}_i, j \neq i, \{i,j\} \in \mathcal{N}$, the following LMIs hold:

$$\Omega_i^{ll} < 0, l \in \mathcal{L}_i \tag{28}$$

$$\Omega_i^{lf} + \Omega_i^{fl} < 0, l \leq f \tag{29}$$

where

$$\begin{cases} \Omega_i^{lf} = \begin{bmatrix} \mathrm{Sym}\left\{P_iA_i^l + T_{Bi}^T \begin{bmatrix} \bar{K}_i^f \\ 0 \end{bmatrix} C_i\right\} + \sum\limits_{j=1,j\neq i}^{N} W_{ji} & \mathbb{A}_i \\ \star & \mathbb{W}_i \end{bmatrix} \\ \mathbb{A}_i = [\underbrace{\mathcal{A}_{i1} \cdots \mathcal{A}_{ij,j\neq i} \cdots \mathcal{A}_{iN}}_{N-1}], \mathcal{A}_{ij} = [\underbrace{P_i\bar{A}_{ij}^{l1} \cdots P_i\bar{A}_{ij}^{ls} \cdots P_i\bar{A}_{ij}^{lr_j}}_{r_j}] \\ \mathbb{W}_i = \mathrm{diag}\{\underbrace{\mathcal{W}_{i1} \cdots \mathcal{W}_{ij,j\neq i} \cdots \mathcal{W}_{iN}}_{N-1}\}, \mathcal{W}_{ij} = \mathrm{diag}\{\underbrace{W_{ij} \cdots W_{ij} \cdots W_{ij}}_{r_j}\} \\ P_i = T_{Bi}^T \begin{bmatrix} P_{i(1)} & 0 \\ 0 & P_{i(3)} \end{bmatrix} T_{Bi} \end{cases} \tag{30}$$

In that case, the decentralized SOF fuzzy controller gains can be obtained as

$$K_i^f = P_{i(1)}^{-1}\bar{K}_i^f, f \in \mathcal{L}_i, i \in \mathcal{N}. \tag{31}$$

Proof. Firstly, we define

$$P_i = T_{Bi}^T \begin{bmatrix} P_{i(1)} & 0 \\ 0 & P_{i(3)} \end{bmatrix} T_{Bi}, \tag{32}$$

where $P_{i(1)} \in \mathfrak{R}^{n_{ui} \times n_{zi}}$ and $P_{i(3)} \in \mathfrak{R}^{n_{ui} \times n_{xi}}$ are symmetric positive definite matrices. Thus, based on (27) and (32), it yields

$$
\begin{aligned}
P_i B_i K_i^f &= T_{Bi}^T \begin{bmatrix} P_{i(1)} & 0 \\ 0 & P_{i(3)} \end{bmatrix} T_{Bi} B_i K_i^f \\
&= T_{Bi}^T \begin{bmatrix} P_{i(1)} K_i^f \\ 0 \end{bmatrix} \\
&= T_{Bi}^T \begin{bmatrix} \bar{K}_i^f \\ 0 \end{bmatrix}
\end{aligned}
\tag{33}
$$

Similar to the processing in Theorem 2.3.1, it has

$$\sum_{l=1}^{r_i} \sum_{f=1}^{r_i} \mu_i^l \mu_i^f \left\{ \Phi_i^{lf} \right\} < 0, \tag{34}$$

where

$$\Phi_i^{lf} = \mathrm{Sym}\left[P_i A_i^l + P_i B_i^l K_i^f C_i \right] + \sum_{j=1, j \neq i}^{N} P_i \left[\sum_{s=1}^{r_j} \bar{A}_{ij}^{ls} M_{ij} \left[\bar{A}_{ij}^{ls} \right]^T \right] P_i + \sum_{j=1, j \neq i}^{N} M_{ji}^{-1}. \tag{35}$$

Define $M_{ij} = W_{ij}^{-1}$, and using Schur complement to $\Phi_i^{lf} < 0$, it yields

$$\begin{bmatrix} \mathrm{Sym}\left\{ P_i A_i^l + P_i B_i^l K_i^f C_i \right\} + \sum_{j=1, j \neq i}^{N} W_{ji} & \mathbb{A}_i \\ \star & \mathbb{W}_i \end{bmatrix} < 0, \tag{36}$$

Where

$$\begin{cases} \mathbb{A}_i = \underbrace{\left[\mathcal{A}_{i1} \cdots \mathcal{A}_{ij, j \neq i} \cdots \mathcal{A}_{iN} \right]}_{N-1}, \mathcal{A}_{ij} = \underbrace{\left[P_i \overline{A}_{ij}^{l1} \cdots P_i \overline{A}_{ij}^{ls} \cdots P_i \overline{A}_{ij}^{lr_j} \right]}_{r_j} \\ \mathbb{W}_i = \underbrace{\mathrm{diag} \left\{ \mathcal{W}_{i1} \cdots \mathcal{W}_{ij, j \neq i} \cdots \mathcal{W}_{iN} \right\}}_{N-1}, \mathcal{W}_{ij} = \underbrace{\mathrm{diag} \left\{ W_{ij} \cdots W_{ij} \cdots W_{ij} \right\}}_{r_j} \end{cases} \tag{37}$$

Based on the relations in (32)-(37), the inequalities in (29) and (30) can be easily obtained. Thus, this proof is completed.

NOTE: It is noted that the LMI-based result in Theorem 3.2.3 is obtained by using the assumption in (20), and the other one in Theorem 3.2.4 is obtained by using the assumption in (27). However, apart from these assumptions, the results in Theorem 3.2.3 and Theorem 3.2.4 cannot be applied for the controller design.

Motivated by Chadli and Guerra (2012), in the following we will propose a descriptor system approach to decentralized SOF fuzzy controller design. By introducing virtual dynamic in the measurement output, the closed-loop fuzzy control system can be rewritten as the following descriptor model,

$$\mathrm{E} \dot{\overline{x}}_i \left(t \right) = \overline{A}_i \left(\mu_i \right) \overline{x}_i \left(t \right) + R \sum_{j=1, j \neq i}^{N} \overline{A}_{ij} \left(\mu_i, \mu_j \right) x_j \left(t \right), \tag{38}$$

where

$$\begin{cases} \mathrm{E} = \begin{bmatrix} \mathrm{I} & 0 \\ 0 & 0 \end{bmatrix}, \overline{x}_i \left(t \right) = \begin{bmatrix} x_i^T \left(t \right) & y_i^T \left(t \right) \end{bmatrix}^T \\ \overline{A}_i \left(\mu_i \right) = \begin{bmatrix} A_i \left(\mu_i \right) & B_i \left(\mu_i \right) K_i \left(\mu_i \right) \\ C_i \left(\mu_i \right) & -\mathrm{I} \end{bmatrix}, R = \begin{bmatrix} \mathrm{I} \\ 0 \end{bmatrix}. \end{cases} \tag{39}$$

Based on the descriptor system in (38), we can obtain the following result.

Theorem 3.2.5 Given the large-scale T-S fuzzy interconnected system in (17) and a SOF fuzzy controller in the form of (18), then the closed-loop fuzzy control system in (19) is asymptotically stable, if there exist symmetric positive definite matrices $\left\{ M_{ij}, X_{i(1)} \right\} \in \mathfrak{R}^{n_{zi} \times n_{zi}}$, and matrices $X_{i(2)} \in \mathfrak{R}^{n_{yi} \times n_{yi}}$, $\bar{K}_i^f \in \mathfrak{R}^{n_{ui} \times n_{zi}}$, $J_i \in \mathfrak{R}^{n_{ui} \times n_{zi}}$, such that for all $\left\{ l, f \right\} \in \mathcal{L}_i, j \neq i, \left\{ i, j \right\} \in \mathcal{N},$ the following LMIs hold:

$$\Omega_i^{ll} < 0, l \in \mathcal{L}_i \tag{40}$$

$$\Omega_i^{lf} + \Omega_i^{fl} < 0, l \leq f \tag{41}$$

where

$$\begin{cases} \Omega_i^{lf} = \begin{bmatrix} \Omega_{i(1)}^{lf} + \Omega_{i(2)}^{lf} & \bar{X}_i^T \mathbb{R} \\ \star & -\mathbb{M}_i \end{bmatrix}, \Omega_{i(1)}^{lf} = \mathrm{Sym} \left\{ \begin{bmatrix} A_i^l X_{i(1)} + B_i^l \bar{K}_i^f J_i & B_i^l \bar{K}_i^f \\ C_i^l X_{i(1)} - X_{i(2)} J_i & -X_{i(2)} \end{bmatrix}^T \right\}, \\ \Omega_{i(2)}^{lf} = \sum_{j=1, j \neq i}^{N} \left(R \left[\sum_{s=1}^{r_j} \bar{A}_{ij}^{ls} M_{ij} \left[\bar{A}_{ij}^{ls} \right]^T \right] R^T \right), \mathbb{M}_i = \mathrm{diag} \underbrace{\left\{ M_{1i} \cdots M_{ji, j \neq i} \cdots M_{Ni} \right\}}_{N-1}, \\ X_i = \begin{bmatrix} X_{i(1)} & 0 \\ X_{i(2)} J_i & X_{i(2)} \end{bmatrix}, \mathbb{R} = \underbrace{\begin{bmatrix} R \cdots R \cdots R \end{bmatrix}}_{N-1}, R = \begin{bmatrix} I \\ 0 \end{bmatrix} \end{cases} \tag{42}$$

In that case, the decentralized SOF fuzzy controller gains can be obtained as

$$K_i^f = \bar{K}_i^f X_{i(2)}^{-1}, f \in \mathcal{L}_i, i \in \mathcal{N}. \tag{43}$$

Proof. Choose the Lyapunov functional as

$$\begin{aligned} V\left(x(t) \right) &= \sum_{i=1}^{N} V_i \left(x_i(t) \right) \\ &= \sum_{i=1}^{N} \bar{x}_i^T(t) \mathrm{E}^T \bar{P}_i \bar{x}_i(t), i \in \mathcal{N} \end{aligned} \tag{44}$$

with

$$\bar{P}_i = \begin{bmatrix} P_{i(1)} & 0 \\ P_{i(2)} & P_{i(3)} \end{bmatrix},$$ (45)

where $0 < P_{i(1)} = P_{i(1)}^T \in \mathfrak{R}^{n_{zi} \times n_{zi}}$, $P_{i(2)} \in \mathfrak{R}^{n_{yi} \times n_{zi}}$, $P_{i(3)} \in \mathfrak{R}^{n_{yi} \times n_{yi}}$.

Taking the time derivative of $V\big(x(t)\big)$ along of the trajectory of the descriptor system in (38), ones has

$$
\begin{aligned}
\dot{V}\big(x(t)\big) &= \sum_{i=1}^{N} 2 \left[\bar{A}_i\big(\mu_i\big)\bar{x}_i(t) + R \sum_{j=1,j\neq i}^{N} \bar{A}_{ij}\big(\mu_i,\mu_j\big)x_j(t) \right]^T \bar{P}_i\bar{x}_i(t) \\
&= \sum_{i=1}^{N}\bar{x}_i^T(t)\Big\{\mathrm{Sym}\big(\bar{A}_i^T\big(\mu_i\big)\bar{P}_i\big)\Big\}\bar{x}_i(t) + 2\left[R\sum_{j=1,j\neq i}^{N}\bar{A}_{ij}\big(\mu_i,\mu_j\big)x_j(t)\right]^T \bar{P}_i\bar{x}_i(t).
\end{aligned}
$$ (46)

Define a positive definite symmetric matrix $M_{ij} \in \mathfrak{R}^{n_{zi} \times n_{zi}}$, it yields

$$
\begin{aligned}
&2\sum_{i=1}^{N}\sum_{j=1,j\neq i}^{N} x_j^T(t)\bar{A}_{ij}^T\big(\mu_i,\mu_j\big)R^T\bar{P}_i\bar{x}_i(t) \\
&\leq \sum_{i=1}^{N}\sum_{j=1,j\neq i}^{N}\Big\{x_j^T(t)M_{ij}^{-1}x_j(t)\Big\} \\
&+ \sum_{i=1}^{N}\sum_{j=1,j\neq i}^{N}\bar{x}_i^T(t)\bar{P}_i^T R\big[\bar{A}_{ij}\big(\mu_i,\mu_j\big)\big]M_{ij}\big[\bar{A}_{ij}\big(\mu_i,\mu_j\big)\big]^T R^T\bar{P}_i\bar{x}_i(t) \\
&\leq \sum_{i=1}^{N}\sum_{j=1,j\neq i}^{N}\Big\{x_i^T(t)M_{ji}^{-1}x_i(t)\Big\} \\
&+ \sum_{i=1}^{N}\sum_{j=1,j\neq i}^{N}\bar{x}_i^T(t)\bar{P}_i^T R\left[\sum_{l=1}^{r_i}\mu_i^l\sum_{s=1}^{r_j}\bar{A}_{ij}^{ls}M_{ij}\big[\bar{A}_{ij}^{ls}\big]^T\right]R^T\bar{P}_i\bar{x}_i(t)
\end{aligned}
$$ (47)

Combined with (46) and (47), it yields

$$\dot{V}\left(x\left(t\right)\right) \le \sum_{i=1}^{N} \overline{x}_i^T\left(t\right)\left\{\mathrm{Sym}\left(\overline{A}_i^T\left(\mu_i\right)\overline{P}_i\right)\right\}\overline{x}_i\left(t\right) + \sum_{i=1}^{N}\sum_{j=1,j\ne i}^{N}\left\{x_i^T\left(t\right)M_{ji}^{-1}x_i\left(t\right)\right\}$$

$$+\sum_{i=1}^{N}\sum_{j=1,j\ne i}^{N}\overline{x}_i^T\left(t\right)\overline{P}_i R\left[\sum_{l=1}^{r_i}\mu_i^l\sum_{s=1}^{r_j}\overline{A}_{ij}^{ls}M_{ij}\left[\overline{A}_{ij}^{ls}\right]^T\right]R^T\overline{P}_i\overline{x}_i\left(t\right)$$

$$\tag{48}$$

It is easy to see that the following inequality implies (48),

$$\mathrm{Sym}\left(\begin{bmatrix}A_i\left(\mu_i\right) & B_i\left(\mu_i\right)K_i\left(\mu_i\right)\\ C_i^l & \_\mathrm{TM}\end{bmatrix}^T\overline{P}_i\right)$$

$$+\sum_{j=1,j\ne i}^{N}\left(\overline{P}_i R\left[\sum_{l=1}^{r_i}\mu_i^l\sum_{s=1}^{r_j}\overline{A}_{ij}^{ls}M_{ij}\left[\overline{A}_{ij}^{ls}\right]^T\right]R^T\overline{P}_i + RM_{ji}^{-1}R^T\right) < 0, i \in \mathcal{N}.$$

$$\tag{49}$$

By using Schur complement lemma, we have

$$\begin{bmatrix}\mathrm{Sym}\left(\begin{bmatrix}A_i\left(\mu_i\right) & B_i\left(\mu_i\right)K_i\left(\mu_i\right)\\ C_i^l & -\mathrm{I}\end{bmatrix}^T\overline{P}_i\right) + \sum_{j=1,j\ne i}^{N}\left(\overline{P}_i R\left[\sum_{l=1}^{r_i}\mu_i^l\sum_{s=1}^{r_j}\overline{A}_{ij}^{ls}M_{ij}\left[\overline{A}_{ij}^{ls}\right]^T\right]R^T\overline{P}_i\right) & \mathbb{R}\\ \star & -\mathbb{M}_i\end{bmatrix} < 0,$$

$$\tag{50}$$

where $\mathbb{R} = \underbrace{\begin{bmatrix}R\cdots R\cdots R\end{bmatrix}}_{N-1}$, $\mathbb{M}_i = \mathrm{diag}\underbrace{\left\{M_{1i}\cdots M_{ji,j\ne i}\cdots M_{Ni}\right\}}_{N-1}$.

Define

$$\overline{X}_i = \overline{P}_i^{-1}$$

$$= \begin{bmatrix}X_{i(1)} & 0\\ X_{i(2)}J_i & X_{i(2)}\end{bmatrix}$$

$$\tag{51}$$

It is easy to see from (40)-(41) that

$$-P_{i(3)} - P_{i(3)} < 0,$$

$$\tag{52}$$

which implies that matrix $\bar{P}_i$ is nonsingular.

We further define

$$\Gamma_i \doteq \operatorname{diag}\left\{ \bar{X}_i \underbrace{I \cdots I \cdots I}_{N-1} \right\}, \bar{K}_i^f = K_i^f X_{i(2)} \tag{53}$$

By performing a congruence transformation to (50) by Γ_i, we have

$$\left[\operatorname{Sym}\left(\bar{X}_i^T \left[\begin{array}{cc} A_i(\mu_i) & B_i(\mu_i) K_i(\mu_i) \\ C_i^l & -I \end{array} \right]^T \right) + \sum_{j=1,j\neq i}^{N} \left[R \left[\sum_{l=1}^{r_i} \mu_i^l \sum_{s=1}^{r_j} \bar{A}_{ij}^{ls} M_{ij} \left[\bar{A}_{ij}^{ls} \right]^T \right] R^T \right] \quad \bar{X}_i^T \mathbb{R} \atop \star \qquad \qquad \qquad \qquad \qquad \qquad \qquad \qquad \qquad \qquad \qquad \qquad \qquad \qquad \qquad -\mathbb{M}_i \right] < 0. \tag{54}$$

Substituting (51) into (54), and taking the relation in (53), and extracting the premise variables, the LMI-based results in (40) and (41) can be obtained. Thus, completing this proof.

NOTE: It is noted that the LMI-based result in Theorem 3.2.5 is obtained by using the descriptor system in (38). However, motivated by (Chadli & Guerra, 2012), we can also use the augmented system $\bar{x}_i(t) = \left[x_i^T(t) \quad u_i^T(t) \right]^T$.

In that case, the closed-loop fuzzy control system in (12) can be rewritten as

$$\mathrm{E}\bar{x}_i(t) = \bar{A}_i(\mu_i) \bar{x}_i(t) + R \sum_{j=1,j\neq i}^{N} \bar{A}_{ij}(\mu_i,\mu_j) x_j(t), \tag{55}$$

where

$$\left\{ \begin{array}{l} \mathrm{E} = \left[\begin{array}{cc} I & 0 \\ 0 & 0 \end{array} \right], \bar{x}_i(t) = \left[x_i^T(t) \quad u_i^T(t) \right]^T \\[2ex] \bar{A}_i(\mu_i) = \left[\begin{array}{cc} A_i(\mu_i) & B_i(\mu_i) \\ K_i(\mu_i) C_i(\mu_i) & -I \end{array} \right], R = \left[\begin{array}{c} I \\ 0 \end{array} \right] \end{array} \right. \tag{56}$$

Based on the descriptor system in (55), we can obtain the design result on the SOF control.

Theorem 3.2.6 Given the large-scale T-S fuzzy interconnected system in (17) and a SOF fuzzy controller in the form of (18), then the closed-loop fuzzy control system in (19) is asymptotically stable, if there exist symmetric positive definite matrices $\left\{ P_{i(1)}, M_{ij} \right\} \in \mathfrak{R}^{n_{zi} \times n_{zi}}$, and matrices $P_{i(2)} \in \mathfrak{R}^{n_{yi} \times n_{yi}}$, $\bar{K}_i^l \in \mathfrak{R}^{n_{ui} \times n_{zi}}$, $J_i \in \mathfrak{R}^{n_{ui} \times n_{zi}}$, such that for all $\left\{ l, f \right\} \in \mathcal{L}_i, j \neq i, \left\{ i, j \right\} \in \mathcal{N},$ the following LMIs hold:

$$\Omega_i^{ll} < 0, l \in \mathcal{L}_i \tag{57}$$

$$\Omega_i^{lf} + \Omega_i^{fl} < 0, l \leq f \tag{58}$$

where

$$
\begin{bmatrix}
\Omega_i^{lf} = \begin{bmatrix} \mathrm{Sym}\left(\begin{bmatrix} \left[A_i^l \right]^T P_{i(1)} + \left[\bar{K}_i^f C_i^l \right]^T J & \left[\bar{K}_i^f C_i^l \right]^T \\ \left[B_i^l \right]^T P_{i(1)} - P_{i(3)} J & -P_{i(3)} \end{bmatrix} \right) + \sum_{j=1, j \neq i}^{N} \left(R W_{ji} R^T \right) & \mathbb{A}_i \\ \star & -\mathbb{W}_i \end{bmatrix} \\
\mathbb{A}_i = \begin{bmatrix} \mathcal{A}_{i1} \cdots \underbrace{\mathcal{A}_{ij, j \neq i}}_{N-1} \cdots \mathcal{A}_{iN} \end{bmatrix}, \mathcal{A}_{ij} = \begin{bmatrix} \bar{P}_i R \bar{A}_{ij}^{l1} \cdots \bar{P}_i R \bar{A}_{ij}^{ls} \cdots \underbrace{\bar{P}_i R \bar{A}_{ij}^{lr_j}}_{r_j} \end{bmatrix}, R = \begin{bmatrix} I \\ 0 \end{bmatrix}, \\
\mathbb{W}_i = \mathrm{diag}\left\{ \mathcal{W}_{i1} \cdots \underbrace{\mathcal{W}_{ij, j \neq i}}_{N-1} \cdots \mathcal{W}_{iN} \right\}, \mathcal{W}_{ij} = \mathrm{diag}\left\{ \underbrace{W_{ij} \cdots W_{ij} \cdots W_{ij}}_{r_j} \right\}, \bar{P}_i = \begin{bmatrix} P_{i(1)} & 0 \\ P_{i(3)} J & P_{i(3)} \end{bmatrix}
\end{bmatrix}
\tag{59}
$$

In that case, the decentralized SOF fuzzy controller gains can be obtained as

$$K_i^f = P_{i(3)}^{-T} \bar{K}_i^f, f \in \mathcal{L}_i, i \in \mathcal{N}. \tag{60}$$

Proof. Recalling the result in (48),

$$\text{Sym}\left(\overline{A}_i^T\left(\mu_i\right)\overline{P}_i\right) + \sum_{j=1,j\neq i}^{N}\left(\overline{P}_i R\left[\sum_{l=1}^{r_i}\mu_i^l \sum_{s=1}^{r_j}\overline{A}_{ij}^{ls} M_{ij}\left[\overline{A}_{ij}^{ls}\right]^T\right]R^T\overline{P}_i + RM_{ji}^{-1}R^T\right) < 0.$$

(61)

Define $M_{ij} = W_{ij}^{-1}$, and by using Schur complement, it yields

$$\sum_{l=1}^{r_i}\sum_{f=1}^{r_i}\mu_i^l\mu_i^f\left\{\Phi_i^{lf}\right\} < 0,$$

(62)

where

$$\begin{cases}
\Phi_i^{lf} = \begin{bmatrix}
\text{Sym}\left(\begin{bmatrix} A_i^l & B_i^l \\ K_i^f C_i^l & -I \end{bmatrix}^T \overline{P}_i\right) + \sum_{j=1,j\neq i}^{N}\left(RW_{ji}R^T\right) & \mathbb{A}_i \\
\star & -\mathbb{W}_i
\end{bmatrix} \\
\mathbb{A}_i = \underbrace{\left[\mathcal{A}_{i1}\cdots\mathcal{A}_{ij,j\neq i}\cdots\mathcal{A}_{iN}\right]}_{N-1}, \mathcal{A}_{ij} = \underbrace{\left[\overline{P}_i R\overline{A}_{ij}^{l1}\cdots\overline{P}_i R\overline{A}_{ij}^{ls}\cdots\overline{P}_i R\overline{A}_{ij}^{lr_j}\right]}_{r_j} \\
\mathbb{W}_i = \text{diag}\underbrace{\left\{\mathcal{W}_{i1}\cdots\mathcal{W}_{ij,j\neq i}\cdots\mathcal{W}_{iN}\right\}}_{N-1}, \mathcal{W}_{ij} = \text{diag}\underbrace{\left\{W_{ij}\cdots W_{ij}\cdots W_{ij}\right\}}_{r_j}
\end{cases}$$

(63)

Here, in order to cast the inequality (62) into LMI-based condition, we define

$$\overline{P}_i = \begin{bmatrix} P_{i(1)} & 0 \\ P_{i(3)}J & P_{i(3)} \end{bmatrix}\overline{K}_i^f = P_{i(3)}K_i^f,$$

(64)

where $P_{i(1)} \in \mathfrak{R}^{n_{xi}\times n_{xi}}, P_{i(3)} \in \mathfrak{R}^{n_{ui}\times n_{ui}}, J_i \in \mathfrak{R}^{n_{xi}\times n_{ui}}$.

Submitting (64) into (62), the inequality in (57) and (58) is obtained. Thus, completing this proof.

3.2.5 Output Feedback Stabilizing for Discrete-Time Systems

Consider a discrete-time large-scale T-S fuzzy interconnected system,

$$x_i\left(t+1\right) = \left(A_i\left(\mu_i\right) + B_i\left(\mu_i\right)K_i\left(\mu_i\right)\right)x_i\left(t\right) + \sum_{j=1, j\neq i}^{N}\overline{A}_{ij}\left(\mu_i, \mu_j\right)x_j\left(t\right). \tag{65}$$

Based on the model in (65) and the assumption in (20), we can directly obtain the following result.

Theorem 3.2.7 Given a large-scale T-S fuzzy interconnected system and a SOF fuzzy controller, then the closed-loop fuzzy control system in (65) is asymptotically stable, if there exist symmetric positive definite matrices $\left\{\overline{P}_i, M_{ij}\right\} \in \mathfrak{R}^{n_{zi}\times n_{zi}}$, and matrices $G_i \in \mathfrak{R}^{n_{zi}\times n_{zi}}$, such that for all $\left\{l, f\right\} \in \mathcal{L}_i, j \neq i, \left\{i, j\right\} \in \mathcal{N}$, the following LMIs hold:

$$\Omega_i^{ll} < 0, l \in \mathcal{L}_i \tag{66}$$

$$\Omega_i^{lf} + \Omega_i^{fl} < 0, l \leq f \tag{67}$$

where

$$\left\{\begin{array}{l}\Omega_i^{lf} = \begin{bmatrix}\overline{P}_i - G_i - G_i^T + \displaystyle\sum_{j=1, j\neq i}^{N}\left[\displaystyle\sum_{s=1}^{r_j}\overline{A}_{ij}^{ls}M_{ij}\left[\overline{A}_{ij}^{ls}\right]^T\right] & A_i^lG_i^T + B_i^l\begin{bmatrix}\overline{K}_i^f & 0\end{bmatrix}T_{Ci}^T & 0 \\ \star & -\overline{P}_i & G_i\mathbb{I} \\ \star & \star & -\mathbb{M}_i\end{bmatrix} \\ \mathbb{I} = \underbrace{\begin{bmatrix}I\cdots I\cdots I\end{bmatrix}}_{N-1}, \mathbb{M}_i = \mathrm{diag}\underbrace{\left\{M_{1i}\cdots M_{ji, j\neq i}\cdots M_{Ni}\right\}}_{N-1}, G_i^T = T_{Ci}\begin{bmatrix}G_{i(1)} & 0 \\ 0 & G_{i(3)}\end{bmatrix}T_{Ci}^T.\end{array}\right. \tag{68}$$

In that case, the decentralized SOF fuzzy controller gains can be obtained as

$$K_i^f = \overline{K}_i^f G_{i(1)}^{-1}, f \in \mathcal{L}_i, i \in \mathcal{N}. \tag{69}$$

Besides, based on the assumption (27), the corresponding design result can be derived as below.

Theorem 3.2.8 The closed-loop fuzzy control system in (65) is asymptotically stable, if there exist symmetric positive definite matrices $\left\{P_i, M_{ij}\right\} \in \mathfrak{R}^{n_{zi} \times n_{zi}}$, and matrices $G_i \in \mathfrak{R}^{n_{zi} \times n_{zi}}$, $\bar{K}_i^f \in \mathfrak{R}^{n_{ui} \times n_{zi}}$, such that for all $l \in \mathcal{L}_i, j \neq i, \{i, j\} \in \mathcal{N}$, the following LMIs hold:

$$\Omega_i^{ll} < 0, l \in \mathcal{L}_i \tag{70}$$

$$\Omega_i^{lf} + \Omega_i^{fl} < 0, l \leq f \tag{71}$$

Where

$$
\left\{
\begin{aligned}
&\Omega_i^{lf} = \begin{bmatrix} P_i - G_i - G_i^T & G_i A_i^l + T_{Bi}^T \begin{bmatrix} \bar{K}_i^l \\ 0 \end{bmatrix} C_i^f & \mathbb{G}_i \\ \star & -P_i + \sum\limits_{j=1, j \neq i}^N W_{ji} & 0 \\ \star & \star & \mathbb{W}_i \end{bmatrix}, G_i = T_{Bi}^T \begin{bmatrix} G_{i(1)} & G_{i(2)} \\ 0 & G_{i(3)} \end{bmatrix} T_{Bi} \\
&\mathbb{G}_i = \underbrace{\left[\mathcal{G}_{i1} \cdots \mathcal{G}_{ij, j \neq i} \cdots \mathcal{G}_{iN} \right]}_{N-1}, \mathcal{G}_{ij} = \underbrace{\left[G_i \bar{A}_{ij}^{l1} \cdots G_i \bar{A}_{ij}^{ls} \cdots G_i \bar{A}_{ij}^{lr_j} \right]}_{r_j}, \\
&\mathbb{W}_i = \operatorname{diag} \underbrace{\left\{ \mathcal{W}_{i1} \cdots \mathcal{W}_{ij, j \neq i} \cdots \mathcal{W}_{iN} \right\}}_{N-1}, \mathcal{W}_{ij} = \operatorname{diag} \underbrace{\left\{ W_{ij} \cdots W_{ij} \cdots W_{ij} \right\}}_{r_j}
\end{aligned}
\right.
\tag{72}
$$

In that case, the decentralized SOF fuzzy controller gains can be obtained as

$$K_i^l = G_{i(1)}^{-1} \bar{K}_i^l, l \in \mathcal{L}_i, i \in \mathcal{N}. \tag{73}$$

In the following, by using descriptor system approach, the closed-loop fuzzy control system is rewritten as

$$\mathrm{E}\bar{x}_i\left(t+1\right) = \bar{A}_i\left(\mu_i\right)\bar{x}_i\left(t\right) + R\sum_{j=1,j\neq i}^{N}\bar{A}_{ij}\left(\mu_i,\mu_j\right)x_j\left(t\right), \tag{74}$$

where

$$\begin{cases} \mathrm{E} = \begin{bmatrix} \mathrm{I} & 0 \\ 0 & 0 \end{bmatrix}, \bar{x}_i\left(t\right) = \begin{bmatrix} x_i^T\left(t\right) & u_i^T\left(t\right) \end{bmatrix}^T \\ \bar{A}_i\left(\mu_i\right) = \begin{bmatrix} A_i\left(\mu_i\right) & B_i\left(\mu_i\right) \\ K_i\left(\mu_i\right)C_i\left(\mu_i\right) & -I \end{bmatrix}, R = \begin{bmatrix} \mathrm{I} \\ 0 \end{bmatrix} \end{cases} \tag{75}$$

Based on the new model in (74), we obtain the design result on decentralized SOF control as below.

Theorem 3.2.9 Given a large-scale T-S fuzzy interconnected system and a SOF fuzzy controller, then the closed-loop fuzzy control system in (65) is asymptotically stable, if there exist symmetric positive definite matrices $\left\{P_i, M_{ij}\right\} \in \Re^{n_{zi} \times n_{zi}}$, and matrices $G_i \in \Re^{n_{zi} \times n_{zi}}$, $\bar{K}_i^f \in \Re^{n_{ui} \times n_{zi}}$, such that for all $l \in \mathcal{L}_i, j \neq i, \left\{i,j\right\} \in \mathcal{N}$, the following LMIs hold:

$$\Omega_i^{ll} < 0, l \in \mathcal{L}_i \tag{76}$$

$$\Omega_i^{lf} + \Omega_i^{fl} < 0, l \leq f \tag{77}$$

where

$$
\left[
\begin{aligned}
&\Omega_i^{lf} = \begin{bmatrix} \Omega_{i(1)}^{lf} + \mathrm{Sym}\left\{\Omega_{i(2)}^{lf}\right\} & \mathbb{G}_i \\ \star & -\mathbb{M}_i \end{bmatrix}, \Omega_{i(1)}^{lf} = \begin{bmatrix} E^T \bar{P}_i E + \displaystyle\sum_{j=1,j\neq i}^{N} M_{ji} & 0 \\ 0 & \bar{P}_i \end{bmatrix} \\
&\Omega_{i(2)}^{lf} = \begin{bmatrix} G_{i(1)} A_i^l + J_i \bar{K}_i^l C_i^f & G_{i(1)} B_i^l - J_i G_{i(3)} & -G_{i(1)} & -J_i G_{i(3)} \\ G_{i(2)} A_i^l + \bar{K}_i^l C_i^f & G_{i(2)} B_i^l - G_{i(3)} & -G_{i(2)} & -G_{i(3)} \\ G_{i(1)} A_i^l + J_i \bar{K}_i^l C_i^f & G_{i(1)} B_i^l - J_i G_{i(3)} & -G_{i(1)} & -J_i G_{i(3)} \\ G_{i(2)} A_i^l + \bar{K}_i^l C_i^f & G_{i(2)} B_i^l - G_{i(3)} & -G_{i(2)} & -G_{i(3)} \end{bmatrix} \\
&\mathbb{G}_i = \Big[\underbrace{\mathcal{G}_{i1} \cdots \mathcal{G}_{ij,j\neq i} \cdots \mathcal{G}_{iN}}_{N-1} \Big], \mathcal{G}_{ij} = \Big[\underbrace{G_i R \bar{A}_{ij}^{l1} \cdots G_i R \bar{A}_{ij}^{ls} \cdots G_i R \bar{A}_{ij}^{lr_j}}_{r_j} \Big] \\
&\mathbb{M}_i = \mathrm{diag}\Big\{ \underbrace{\mathcal{M}_{i1} \cdots \mathcal{M}_{ij,j\neq i} \cdots \mathcal{M}_{iN}}_{N-1} \Big\}, \mathcal{M}_{ij} = \mathrm{diag}\Big\{ \underbrace{M_{ij} \cdots M_{ij} \cdots M_{ij}}_{r_j} \Big\} \\
&\bar{P}_i = \begin{bmatrix} P_{i(1)} & P_{i(2)} \\ \star & P_{i(3)} \end{bmatrix}, G_i = \begin{bmatrix} G_{i(1)} & J_i G_{i(3)} \\ G_{i(2)} & G_{i(3)} \\ G_{i(1)} & J_i G_{i(3)} \\ G_{i(2)} & G_{i(3)} \end{bmatrix}
\end{aligned}
\right. \tag{78}
$$

In that case, the decentralized SOF fuzzy controller gains can be obtained as

$$
K_i^l = G_{i(3)}^{-1} \bar{K}_i^l, l \in \mathcal{L}_i, i \in \mathcal{N}. \tag{79}
$$

Proof: Choose the Lyapunov functional as

$$
\begin{aligned}
V\big(x(t)\big) &= \sum_{i=1}^{N} V_i\big(x_i(t)\big) \\
&= \sum_{i=1}^{N} \bar{x}_i^T(t) E^T \bar{P}_i E \bar{x}_i(t), i \in \mathcal{N}
\end{aligned} \tag{80}
$$

with

$$
\bar{P}_i = \begin{bmatrix} P_{i(1)} & P_{i(2)} \\ \star & P_{i(3)} \end{bmatrix}, \tag{81}
$$

where $0 < P_{i(1)} = P_{i(1)}^T \in \mathfrak{R}^{n_{xi} \times n_{xi}}, P_{i(2)} \in \mathfrak{R}^{n_{xi} \times n_{ui}}, P_{i(3)} = P_{i(3)}^T \in \mathfrak{R}^{n_{ui} \times n_{ui}}$.

Define $\Delta V\left(x\left(t\right)\right) = V\left(x\left(t+1\right)\right) - V\left(x\left(t\right)\right)$ one has

$$
\begin{aligned}
\Delta V\left(x\left(t\right)\right) &= \sum_{i=1}^{N} \left\{ \bar{x}_i^T\left(t+1\right) E^T \bar{P}_i E \bar{x}_i\left(t+1\right) - \bar{x}_i^T\left(t\right) E^T \bar{P}_i E \bar{x}_i\left(t\right) \right\} \\
&= \sum_{i=1}^{N} \begin{bmatrix} \bar{x}_i\left(t\right) \\ E\bar{x}_i\left(t+1\right) \end{bmatrix}^T \begin{bmatrix} E^T \bar{P}_i E & 0 \\ 0 & \bar{P}_i \end{bmatrix} \begin{bmatrix} \bar{x}_i\left(t\right) \\ E\bar{x}_i\left(t+1\right) \end{bmatrix}
\end{aligned}
\tag{82}
$$

Define the symmetric positive definite matrix $G_i \in \mathfrak{R}^{n_{xi} \times n_{xi}}$, it yields

$$
\begin{aligned}
0 &= 2\sum_{i=1}^{N} \begin{bmatrix} \bar{x}_i\left(t\right) \\ E\bar{x}_i\left(t+1\right) \end{bmatrix}^T G_i \left[\bar{A}_i\left(\mu_i\right)\bar{x}_i\left(t\right) - E\bar{x}_i\left(t+1\right) + R\sum_{j=1,j\neq i}^{N} \bar{A}_{ij}\left(\mu_i,\mu_j\right)x_j\left(t\right) \right] \\
&\leq 2\sum_{i=1}^{N} \begin{bmatrix} \bar{x}_i\left(t\right) \\ E\bar{x}_i\left(t+1\right) \end{bmatrix}^T G_i \left[\bar{A}_i\left(\mu_i\right)\bar{x}_i\left(t\right) - E\bar{x}_i\left(t+1\right) \right] \\
&\quad + \sum_{i=1}^{N}\sum_{j=1,j\neq i}^{N} \begin{bmatrix} \bar{x}_i\left(t\right) \\ E\bar{x}_i\left(t+1\right) \end{bmatrix}^T \left(G_i R \left[\sum_{l=1}^{r_i}\mu_i^l\sum_{s=1}^{r_j}\bar{A}_{ij}^{ls} M_{ij}^{-1}\left[\bar{A}_{ij}^{ls}\right]^T \right] R^T G_i^T \right) \begin{bmatrix} \bar{x}_i\left(t\right) \\ E\bar{x}_i\left(t+1\right) \end{bmatrix} \\
&\quad + \sum_{i=1}^{N}\sum_{j=1,j\neq i}^{N} \left\{ x_i^T\left(t\right) M_{ji} x_i\left(t\right) \right\}
\end{aligned}
\tag{83}
$$

Combined with (82) and (83), it yields

$$
\begin{aligned}
\Delta V\left(x\left(t\right)\right) &\leq \sum_{i=1}^{N} \begin{bmatrix} \bar{x}_i\left(t\right) \\ E\bar{x}_i\left(t+1\right) \end{bmatrix}^T \left[\begin{bmatrix} E^T \bar{P}_i E + \sum_{j=1,j\neq i}^{N} M_{ji} & 0 \\ 0 & \bar{P}_i \end{bmatrix} + \mathrm{Sym}\left(G_i \begin{bmatrix} \bar{A}_i\left(\mu_i\right) & -I \end{bmatrix} \right) \right. \\
&\quad \left. + G_i R\left[\sum_{l=1}^{r_i}\mu_i^l\sum_{s=1}^{r_j}\bar{A}_{ij}^{ls} M_{ij}^{-1}\left[\bar{A}_{ij}^{ls}\right]^T\right]R^T G_i^T \right] \begin{bmatrix} \bar{x}_i\left(t\right) \\ E\bar{x}_i\left(t+1\right) \end{bmatrix}
\end{aligned}
\tag{84}
$$

By using Schur complement, it is easy to see that the following inequality implies (84),

$$
\left[\begin{bmatrix} E^T \bar{P}_i E + \sum_{j=1,j\neq i}^{N} M_{ji} & 0 \\ 0 & \bar{P}_i \end{bmatrix} + G_i \begin{bmatrix} \bar{A}_i(\mu_i) & -I \end{bmatrix} \quad \mathbb{G}_i \\ \star \qquad\qquad\qquad\qquad -\mathbb{M}_i \right] < 0, \tag{85}
$$

where

$$
\begin{cases} \mathbb{G}_i = \underbrace{\left[\mathcal{G}_{i1} \cdots \mathcal{G}_{ij,j\neq i} \cdots \mathcal{G}_{iN} \right]}_{N-1}, \mathcal{G}_{ij} = \underbrace{\left[G_i R \bar{A}_{ij}^{l1} \cdots G_i R \bar{A}_{ij}^{ls} \cdots G_i R \bar{A}_{ij}^{lr_j} \right]}_{r_j}, \\ \mathbb{M}_i = \mathrm{diag} \underbrace{\left\{ \mathcal{M}_{i1} \cdots \mathcal{M}_{ij,j\neq i} \cdots \mathcal{M}_{iN} \right\}}_{N-1}, \mathcal{M}_{ij} = \mathrm{diag} \underbrace{\left\{ M_{ij} \cdots M_{ij} \cdots M_{ij} \right\}}_{r_j} \end{cases} \tag{86}
$$

In order to cast the inequality (84) into LMIs, G_i is directly specified as

$$
G_i = \begin{bmatrix} G_{i(1)} & J_i G_{i(3)} \\ G_{i(2)} & G_{i(3)} \\ G_{i(1)} & J_i G_{i(3)} \\ G_{i(2)} & G_{i(3)} \end{bmatrix}, \tag{87}
$$

where $G_{i(1)} \in \mathfrak{R}^{n_{zi} \times n_{zi}}, G_{i(2)} \in \mathfrak{R}^{n_{ui} \times n_{zi}}, J_i \in \mathfrak{R}^{n_{zi} \times n_{ui}}, G_{i(3)} \in \mathfrak{R}^{n_{ui} \times n_{ui}}$ is nonsingular matrix.

Now, by submitting (87) into (85), the inequality in (76) and (77) can be easily obtained. Thus, completing this proof.

3.3 DISTRIBUTED STABILIZATION DESIGN

In this section, we will study distributed stabilization for large-scale T-S fuzzy interconnected systems.

3.3.1 Problem Formulation

Due to the fact that the decentralized control strategy appears weaker stability margins and performance, especially when the interconnections among subsystems are strong. The distributed control provides the supplemental feedbacks with the interconnected information for the local controllers to enhance the requirements of stability and performance (Kazempour & Ghaisari, 2013). As a result, the distributed control avoids those shortages appearing in both the centralized and decentralized controls.

Consider a large-scale fuzzy interconnected system as below:

Plant Rule R_i^l: IF $\varsigma_{i1}(t)$ is F_{i1}^l and $\varsigma_{i2}(t)$ is F_{i2}^l and $\cdots$ and $\varsigma_{ig}(t)$ is F_{ig}^l,

   THEN

$$\dot{x}_i(t) = A_i^l x_i(t) + B_i^l u_i(t) + \sum_{j=1,j\neq i}^{N} \bar{A}_{ij}^l x_j(t), l \in \mathcal{L}_i := \{1,2,\cdots,r_i\} \tag{88}$$

where $i \in \mathcal{N} := \{1,2,\cdots,N\}$, N is the number of the subsystems. For the i-th subsystem, R_i^l is the l-th fuzzy inference rule; r_i is the number of inference rules; $F_{i\varnothing}^l$ $(\varnothing = 1,2,\cdots,g)$ are fuzzy sets; $x_i(t) \in \mathfrak{R}^{n_{xi}}$ and $u(t) \in \mathfrak{R}^{n_{ui}}$ denote the system state, respectively; $\varsigma_i(t) := \left[\varsigma_{i1}(t), \varsigma_{i2}(t), \cdots, \varsigma_{ig}(t)\right]$ are the measurable variables; A_i^l is the l-th local model; $\bar{A}_{ij}^l$ denotes the nonlinear interconnection of the i-th and j-th subsystems for the l-th local model.

Define the inferred fuzzy set $F_i^l := \Pi_{\varnothing=1}^g F_{i\varnothing}^l$ and normalized membership function $\mu_i^l\left[\varsigma(t)\right]$, it yields

$$\mu_i^l\left[\varsigma_i(t)\right] := \frac{\Pi_{\varnothing=1}^g \mu_{i\varnothing}^l\left[\varsigma_{i\varnothing}(t)\right]}{\sum_{\varsigma=1}^{r_i} \Pi_{\varnothing=1}^g \mu_{i\varnothing}^\varsigma\left[\varsigma_{i\varnothing}(t)\right]} \geq 0, \sum_{l=1}^{r_i} \mu_i^l\left[\varsigma_i(t)\right] := 1, \tag{89}$$

where $\mu_{i\varnothing}^l\left[\varsigma_{i\varnothing}(t)\right]$ is the grade of membership of $\varsigma_{i\varnothing}(t)$ in $F_{i\varnothing}^l$. Here we will denote $\mu_i^l := \mu_i^l\left[\varsigma_i(t)\right]$ for brevity.

By fuzzy blending, the i-th global T-S fuzzy dynamic model is obtained by

$$\dot{x}_i(t) = A_i(\mu_i) x_i(t) + B_i(\mu_i) u_i(t) + \sum_{j=1,j\neq i}^{N} \bar{A}_{ij}(\mu_i) x_j(t), \tag{90}$$

where

$$A_i\left(\mu_i\right) := \sum_{l=1}^{r_i}\mu_i^l A_i^l, B_i\left(\mu_i\right) := \sum_{l=1}^{r_i}\mu_i^l B_i^l, \bar{A}_{ij}\left(\mu_i\right) := \sum_{l=1}^{r_i}\mu_i^l A_{ij}^l. \tag{91}$$

Now, consider the following distributed state-feedback fuzzy controller

$$u_i\left(t\right) = K_i\left(\mu_i\right)x_i\left(t\right) + \sum_{j=1,j\neq i}^{N} K_{ij}\left(\mu_i\right)x_j\left(t\right), i \in \mathcal{N} \tag{92}$$

where the proposed controller shares the same premise variables of the system in (90); $K_i\left(\mu_i\right) := \sum_{l=1}^{r_i}\mu_i^l K_i^l, K_{ij}\left(\mu_i\right) := \sum_{l=1}^{r_i}\mu_i^l K_{ij}^l, \left\{K_i^l, K_{ij}^l\right\} \in \mathfrak{R}^{n_{ui}\times n_{xi}}$ is controller gains to be determined.

Combined with the system in (90) and the controller in (92), the closed-loop fuzzy control system can be given by

$$\dot{x}_i\left(t\right) = A_i\left(\mu_i\right)x_i\left(t\right) + B_i\left(\mu_i\right)K_i\left(\mu_i\right)x_i\left(t\right) +$$
$$\sum_{j=1,j\neq i}^{N}\left[B_i\left(\mu_i\right)K_{ij}\left(\mu_i\right) + \bar{A}_{ij}\left(\mu_i\right)\right]x_j\left(t\right). \tag{93}$$

This chapter focuses on the distributed stabilization problem for large-scale T-S fuzzy systems. In particular, it aims to present distributed fuzzy controller design of state feedback and SOF stabilizing for the considered system. The obtained results will be extended to the discrete-time systems.

3.3.2 State Feedback Stabilizing for Continuous-Time Systems

Similar to a processing the decentralized case in Theorem 3.2.1, we can directly obtain the following design result on the distributed control.

Theorem 3.3.1 Given the large-scale T-S fuzzy interconnected system in (90) and a distributed fuzzy controller in the form of (92), then the closed-loop fuzzy control system in (93) is asymptotically stable, if there exist symmetric positive definite matrices $\left\{ Q_i, M_{ij} \right\} \in \mathfrak{R}^{n_{zi} \times n_{zi}}$, and matrix $\left\{ \bar{K}_i^f, \bar{K}_{ij}^f \right\} \in \mathfrak{R}^{n_{ui} \times n_{zi}}$, such that for all $\left\{ l, f \right\} \in \mathcal{L}_i, j \neq i, \left\{ i, j \right\} \in \mathcal{N}$, the following LMIs hold:

$$\Omega_i^{ll} < 0, l \in \mathcal{L}_i \tag{94}$$

$$\Omega_i^{lf} + \Omega_i^{fl} < 0, l \leq f \tag{95}$$

where

$$
\begin{cases}
\Omega_i^{lf} = \begin{bmatrix}
\mathrm{Sym}\left\{ \left(A_i^l Q_i + B_i^l \bar{K}_i^f \right) \right\} & \mathbb{A}_i^{lf} & Q_i \mathbb{I} \\
\star & \mathbb{M}_i - \mathbb{Q}_i - \mathbb{Q}_i^T & 0 \\
\star & \star & -\bar{\mathbb{M}}_i
\end{bmatrix} \\
\mathbb{A}_i^{lf} = \underbrace{\left[\mathcal{A}_{i1}^{lf} \cdots \mathcal{A}_{ij,j\neq i}^{lf} \cdots \mathcal{A}_{iN}^{lf} \right]}_{N-1}, \mathcal{A}_{ij}^{lf} = B_i^l \bar{K}_{ij}^f + \bar{A}_{ij}^l Q_i, \\
\bar{\mathbb{M}}_i = \mathrm{diag}\underbrace{\left\{ M_{1i} \cdots M_{ji,j\neq i} \cdots M_{Ni} \right\}}_{N-1}, \mathbb{I} = \underbrace{\left[I \cdots I \cdots I \right]}_{N-1}, \\
\mathbb{M}_i = \mathrm{diag}\underbrace{\left\{ M_{i1} \cdots M_{ij,j\neq i} \cdots M_{iN} \right\}}_{N-1}, \mathbb{Q}_i = \mathrm{diag}\underbrace{\left\{ Q_i \cdots Q_i \cdots Q_i \right\}}_{N-1}
\end{cases} \tag{96}
$$

In that case, the distributed state feedback fuzzy controller gains can be obtained as

$$K_i^f = \bar{K}_i^f Q_i^{-1}, K_{ij}^f = \bar{K}_{ij}^f Q_i^{-1}, f \in \mathcal{L}_i, i \in \mathcal{N}. \tag{97}$$

Proof: Compared with the decentralized fuzzy controller (6), the extra interconnected term $\sum_{j=1,j\neq i}^{N} B_i\left(\mu_i\right) K_{ij}\left(\mu_i\right) x_j\left(t\right)$ is introduced for the distributed one. Define the symmetric positive definite matrix $M_{ij} \in \mathfrak{R}^{n_{zi} \times n_{zi}}$, it yields

$$\sum_{i=1}^{N} 2x_i^T(t) P_i \sum_{j=1, j\neq i}^{N} \left[B_i(\mu_i) K_{ij}(\mu_i) + \bar{A}_{ij}(\mu_i) \right] x_j(t)$$

$$\leq \sum_{i=1}^{N} \sum_{j=1, j\neq i}^{N} x_i^T(t) P_i \left[B_i(\mu_i) K_{ij}(\mu_i) + \bar{A}_{ij}(\mu_i) \right] M_{ij} \left[B_i(\mu_i) K_{ij}(\mu_i) + \bar{A}_{ij}(\mu_i) \right]^T P_i x_i(t)$$

$$+ \sum_{i=1}^{N} \sum_{j=1, j\neq i}^{N} \left\{ x_j^T(t) M_{ij}^{-1} x_j(t) \right\}$$

$$= \sum_{i=1}^{N} \sum_{j=1, j\neq i}^{N} x_i^T(t) P_i \left[B_i(\mu_i) K_{ij}(\mu_i) + \bar{A}_{ij}(\mu_i) \right] M_{ij} \left[B_i(\mu_i) K_{ij}(\mu_i) + \bar{A}_{ij}(\mu_i) \right]^T P_i x_i(t)$$

$$+ \sum_{i=1}^{N} \sum_{j=1, j\neq i}^{N} \left\{ x_i^T(t) M_{ji}^{-1} x_i(t) \right\}$$

$$\tag{98}$$

Similar the processing in Theorem 2.3.1, we have

$$\begin{bmatrix} \mathrm{Sym}\left\{ P_i\left(A_i(\mu_i) + B_i(\mu_i) K_i(\mu_i) \right) \right\} & P_i \bar{\mathbb{A}}_i(\mu_i) & \mathbb{I} \\ \star & -\mathbb{M}_i^{-1} & 0 \\ \star & \star & -\bar{\mathbb{M}}_i \end{bmatrix} < 0, \tag{99}$$

where

$$\bar{\mathbb{A}}_i(\mu_i) = \underbrace{\left[\mathcal{A}_{i1}(\mu_i) \cdots \mathcal{A}_{ij, j\neq i}(\mu_i) \cdots \mathcal{A}_{iN}(\mu_i) \right]}_{N-1}, \mathcal{A}_{ij}(\mu_i) = B_i(\mu_i) K_{ij}(\mu_i) + \bar{A}_{ij}(\mu_i),$$

$$\mathbb{I} = \underbrace{\left[\mathrm{I} \cdots \mathrm{I} \cdots \mathrm{I} \right]}_{N-1}, \mathbb{M}_i = \mathrm{diag}\underbrace{\left\{ M_{i1} \cdots M_{ij, j\neq i} \cdots M_{iN} \right\}}_{N-1},$$

$$\bar{\mathbb{M}}_i = \mathrm{diag}\underbrace{\left\{ M_{1i} \cdots M_{ji, j\neq i} \cdots M_{Ni} \right\}}_{N-1}$$

$$\tag{100}$$

Note that

$$M_i - \left[Q_i \right] - \left[Q_i \right]^T + \left[Q_i \right]^T M_i^{-1} \left[Q_i \right] = \left[M_i - Q_i \right] M_i^{-1} \left[M_i - Q_i \right]^T \geq 0. \tag{101}$$

We define $P_i^{-1} = Q_i$, and perform a congruence transformation into (99) by

$$\Gamma_i = \text{diag}\left\{\underbrace{Q_i \cdots Q_i \cdots Q_i}_{N} \underbrace{I \cdots I \cdots I}_{N-1}\right\}, \bar{K}_{ij}^l = K_{ij}^l Q_i \tag{102}$$

Now, by extracting the premise variables and taking the relation in (101), the LMI-based result can be directly obtained. Thus, completing this proof.

3.3.3 State Feedback Stabilizing for Discrete-Time Systems

For the discrete-time case, the closed-loop fuzzy control system can be obtained as

$$x_i(t+1) = \left(A_i(\mu_i) + B_i(\mu_i)K_i(\mu_i)\right)x_i(t) +$$
$$\sum_{j=1,j\neq i}^{N}\left[B_i(\mu_i)K_{ij}(\mu_i) + \bar{A}_{ij}(\mu_i)\right]x_j(t). \tag{103}$$

Similar to a processing in Theorem 2.4.1, we can directly obtain the following results,

Theorem 3.3.2 Given a large-scale T-S fuzzy interconnected system and a distributed fuzzy controller, then the closed-loop fuzzy control system in (103) is asymptotically stable, if there exist symmetric positive definite matrices $\left\{\bar{P}_i, M_{ij}\right\} \in \mathfrak{R}^{n_{zi} \times n_{zi}}$, and matrices $G_i \in \mathfrak{R}^{n_{zi} \times n_{zi}}$, $\left\{\bar{K}_i^f, \bar{K}_{ij}^f\right\} \in \mathfrak{R}^{n_{ui} \times n_{zi}}$, such that for all $\{l, f\} \in \mathcal{L}_i, j \neq i, \{i, j\} \in \mathcal{N}$, the following LMIs hold:

$$\Omega_i^{ll} < 0, l \in \mathcal{L}_i \tag{104}$$

$$\Omega_i^{lf} + \Omega_i^{fl} < 0, l \leq f \tag{105}$$

where

$$
\begin{cases}
\Omega_i^{lf} = \begin{bmatrix} \Omega_{i(1)}^l & A_i^l G_i^T + B_i^l \bar{K}_i^f & \mathbb{A}_i^{lf} & 0 \\ \star & -\bar{P}_i & 0 & G_i^T \mathbb{I} \\ \star & \star & \mathbb{M}_i - \mathbb{G}_i - \mathbb{G}_i^T & 0 \\ \star & \star & \star & -\bar{\mathbb{M}}_i \end{bmatrix} \\
\Omega_{i(1)}^l = \bar{P}_i - G_i - G_i^T, \\
\mathbb{A}_i^{lf} = \underbrace{\left[\mathcal{A}_{i1}^{lf} \cdots \mathcal{A}_{ij,j\neq i}^{lf} \cdots \mathcal{A}_{iN}^{lf} \right]}_{N-1}, \mathcal{A}_{ij}^{lf} = B_i^l \bar{K}_{ij}^f + \bar{A}_{ij}^l G_i, \\
\mathbb{I}, = \underbrace{\left[I \cdots I \cdots I \right]}_{N-1}, \mathbb{M}_i = \mathrm{diag}\underbrace{\left\{ M_{i1} \cdots M_{ij,j\neq i} \cdots M_{iN} \right\}}_{N-1} \\
\bar{\mathbb{M}}_i = \mathrm{diag}\underbrace{\left\{ M_{1i} \cdots M_{ji,j\neq i} \cdots M_{Ni} \right\}}_{N-1}
\end{cases}
\tag{106}
$$

In that case, the distributed state-feedback fuzzy controller gains can be obtained as

$$
K_i^f = \bar{K}_i^f G_i^{-T}, K_{ij}^f = \bar{K}_{ij}^f G_i^{-T}, f \in \mathcal{L}_i, i \in \mathcal{N}.
\tag{107}
$$

3.3.4 Output Feedback Stabilizing for Continuous-Time Systems

Consider a distributed SOF fuzzy controller

$$
u_i(t) = K_i(\mu_i) y_i(t) + \sum_{j=1,j\neq i}^{N} K_{ij}(\mu_i) y_j(t), i \in \mathcal{N}
\tag{108}
$$

where $K_i(\mu_i) := \sum_{l=1}^{r_i} \mu_i^l K_i^l, K_{ij}(\mu_i) := \sum_{l=1}^{r_i} \mu_i^l K_{ij}^l.$

Combined with the fuzzy system in (90) and the controller in (108), the closed-loop fuzzy control system can be given by

$$
\begin{aligned}
\dot{x}_i(t) = &A_i(\mu_i) x_i(t) + B_i(\mu_i) K_i(\mu_i) C_i(\mu_i) x_i(t) \\
&+ \sum_{j=1,j\neq i}^{N} \left[B_i(\mu_i) K_{ij}(\mu_i) C_j(\mu_j) + \bar{A}_{ij}(\mu_i) \right] x_j(t).
\end{aligned}
\tag{109}
$$

Based on the assumption in (20), we can directly obtain the design result on distributed SOF fuzzy controller as below.

Theorem 3.3.3 Given a large-scale T-S fuzzy interconnected system and a distributed fuzzy controller, then the closed-loop fuzzy control system in (109) is asymptotically stable, if there exist symmetric positive definite matrices

$$M_{ij} \in \mathfrak{R}^{n_{zi} \times n_{zi}}, Q_{i(1)} \in \mathfrak{R}^{n_{yi} \times n_{yi}}, Q_{i(2)} \in \mathfrak{R}^{\left(n_{zi} - n_{yi}\right) \times \left(n_{zi} - n_{yi}\right)},$$

and matrices $G_i \in \mathfrak{R}^{n_{zi} \times n_{zi}}$, $\left\{ \bar{K}_i^f, \bar{K}_{ij}^f \right\} \in \mathfrak{R}^{n_{ui} \times n_{zi}}$, such that for all $\{l, f\} \in \mathcal{L}_i, j \neq i, \{i, j\} \in \mathcal{N}$, the following LMIs hold:

$$\Omega_i^{ll} < 0, l \in \mathcal{L}_i \tag{110}$$

$$\Omega_i^{lf} + \Omega_i^{fl} < 0, l \leq f \tag{111}$$

Where

$$
\begin{cases}
\Omega_i^{lf} = \begin{bmatrix} \Omega_{i(1)}^{lf} & \mathbb{A}_i^{lf} & Q_i \mathbb{I} \\ \star & \mathbb{M}_i - \mathbb{G}_i - \mathbb{G}_i^T & 0 \\ \star & \star & -\bar{\mathbb{M}}_i \end{bmatrix} \\
\Omega_{i(1)}^{lf} = \mathrm{Sym}\left\{ A_i^l Q_i + B_i^l \begin{bmatrix} \bar{K}_i^f & 0 \end{bmatrix} T_{Ci}^T \right\}, \\
\mathbb{A}_i^{lf} = \underbrace{\begin{bmatrix} \mathcal{A}_{i1}^{lf} \cdots \mathcal{A}_{ij,j\neq i}^{lf} \cdots \mathcal{A}_{iN}^{lf} \end{bmatrix}}_{N-1}, \mathcal{A}_{ij}^{lf} = B_i^l \begin{bmatrix} \bar{K}_{ij,j\neq i}^f & 0 \end{bmatrix} T_{Cj}^T + \bar{A}_{ij}^l Q_i, \\
G_j = T_{Cj} \begin{bmatrix} G_{j(1)} & 0 \\ G_{j(2)} & G_{j(3)} \end{bmatrix} T_{Cj}^T, Q_i = T_{Ci} \begin{bmatrix} Q_{i(1)} & 0 \\ 0 & Q_{i(3)} \end{bmatrix} T_{Ci}^T, \mathbb{I} = \underbrace{\begin{bmatrix} \mathrm{I} \cdots \mathrm{I} \cdots \mathrm{I} \end{bmatrix}}_{N-1} \\
\mathbb{M}_i = \mathrm{diag}\underbrace{\left\{ M_{i1} \cdots M_{ij,j\neq i} \cdots M_{iN} \right\}}_{N-1}, \mathbb{G}_i = \mathrm{diag}\underbrace{\left\{ G_1 \cdots G_{j,j\neq i} \cdots G_N \right\}}_{N-1} \\
\bar{\mathbb{M}}_i = \mathrm{diag}\underbrace{\left\{ M_{1i} \cdots M_{ji,j\neq i} \cdots M_{Ni} \right\}}_{N-1}
\end{cases}
\tag{112}
$$

In that case, the distributed SOF fuzzy controller gains can be obtained as

$$K_i^f = \bar{K}_i^f \left[Q_{i(1)} \right]^{-1}, K_{ij}^f = \bar{K}_{ij}^f \left[G_{j(1)} \right]^{-1}, f \in \mathcal{L}_i, i \in \mathcal{N}. \tag{113}$$

Based on the assumption in (27), the LMI-based result can be obtained as below,

Theorem 3.3.4 Given a large-scale T-S fuzzy interconnected system with the assumption in (27) and a distributed fuzzy controller, then the closed-loop fuzzy control system in (109) is asymptotically stable, if there exist symmetric positive definite matrices $M_{ij} \in \mathfrak{R}^{n_{zi} \times n_{zi}}$, $P_{i(1)} \in \mathfrak{R}^{n_{ui} \times n_{ui}}$, $P_{i(2)} \in \mathfrak{R}^{(n_{zi} - n_{ui}) \times (n_{zi} - n_{ui})}$, and matrices $\left\{ \bar{K}_i^f, \bar{K}_{ij}^f \right\} \in \mathfrak{R}^{n_{ui} \times n_{zi}}$, such that for all $\left\{ l, f \right\} \in \mathcal{L}_i, j \neq i, \left\{ i, j \right\} \in \mathcal{N}$, the following LMIs hold:

$$\Omega_i^{ll} < 0, l \in \mathcal{L}_i \tag{114}$$

$$\Omega_i^{lf} + \Omega_i^{fl} < 0, l \leq f \tag{115}$$

where

$$\begin{bmatrix} \Omega_i^{lf} = \begin{bmatrix} \mathrm{Sym} \left\{ P_i A_i^l + T_{Bi}^T \begin{bmatrix} \bar{K}_i^f \\ 0 \end{bmatrix} C_i \right\} + \displaystyle\sum_{j=1, j \neq i}^{N} M_{ji} & \mathbb{A}_i^{lf} \\ \star & -\mathbb{M}_i \end{bmatrix} \\ \mathbb{A}_i^{lf} = \underbrace{\begin{bmatrix} \mathcal{A}_{i1}^{lf} \cdots \mathcal{A}_{ij, j \neq i}^{lf} \cdots \mathcal{A}_{iN}^{lf} \end{bmatrix}}_{N-1}, \mathcal{A}_{ij}^{lf} = P_i \bar{A}_{ij}^l + T_{Bi}^T \begin{bmatrix} \bar{K}_{ij}^f \\ 0 \end{bmatrix} C_j, \\ \mathbb{M}_i = \mathrm{diag} \underbrace{\left\{ M_{i1} \cdots M_{ij, j \neq i} \cdots M_{iN} \right\}}_{N-1}, P_i = T_{Bi}^T \begin{bmatrix} P_{i(1)} & 0 \\ 0 & P_{i(3)} \end{bmatrix} T_{Bi} \end{bmatrix} \tag{116}$$

In that case, the distributed SOF fuzzy controller gains can be obtained as

$$K_i^f = P_{i(1)}^{-1} \bar{K}_i^f, K_{ij}^f = P_{i(1)}^{-1} \bar{K}_{ij}^f, f \in \mathcal{L}_i, i \in \mathcal{N}. \tag{117}$$

Similar to the design result on decentralized SOF controller, we will propose a descriptor system approach to distributed SOF fuzzy controller design. By introducing virtual dynamic in the measurement output, the closed-loop fuzzy control system can be rewritten as the following descriptor model,

$$E\dot{\bar{x}}_i(t) = \bar{A}_i(\mu_i)\bar{x}_i(t) + \sum_{j=1, j \neq i}^{N} \tilde{A}_{ij}(\mu_i)\bar{x}_j(t), \tag{118}$$

where

$$\begin{cases} E = \begin{bmatrix} I & 0 \\ 0 & 0 \end{bmatrix}, \bar{x}_i(t) = \begin{bmatrix} x_i^T(t) & y_i^T(t) \end{bmatrix}^T, \\ \bar{A}_i(\mu_i) = \begin{bmatrix} A_i(\mu_i) & B_i(\mu_i)K_i(\mu_i) \\ C_i(\mu_i) & -I \end{bmatrix}, \tilde{A}_{ij}(\mu_i) = \begin{bmatrix} \bar{A}_{ij}(\mu_i) & 0 \\ 0 & B_i(\mu_i)K_{ij}(\mu_i) \end{bmatrix}. \end{cases} \tag{119}$$

Based on the descriptor system in (118), we can obtain the following result.

Theorem 3.3.5 Given a large-scale T-S fuzzy interconnected system and a distributed fuzzy controller, then the closed-loop fuzzy control system in (109) is asymptotically stable, if there exist symmetric positive definite matrices $M_{ij} \in \Re^{n_{zi} \times n_{zi}}$, and matrices

$$X_{i(1)} \in \Re^{n_{zi} \times n_{zi}}, X_{i(2)} \in \Re^{n_{yi} \times n_{yi}},$$

$$\left\{ \bar{K}_i^f, \bar{K}_{ij}^f \right\} \in \Re^{n_{ui} \times n_{zi}},$$

$$J_i \in \Re^{n_{ui} \times n_{zi}},$$

such that for all $\{l, f\} \in \mathcal{L}_i, j \neq i, \{i, j\} \in \mathcal{N}$, the following LMIs hold:

$$\Omega_i^{ll} < 0, l \in \mathcal{L}_i \tag{120}$$

$$\Omega_i^{lf} + \Omega_i^{fl} < 0, l \leq f \tag{121}$$

where

$$
\left\{
\begin{aligned}
\Omega_i^{lf} &=
\begin{bmatrix}
\mathrm{Sym}\left\{\Omega_{i(1)}^{lf}\right\} & \overline{\mathbb{A}}_i^{lf} & \overline{X}_i^T \mathbb{I} \\
\star & \mathbb{M}_i - \mathbb{X}_i - \mathbb{X}_i^T & 0 \\
\star & \star & -\overline{\mathbb{M}}_i
\end{bmatrix} \\
\Omega_{i(1)}^{lf} &=
\begin{bmatrix}
A_i^l X_{i(1)} + B_i^l \overline{K}_i^f J_i & B_i^l \overline{K}_i^f \\
C_i^l X_{i(1)} - X_{i(2)} J_i & -X_{i(2)}
\end{bmatrix}, \mathbb{I} = \underbrace{\begin{bmatrix} I \cdots I \cdots I \end{bmatrix}}_{N-1} \\
\overline{\mathbb{A}}_i^{lf} &= \underbrace{\begin{bmatrix} \overline{\mathcal{A}}_{i1}^{lf} \cdots \overline{\mathcal{A}}_{ij,j\neq i}^{lf} \cdots \overline{\mathcal{A}}_{iN}^{lf} \end{bmatrix}}_{N-1}, \overline{\mathcal{A}}_{ij}^{lf} = \begin{bmatrix} \overline{A}_{ij}^l X_{i(1)} & 0 \\ B_i^l \overline{K}_{ij}^f J_i & B_i^l \overline{K}_{ij}^f \end{bmatrix} \\
\mathbb{M}_i &= \mathrm{diag}\underbrace{\left\{ M_{ij} \cdots M_{ij} \cdots M_{ij} \right\}}_{N-1}, \overline{\mathbb{M}}_i = \mathrm{diag}\underbrace{\left\{ M_{1i} \cdots M_{ji,j\neq i} \cdots M_{Ni} \right\}}_{N-1}
\end{aligned}
\right.
\tag{122}
$$

In that case, the distributed SOF fuzzy controller gains can be obtained as

$$
K_i^f = \overline{K}_i^f \left[X_{i(2)} \right]^{-1}, K_{ij}^f = \overline{K}_{ij}^f \left[X_{i(2)} \right]^{-1}, f \in \mathcal{L}_i, i \in \mathcal{N}.
\tag{123}
$$

Proof. Choose the Lyapunov functional

$$
\begin{aligned}
V\left(x(t)\right) &= \sum_{i=1}^N V_i\left(x_i(t)\right) \\
&= \sum_{i=1}^N \overline{x}_i^T(t) \mathrm{E}^T \overline{P}_i \overline{x}_i(t), i \in \mathcal{N}
\end{aligned}
\tag{124}
$$

with

$$
\overline{P}_i = \begin{bmatrix} P_{i(1)} & 0 \\ P_{i(2)} & P_{i(3)} \end{bmatrix},
\tag{125}
$$

where $0 < P_{i(1)} = \left[P_{i(1)} \right]^T \in \mathfrak{R}^{n_{xi} \times n_{xi}}, P_{i(2)} \in \mathfrak{R}^{n_{yi} \times n_{xi}}, P_{i(3)} \in \mathfrak{R}^{n_{yi} \times n_{yi}}$.

Taking the time derivative of $V\left(x(t)\right)$ along of the trajectory of the descriptor system in (118), it yields

$$
\begin{cases}
\dot{V}\left(x\left(t\right)\right) \leq \sum_{i=1}^{N} \overline{x}_i^T\left(t\right)\left\{\mathrm{Sym}\left(\overline{A}_i^T\left(\mu_i\right)\overline{P}_i\right)\right\}\overline{x}_i\left(t\right) \\
+\sum_{i=1}^{N}\sum_{j=1,j\neq i}^{N} \overline{x}_i^T\left(t\right)\overline{P}_i^T\left[\tilde{A}_{ij}\left(\mu_i\right)\right]M_{ij}\left[\tilde{A}_{ij}\left(\mu_i\right)\right]^T\overline{P}_i\overline{x}_i\left(t\right) \\
+\sum_{i=1}^{N}\sum_{j=1,j\neq i}^{N}\left\{\overline{x}_i^T\left(t\right)M_{ji}^{-1}\overline{x}_i\left(t\right)\right\}
\end{cases} \tag{126}
$$

By using the Schur complement, the following inequality implies $\dot{V}\left(x\left(t\right)\right)<0$,

$$
\begin{bmatrix}
\mathrm{Sym}\left\{\overline{A}_i^T\left(\mu_i\right)\overline{P}_i\right\} & \mathbb{A}_i\left(\mu_i\right) & \mathbb{I} \\
\star & -\mathbb{M}_i^{-1} & 0 \\
\star & \star & -\overline{\mathbb{M}}_i
\end{bmatrix} < 0, \tag{127}
$$

where

$$
\begin{aligned}
\mathbb{M}_i &= \mathrm{diag}\underbrace{\left\{M_{i1}\cdots M_{ij,j\neq i}\cdots M_{iN}\right\}}_{N-1} \\
\overline{\mathbb{M}}_i &= \mathrm{diag}\underbrace{\left\{M_{1i}\cdots M_{ji,j\neq i}\cdots M_{Ni}\right\}}_{N-1}, \mathbb{I} = \underbrace{\left[\mathrm{I}\cdots\mathrm{I}\cdots\mathrm{I}\right]}_{N-1} \\
\mathbb{A}_i\left(\mu_i\right) &= \underbrace{\left[\mathcal{A}_{ij}\left(\mu_i\right)\cdots\mathcal{A}_{ij,j\neq i}\left(\mu_i\right)\cdots\mathcal{A}_{ij}\left(\mu_i\right)\right]}_{N-1} \\
\mathcal{A}_{ij}\left(\mu_i\right) &= \overline{P}_i^T\left[\tilde{A}_{ij}\left(\mu_i\right)\right]
\end{aligned} \tag{128}
$$

Define

$$
\begin{aligned}
\overline{X}_i &= \overline{P}_i^{-1} \\
&= \begin{bmatrix} X_{i(1)} & 0 \\ X_{i(2)}J_i & X_{i(2)} \end{bmatrix}
\end{aligned} \tag{129}
$$

And

$$\Gamma_i \doteq \mathrm{diag}\left\{\bar{X}_i \mathbb{X}_i \underbrace{\mathrm{I}\cdots \mathrm{I}\cdots \mathrm{I}}_{N-1}\right\}, \mathbb{X}_i = \mathrm{diag}\left\{\underbrace{\bar{X}_i \cdots \bar{X}_i \cdots \bar{X}_i}_{N-1}\right\},$$

$$\bar{K}_i^f = \mathrm{K}_i^f X_{i(2)}, \bar{K}_{ij}^f = \mathrm{K}_{ij}^f X_{i(2)} \tag{130}$$

It follows from (120) and (121) that

$$-\mathrm{Sym}\left\{X_{i(2)}\right\} < 0, \tag{131}$$

which implies the matrix $X_{i(2)}$ is nonsingular.

By performing a congruence transformation to (127) by " $_i$, and taking the relation in (101), we have

$$\begin{bmatrix} \mathrm{Sym}\left\{\bar{A}_i^T\left(\mu_i\right)\bar{P}_i\right\} & \bar{\mathbb{A}}_i\left(\mu_i\right) & \bar{X}_i^T \mathbb{I} \\ \star & \mathbb{M}_i - \mathbb{X}_i - \mathbb{X}_i^T & 0 \\ \star & \star & -\bar{\mathbb{M}}_i \end{bmatrix} < 0, \tag{132}$$

where $\bar{\mathbb{A}}_i\left(\mu_i\right) = \underbrace{\left[\bar{\mathcal{A}}_{ij}\left(\mu_i\right)\cdots \bar{\mathcal{A}}_{ij,j\neq i}\left(\mu_i\right)\cdots \bar{\mathcal{A}}_{ij}\left(\mu_i\right)\right]}_{N-1}, \bar{\mathcal{A}}_{ij}\left(\mu_i\right) = \left[\tilde{A}_{ij}\left(\mu_i\right)\right]\bar{X}_i.$

By extracting the premise variables, the LMI-based results in (120) and (121) can be obtained. Thus, completing this proof.

NOTE: It is noted that the LMI-based result in Theorem 3.3.5 is obtained by using the descriptor system in (118). However, we can also use augmented system $\bar{x}_i\left(t\right) = \left[x_i^T\left(t\right) \quad u_i^T\left(t\right)\right]^T$. In that case, the closed-loop fuzzy control system in (109) can be rewritten as

$$\mathrm{E}\bar{\dot{x}}_i\left(t\right) = \bar{A}_i\left(\mu_i\right)\bar{x}_i\left(t\right) + \sum_{j=1,j\neq i}^{N} \bar{\mathcal{A}}_{ij}\left(\mu_i,\mu_j\right)x_j\left(t\right), \tag{133}$$

where

$$
\begin{cases}
\mathrm{E} = \begin{bmatrix} \mathrm{I} & 0 \\ 0 & 0 \end{bmatrix}, \bar{x}_i\left(t\right) = \begin{bmatrix} x_i^T\left(t\right) & u_i^T\left(t\right) \end{bmatrix}^T, \\[2mm]
\bar{A}_i\left(\mu_i\right) = \begin{bmatrix} A_i\left(\mu_i\right) & B_i\left(\mu_i\right) \\ K_i\left(\mu_i\right)C_i\left(\mu_i\right) & -I \end{bmatrix}, \mathcal{A}_{ij}\left(\mu_i\right) = \begin{bmatrix} \bar{A}_{ij}\left(\mu_i\right) \\ K_{ij}\left(\mu_i\right)C_j\left(\mu_j\right) \end{bmatrix}.
\end{cases}
\tag{134}
$$

Based on the descriptor system in (133), we can obtain the following result.

Theorem 3.3.6 Given a large-scale T-S fuzzy interconnected system and a distributed fuzzy controller, then the closed-loop fuzzy control system in (109) is asymptotically stable, if there exist symmetric positive definite matrices $M_{ij} \in \mathfrak{R}^{n_{zi} \times n_{zi}}$, and $P_{i(1)} \in \mathfrak{R}^{n_{zi} \times n_{zi}}, P_{i(2)} \in \mathfrak{R}^{n_{ui} \times n_{ui}}, J_i \in \mathfrak{R}^{n_{zi} \times n_{ui}}$, $\left\{\bar{K}_i^f, \bar{K}_{ij}^f\right\} \in \mathfrak{R}^{n_{ui} \times n_{zi}}$, , such that for all $\left\{l, f\right\} \in \mathcal{L}_i, j \neq i, \left\{i, j\right\} \in \mathcal{N}$, the following LMIs hold:

$$
\Omega_i^{ll} < 0, l \in \mathcal{L}_i
\tag{135}
$$

$$
\Omega_i^{lf} + \Omega_i^{fl} < 0, l \leq f
\tag{136}
$$

where

$$
\begin{cases}
\Omega_i^{lf} = \begin{bmatrix} \Omega_{i(1)}^{lf} + R \displaystyle\sum_{j=1, j \neq i}^{N} M_{ji} R^T & \bar{\mathbb{A}}_i^{lf} \\ \star & -\mathbb{M}_i \end{bmatrix} \\[6mm]
\Omega_{i(1)}^{lf} = \mathrm{Sym}\left\{ \begin{bmatrix} \left[P_{i(1)}\right]^T A_i^l + J^T \bar{K}_i^f C_i^l & \left[P_{i(1)}\right]^T B_i^l - J^T \left[P_{i(2)}\right]^T \\ \bar{K}_i^f C_i^l & -\left[P_{i(2)}\right]^T \end{bmatrix} \right\} \\[6mm]
\mathbb{M}_i = \mathrm{diag}\underbrace{\left\{ M_{i1} \cdots M_{ij, j \neq i} \cdots M_{iN} \right\}}_{N-1}, R = \begin{bmatrix} I \\ 0 \end{bmatrix}, \mathbb{I} = \underbrace{\begin{bmatrix} I \cdots I \cdots I \end{bmatrix}}_{N-1} \\[6mm]
\bar{\mathbb{A}}_i^{lf} = \underbrace{\begin{bmatrix} \bar{\mathcal{A}}_{i1}^{lf} \cdots \bar{\mathcal{A}}_{ij, j \neq i}^{lf} \cdots \bar{\mathcal{A}}_{iN}^{lf} \end{bmatrix}}_{N-1}, \bar{\mathcal{A}}_{ij}^{lf} = \begin{bmatrix} \left[P_{i(1)}\right]^T \bar{A}_{ij}^l + J^T \bar{K}_{ij}^f C_i^l \\ \bar{K}_{ij}^f C_i^l \end{bmatrix}
\end{cases}
\tag{137}
$$

In that case, the distributed SOF fuzzy controller gains can be obtained as

$$K_i^f = \left[P_{i(2)}\right]^{-1} \bar{K}_i^f, K_i^f = \left[P_{i(2)}\right]^{-1} K_{ij}^f, f \in \mathcal{L}_i, i \in \mathcal{N}. \tag{138}$$

Proof. Similar to (127), we obtain the result

$$\left[\begin{array}{cc} \mathrm{Sym}\left\{\bar{A}_i^T\left(\mu_i\right)\bar{P}_i\right\} + R \displaystyle\sum_{j=1,j\neq i}^{N} M_{ji}R^T & \mathbb{A}_i\left(\mu_i\right) \\ \star & -\mathbb{M}_i^{-1} \end{array} \right] < 0, \tag{139}$$

where

$$\begin{aligned} \mathbb{M}_i &= \mathrm{diag}\underbrace{\left\{M_{i1} \cdots M_{ij,j\neq i} \cdots M_{iN}\right\}}_{N-1} \\ \mathbb{A}_i\left(\mu_i\right) &= \underbrace{\left[\mathcal{A}_{ij}\left(\mu_i\right)\cdots \mathcal{A}_{ij,j\neq i}\left(\mu_i\right)\cdots \mathcal{A}_{ij}\left(\mu_i\right)\right]}_{N-1} \end{aligned} \tag{140}$$

Here, in order to cast (139) into LMI-based condition, we define

$$\bar{P}_i = \begin{bmatrix} P_{i(1)} & 0 \\ P_{i(2)}J & P_{i(2)} \end{bmatrix}, \bar{K}_i^l = \left[P_{i(2)}\right]^T K_i^l, \bar{K}_{ij}^l = \left[P_{i(2)}\right]^T K_{ij}^l, \tag{141}$$

where $P_{i(1)} \in \mathfrak{R}^{n_{xi} \times n_{xi}}, P_{i(2)} \in \mathfrak{R}^{n_{ui} \times n_{ui}}, J_i \in \mathfrak{R}^{n_{xi} \times n_{ui}}$.

Submitting (141) into (139), the inequality in (135) and (136) is obtained. Thus, completing this proof.

3.3.5 Output Feedback Stabilizing for Discrete-Time Systems

Consider a discrete-time large-scale fuzzy interconnected system

$$x_i\left(t+1\right) = A_i\left(\mu_i\right)x_i\left(t\right) + B_i\left(\mu_i\right)u_i\left(t\right) + \sum_{j=1,j\neq i}^{N} \bar{A}_{ij}\left(\mu_i\right)x_j\left(t\right), \tag{142}$$

and a distributed SOF fuzzy controller

$$u_i(t) = K_i(\mu_i) y_i(t) + \sum_{j=1, j \neq i}^{N} K_{ij}(\mu_i) y_j(t), i \in \mathcal{N} \tag{143}$$

where $K_i(\mu_i) := \sum_{l=1}^{r_i} \mu_i^l K_i^l, K_{ij}(\mu_i) := \sum_{l=1}^{r_i} \mu_i^l K_{ij}^l$.

Based on the system in (142) and the assumption in (20), we can directly obtain the following design result on the distributed control.

Theorem 3.3.7 Given the large-scale T-S fuzzy interconnected system in (142) and the distributed fuzzy controller in (143), then the resulting closed-loop fuzzy control system is asymptotically stable, if there exist symmetric positive definite matrices $\{\bar{P}_i, M_{ij}\} \in \mathfrak{R}^{n_{zi} \times n_{zi}}$, and matrices $G_i \in \mathfrak{R}^{n_{zi} \times n_{zi}}$, $\{\bar{K}_i^f, \bar{K}_{ij}^f\} \in \mathfrak{R}^{n_{ui} \times n_{zi}}$, such that for all $\{l, f\} \in \mathcal{L}_i, j \neq i, \{i, j\} \in \mathcal{N}$, the following LMIs hold:

$$\Omega_i^{ll} < 0, l \in \mathcal{L}_i \tag{144}$$

$$\Omega_i^{lf} + \Omega_i^{fl} < 0, l \leq f \tag{145}$$

where

$$\begin{cases} \Omega_i^{lf} = \begin{bmatrix} \Omega_{i(1)}^{lf} & A_i^l G_i^T + B_i^l [\bar{K}_i^f \quad 0] T_{Ci}^T & \mathbb{B}_i^{lf} & 0 \\ \star & -\bar{P}_i & 0 & G_i^T \mathbb{I} \\ \star & \star & \mathbb{M}_i - \mathbb{G}_i - \mathbb{G}_i^T & 0 \\ \star & \star & \star & -\bar{\mathbb{M}}_i \end{bmatrix} \\ \Omega_{i(1)}^{lf} = \bar{P}_i - G_i - G_i^T, \mathbb{I} = \underbrace{[I \cdots I \cdots I]}_{N-1}, \mathbb{G}_i = \underbrace{[G_i \cdots G_i \cdots G_i]}_{N-1} \\ \bar{\mathbb{M}}_i = \text{diag}\underbrace{\{M_{1i} \cdots M_{ji, j \neq i} \cdots M_{Ni}\}}_{N-1}, G_i^T = T_{Ci} \begin{bmatrix} G_{i(1)} & 0 \\ G_{i(2)} & G_{i(3)} \end{bmatrix} T_{Ci}^T \\ \mathbb{B}_i^{lf} = \underbrace{[\mathcal{B}_{i1}^{lf} \cdots \mathcal{B}_{ij, j \neq i}^{lf} \cdots \mathcal{B}_{iN}^{lf}]}_{N-1}, \mathcal{B}_{ij}^{lf} = B_i^l [\bar{K}_{ij}^f \quad 0] T_{Cj}^T + \bar{A}_{ij}^l G_i^T \\ \mathbb{M}_i = \text{diag}\underbrace{\{M_1 \cdots M_{j, j \neq i} \cdots M_N\}}_{N-1} \end{cases} \tag{146}$$

In that case, the state-feedback fuzzy controller gains can be obtained as

$$K_i^f = \bar{K}_i^f G_{i(1)}^{-T}, K_{ij}^f = \bar{K}_{ij}^f G_{i(1)}^{-T}, f \in \mathcal{L}_i, i \in \mathcal{N}. \tag{147}$$

Similarly, based on the assumption (27), the corresponding design result can be derived as below:

Theorem 3.3.8 Given the large-scale T-S fuzzy interconnected system in (142) and the distributed fuzzy controller in (143), then the resulting closed-loop fuzzy control system is asymptotically stable, if there exist symmetric positive definite matrices $\{P_i, M_{ij}\} \in \mathfrak{R}^{n_{zi} \times n_{zi}}$, and matrices $G_i \in \mathfrak{R}^{n_{zi} \times n_{zi}}, \{\bar{K}_i^f, \bar{K}_{ij}^f\} \in \mathfrak{R}^{n_{ui} \times n_{zi}}$, such that for all $l \in \mathcal{L}_i, , j \neq i, \{i, j\} \in \mathcal{N}$, the following LMIs hold:

$$\Omega_i^{ll} < 0, l \in \mathcal{L}_i \tag{148}$$

$$\Omega_i^{lf} + \Omega_i^{fl} < 0, l \le f \tag{149}$$

where

$$\begin{bmatrix} \Omega_i^{lf} = \begin{bmatrix} P_i - G_i - G_i^T & G_i A_i^l + T_{Bi}^T \begin{bmatrix} \bar{K}_i^l \\ 0 \end{bmatrix} C_i^f & \mathbb{A}_i^{lf} \\ \star & -P_i + \sum_{j=1, j \neq i}^{N} M_{ji} & 0 \\ \star & \star & -\mathbb{M}_i \end{bmatrix} \\ \mathbb{M}_i = \text{diag}\underbrace{\{M_{i1} \cdots M_{ij, j \neq i} \cdots M_{iN}\}}_{N-1}, \mathbb{A}_i^{lf} = \underbrace{[\bar{A}_{i1}^{lf} \cdots \bar{A}_{ij, j \neq i}^{lf} \cdots \bar{A}_{iN}^{lf}]}_{N-1} \\ G_i = T_{Bi}^T \begin{bmatrix} G_{i(1)} & G_{i(2)} \\ 0 & G_{i(3)} \end{bmatrix} T_{Bi}, \bar{A}_{ij}^{lf} = T_{Bi}^T \begin{bmatrix} \bar{K}_{ij}^l \\ 0 \end{bmatrix} C_i^f + G_i \bar{A}_{ij}^l \end{bmatrix} \tag{150}$$

In that case, the distributed state-feedback fuzzy controller gains can be obtained as

$$K_i^l = G_{i(1)}^{-1} \bar{K}_i^l, K_{ij}^l = G_{i(1)}^{-1} \bar{K}_{ij}^l, l \in \mathcal{L}_i, i \in \mathcal{N}. \tag{151}$$

In the following, by using descriptor system approach, the closed-loop fuzzy control system is rewritten as

$$\mathrm{E}\bar{x}_i(t+1) = \bar{A}_i(\mu_i)\bar{x}_i(t) + \sum_{j=1, j\neq i}^{N} \bar{A}_{ij}(\mu_i, \mu_j) x_j(t), \tag{152}$$

where

$$\begin{cases}
\mathrm{E} = \begin{bmatrix} \mathrm{I} & 0 \\ 0 & 0 \end{bmatrix}, \bar{x}_i(t) = \begin{bmatrix} x_i^T(t) & u_i^T(t) \end{bmatrix}^T, \\
\bar{A}_i(\mu_i) = \begin{bmatrix} A_i(\mu_i) & B_i(\mu_i) \\ K_i(\mu_i)C_i(\mu_i) & -I \end{bmatrix}, \bar{A}_{ij}(\mu_i, \mu_j) = \begin{bmatrix} \bar{A}_{ij}(\mu_i, \mu_j) \\ K_{ij}(\mu_i)C_j(\mu_i) \end{bmatrix}.
\end{cases} \tag{153}$$

Based on the new model in (152), we can also obtain the design result as below.

Theorem 3.3.9 Given the large-scale T-S fuzzy interconnected system in (142) and the distributed fuzzy controller in (143), then the resulting closed-loop fuzzy control system is asymptotically stable, if there exist symmetric positive definite matrices $\{P_i, M_{ij}\} \in \mathfrak{R}^{n_{zi} \times n_{zi}}$, and matrices $G_i \in \mathfrak{R}^{n_{zi} \times n_{zi}}$, $\{\bar{K}_i^f, \bar{K}_{ij}^f\} \in \mathfrak{R}^{n_{ui} \times n_{zi}}$, such that for all $l \in \mathcal{L}_i, j \neq i, \{i, j\} \in \mathcal{N}$, the following LMIs hold:

$$\Omega_i^{ll} < 0, l \in \mathcal{L}_i \tag{154}$$

$$\Omega_i^{lf} + \Omega_i^{fl} < 0, l \leq f \tag{155}$$

Where

$$\Omega_i^{lf} = \begin{bmatrix} \Omega_{i(1)}^{lf} + \mathrm{Sym}\left\{\Omega_{i(2)}^{lf}\right\} & \mathbb{A}_i^{lf} \\ \star & -\mathbb{M}_i \end{bmatrix}, \Omega_{i(1)}^{lf} = \begin{bmatrix} E^T \bar{P}_i E + \sum_{j=1, j\neq i}^{N} M_{ji} & 0 \\ 0 & \bar{P}_i \end{bmatrix}$$

$$\Omega_{i(2)}^{lf} = \begin{bmatrix} G_{i(1)}A_i^l + J_i\bar{K}_i^l C_i^f & G_{i(1)}B_i^l - J_i G_{i(3)} & -G_{i(1)} & -J_i G_{i(3)} \\ G_{i(2)}A_i^l + \bar{K}_i^l C_i^f & G_{i(2)}B_i^l - G_{i(3)} & -G_{i(2)} & -G_{i(3)} \\ G_{i(1)}A_i^l + J_i\bar{K}_i^l C_i^f & G_{i(1)}B_i^l - J_i G_{i(3)} & -G_{i(1)} & -J_i G_{i(3)} \\ G_{i(2)}A_i^l + \bar{K}_i^l C_i^f & G_{i(2)}B_i^l - G_{i(3)} & -G_{i(2)} & -G_{i(3)} \end{bmatrix}$$

$$\mathbb{A}_i^{lf} = \underbrace{\left[\bar{\mathcal{A}}_{i1}^{lf} \cdots \bar{\mathcal{A}}_{ij,j\neq i}^{lf} \cdots \bar{\mathcal{A}}_{iN}^{lf} \right]}_{N-1}, \bar{\mathcal{A}}_{ij}^{lf} = \begin{bmatrix} G_{i(1)}\bar{A}_{ij}^l + J_i\bar{K}_{ij}^l C_i^f \\ G_{i(2)}\bar{A}_{ij}^l + \bar{K}_{ij}^l C_i^f \\ G_{i(1)}\bar{A}_{ij}^l + J_i\bar{K}_{ij}^l C_i^f \\ G_{i(2)}\bar{A}_{ij}^l + \bar{K}_{ij}^l C_i^f \end{bmatrix}, \bar{P}_i = \begin{bmatrix} P_{i(1)} & P_{i(2)} \\ \star & P_{i(3)} \end{bmatrix} \quad (156)$$

In that case, the distributed state-feedback fuzzy controller gains can be obtained as

$$K_i^l = G_{i(3)}^{-1}\bar{K}_i^l, K_{ij}^l = G_{i(3)}^{-1}\bar{K}_{ij}^l, l \in \mathcal{L}, i \in \mathcal{N}. \quad (157)$$

3.4 ILLUSTRATIVE EXAMPLES

In this section, we will demonstrate the validity of the proposed method for controller design by using two numerical examples.

Example 1

Consider a continuous-time large-scale interconnected system with three fuzzy subsystems as below.

Plant Rule R_i^{11}: IF $\varsigma_{i1}(t)$ is F_{i1}^1 and $\varsigma_{j2}(t)$ is F_{j2}^1 and $\varsigma_{k3}(t)$ is F_{k3}^1, THEN

$$\dot{x}_i(t) = A_i^1 x_i(t) + B_i^1 u_i(t) + \bar{A}_{ij,j\neq i}^{11} x_j(t) + \bar{A}_{ik,k\neq i,k\neq j}^{11} x_k(t), i \in \{1,2,3\}$$

Plant Rule R_i^{12}: IF $\varsigma_{i1}(t)$ is F_{i1}^1 and $\varsigma_{j2}(t)$ is F_{j2}^2 and $\varsigma_{k3}(t)$ is F_{k3}^1, THEN

$$\dot{x}_i(t) = A_i^1 x_i(t) + B_i^1 u_i(t) + \bar{A}_{ij,j\neq i}^{12} x_j(t) + \bar{A}_{ik,k\neq i,k\neq j}^{11} x_k(t), i \in \{1,2,3\}$$

Plant Rule R_i^{13}: IF $\varsigma_{i1}(t)$ is F_{i1}^1 and $\varsigma_{j2}(t)$ is F_{j2}^1 and $\varsigma_{k3}(t)$ is F_{k3}^2, THEN

$$\dot{x}_i(t) = A_i^1 x_i(t) + B_i^1 u_i(t) + \bar{A}_{ij,j\neq i}^{11} x_j(t) + \bar{A}_{ik,k\neq i,k\neq j}^{12} x_k(t), i \in \{1,2,3\}$$

Plant Rule R_i^{14}: IF $\varsigma_{i1}(t)$ is F_{i1}^1 and $\varsigma_{j2}(t)$ is F_{j2}^2 and $\varsigma_{k3}(t)$ is F_{k3}^2, THEN

$$\dot{x}_i(t) = A_i^1 x_i(t) + B_i^1 u_i(t) + \bar{A}_{ij,j\neq i}^{12} x_j(t) + \bar{A}_{ik,k\neq i,k\neq j}^{12} x_k(t), i \in \{1,2,3\}$$

Plant Rule R_i^{21}: IF $\varsigma_{i1}(t)$ is F_{i1}^2 and $\varsigma_{j2}(t)$ is F_{j2}^1 and $\varsigma_{k3}(t)$ is F_{k3}^1, THEN

$$\dot{x}_i(t) = A_i^2 x_i(t) + B_i^2 u_i(t) + \bar{A}_{ij,j\neq i}^{11} x_j(t) + \bar{A}_{ik,k\neq i,k\neq j}^{11} x_k(t), i \in \{1,2,3\}$$

Plant Rule R_i^{22}: IF $\varsigma_{i1}(t)$ is F_{i1}^2 and $\varsigma_{j2}(t)$ is F_{j2}^2 and $\varsigma_{k3}(t)$ is F_{k3}^1, THEN

$$\dot{x}_i(t) = A_i^2 x_i(t) + B_i^2 u_i(t) + \bar{A}_{ij,j\neq i}^{12} x_j(t) + \bar{A}_{ik,k\neq i,k\neq j}^{11} x_k(t), i \in \{1,2,3\}$$

Plant Rule R_i^{23}: IF $\varsigma_{i1}(t)$ is F_{i1}^2 and $\varsigma_{j2}(t)$ is F_{j2}^1 and $\varsigma_{k3}(t)$ is F_{k3}^2, THEN

$$\dot{x}_i(t) = A_i^2 x_i(t) + B_i^2 u_i(t) + \bar{A}_{ij,j\neq i}^{11} x_j(t) + \bar{A}_{ik,k\neq i,k\neq j}^{12} x_k(t), i \in \{1,2,3\}$$

Plant Rule R_i^{24}: IF $\xi_{i1}(t)$ is F_{i1}^2 and $\varsigma_{j2}(t)$ is F_{j2}^2 and $\varsigma_{k3}(t)$ is F_{k3}^2, THEN

$$\dot{x}_i(t) = A_i^2 x_i(t) + B_i^2 u_i(t) + \bar{A}_{ij,j\neq i}^{12} x_j(t) + \bar{A}_{ik,k\neq i,k\neq j}^{12} x_k(t), i \in \{1,2,3\}$$

Where

$$A_1^1 = \begin{bmatrix} 0.1 & 1.8 \\ 0 & 0 \end{bmatrix}, A_1^2 = \begin{bmatrix} 0.1 & 1.6 \\ 0 & 0 \end{bmatrix}, B_1^1 = \begin{bmatrix} 0.5 \\ 0.2 \end{bmatrix}, B_1^2 = \begin{bmatrix} 0.4 \\ 0.5 \end{bmatrix}, A_{12}^{11} = \begin{bmatrix} 0.1 & 0.2 \\ 0 & 0 \end{bmatrix},$$

$$A_{12}^{12} = \begin{bmatrix} 0.3 & 0.1 \\ 0 & 0 \end{bmatrix}, A_{12}^{21} = \begin{bmatrix} 0.2 & 0.1 \\ 0 & 0 \end{bmatrix}, A_{12}^{22} = \begin{bmatrix} 0.1 & 0.2 \\ 0 & 0 \end{bmatrix}, A_{13}^{11} = \begin{bmatrix} 0.1 & 0.3 \\ 0 & 0 \end{bmatrix},$$

$$A_{13}^{12} = \begin{bmatrix} 0.3 & 0.1 \\ 0 & 0 \end{bmatrix}, A_{13}^{21} = \begin{bmatrix} 0.1 & 0.3 \\ 0 & 0 \end{bmatrix}, A_{13}^{22} = \begin{bmatrix} 0.1 & 0.2 \\ 0 & 0 \end{bmatrix}$$

for the subsystem 1, and

$$A_2^1 = \begin{bmatrix} 0.1 & 1.8 \\ 0 & 0 \end{bmatrix}, A_2^2 = \begin{bmatrix} 0.1 & 1.5 \\ 0 & 0 \end{bmatrix}, B_2^1 = \begin{bmatrix} 0.6 \\ 0.3 \end{bmatrix}, B_2^2 = \begin{bmatrix} 0.4 \\ 0.5 \end{bmatrix},$$

$$A_{21}^{11} = \begin{bmatrix} 0.1 & 0.1 \\ 0 & 0 \end{bmatrix}, A_{21}^{12} = \begin{bmatrix} 0.1 & 0.3 \\ 0 & 0 \end{bmatrix}, A_{21}^{21} = \begin{bmatrix} 0.1 & 0.2 \\ 0 & 0 \end{bmatrix}, A_{12}^{22} = \begin{bmatrix} 0.2 & 0.2 \\ 0 & 0 \end{bmatrix},$$

$$A_{23}^{11} = \begin{bmatrix} 0.1 & 0.2 \\ 0 & 0 \end{bmatrix}, A_{23}^{12} = \begin{bmatrix} 0.2 & 0.1 \\ 0 & 0 \end{bmatrix}, A_{23}^{21} = \begin{bmatrix} 0.1 & 0.2 \\ 0 & 0 \end{bmatrix}, A_{23}^{22} = \begin{bmatrix} 0.1 & 0.1 \\ 0 & 0 \end{bmatrix},$$

for the subsystem 2, and

$$A_3^1 = \begin{bmatrix} 0.1 & 1.7 \\ 0 & 0 \end{bmatrix}, A_3^2 = \begin{bmatrix} 0.1 & 1.5 \\ 0 & 0 \end{bmatrix}, B_3^1 = \begin{bmatrix} 0.5 \\ 0.3 \end{bmatrix}, B_3^2 = \begin{bmatrix} 0.4 \\ 0.5 \end{bmatrix},$$

$$A_{31}^{11} = \begin{bmatrix} 0.2 & 0.1 \\ 0 & 0 \end{bmatrix}, A_{31}^{12} = \begin{bmatrix} 0.1 & 0 \\ 0 & 0 \end{bmatrix}, A_{31}^{21} = \begin{bmatrix} 0.1 & 0.1 \\ 0 & 0 \end{bmatrix}, A_{31}^{22} = \begin{bmatrix} 0.1 & 0 \\ 0 & 0 \end{bmatrix},$$

$$A_{32}^{11} = \begin{bmatrix} 0.1 & 0.1 \\ 0 & 0 \end{bmatrix}, A_{32}^{12} = \begin{bmatrix} 0.1 & 0 \\ 0 & 0 \end{bmatrix}, A_{32}^{21} = \begin{bmatrix} 0.1 & 0.1 \\ 0 & 0 \end{bmatrix}, A_{32}^{22} = \begin{bmatrix} 0.1 & 0 \\ 0 & 0 \end{bmatrix},$$

for the subsystem 3.

The normalized membership functions are shown in Figure 1, where $r_i = 5$. It is noted that the open-loop system is unstable. Here, the objective is to design a decentralized fuzzy controller such that the resulting closed-loop control system is asymptotically stable. By using Theorem 3.2.1, we find a feasible solution to the stability problem for the considered system, and the corresponding controller gains are

$$K_1^1 = \begin{bmatrix} -6.6526 & -3.8335 \end{bmatrix}, K_1^2 = \begin{bmatrix} -6.3185 & -2.6909 \end{bmatrix},$$
$$K_2^1 = \begin{bmatrix} -5.0860 & -3.1953 \end{bmatrix}, K_2^2 = \begin{bmatrix} -5.7107 & -2.6693 \end{bmatrix},$$
$$K_3^1 = \begin{bmatrix} -4.9885 & -3.5170 \end{bmatrix}, K_3^2 = \begin{bmatrix} -5.0181 & -2.8287 \end{bmatrix}.$$

Taken the above controller gains, under the initial conditions $x_1(0) = \begin{bmatrix} 1.1 & -0.8 \end{bmatrix}^T$, $x_2(0) = \begin{bmatrix} 1.4 & -0.6 \end{bmatrix}^T$, and $x_3(0) = \begin{bmatrix} 1.5 & -1.1 \end{bmatrix}^T$. Figures 2, 3, and 4 show the state responses for the closed-loop large-scale fuzzy interconnected system. Thus, showing the effectiveness of the decentralized fuzzy controller design methods.

Figure 1. Membership functions

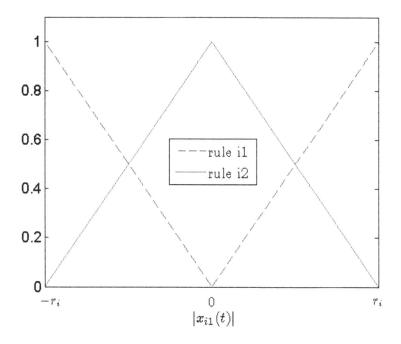

Figure 2. Response of closed-loop subsystem 1

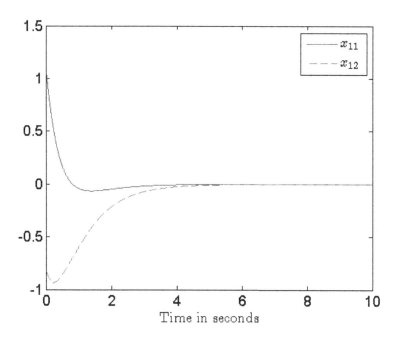

Figure 3. Response of closed-loop subsystem 2

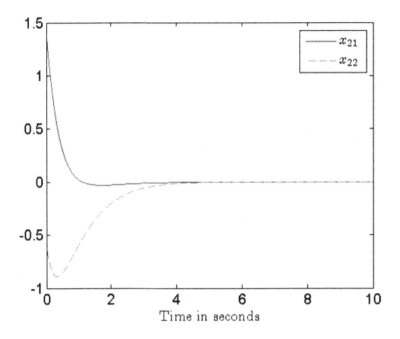

Figure 4. Response of closed-loop subsystem 3

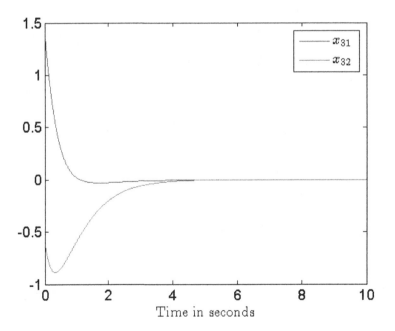

Example 2

Consider a discrete-time large-scale fuzzy interconnected system with the parameters as below,

$$A_1^1 = \begin{bmatrix} 1.5 & 0 \\ 0.05 & 0.7 \end{bmatrix}, A_1^2 = \begin{bmatrix} 1.8 & 0 \\ 0.09 & 0.7 \end{bmatrix}, B_1^1 = B_1^2 = \begin{bmatrix} 1 \\ 0 \end{bmatrix},$$

$$A_{12}^{11} = \begin{bmatrix} 0.04 & 0 \\ 0.02 & 0.07 \end{bmatrix}, A_{12}^{12} = \begin{bmatrix} 0.03 & 0 \\ 0.01 & 0.08 \end{bmatrix}, A_{12}^{21} = \begin{bmatrix} 0.05 & 0 \\ 0.01 & 0.06 \end{bmatrix}, A_{12}^{22} = \begin{bmatrix} 0.07 & 0 \\ 0.03 & 0.05 \end{bmatrix},$$

$$A_{13}^{11} = \begin{bmatrix} 0.04 & 0 \\ 0.04 & 0.03 \end{bmatrix}, A_{13}^{12} = \begin{bmatrix} 0.03 & 0 \\ 0.03 & 0.04 \end{bmatrix}, A_{13}^{21} = \begin{bmatrix} 0.04 & 0 \\ 0.02 & 0.05 \end{bmatrix}, A_{13}^{22} = \begin{bmatrix} 0.05 & 0 \\ 0.03 & 0.02 \end{bmatrix}$$

for the subsystem 1, and

$$A_2^1 = \begin{bmatrix} 1.8 & 0 \\ 0.05 & 0.7 \end{bmatrix}, A_2^2 = \begin{bmatrix} 1.2 & 0 \\ 0.09 & 0.7 \end{bmatrix}, B_2^1 = B_2^2 = \begin{bmatrix} 1 \\ 0 \end{bmatrix},$$

$$A_{21}^{11} = \begin{bmatrix} 0.04 & 0 \\ 0.02 & 0.05 \end{bmatrix}, A_{21}^{12} = \begin{bmatrix} 0.05 & 0 \\ 0.01 & 0.06 \end{bmatrix}, A_{21}^{21} = \begin{bmatrix} 0.04 & 0 \\ 0.05 & 0.04 \end{bmatrix}, A_{21}^{22} = \begin{bmatrix} 0.05 & 0 \\ 0.06 & 0.02 \end{bmatrix},$$

$$A_{23}^{11} = \begin{bmatrix} 0.03 & 0 \\ 0.05 & 0.03 \end{bmatrix}, A_{23}^{12} = \begin{bmatrix} 0.05 & 0 \\ 0.04 & 0.05 \end{bmatrix}, A_{23}^{21} = \begin{bmatrix} 0.04 & 0 \\ 0.02 & 0.04 \end{bmatrix}, A_{23}^{22} = \begin{bmatrix} 0.06 & 0 \\ 0.03 & 0.03 \end{bmatrix}$$

for the subsystem 2, and

$$A_3^1 = \begin{bmatrix} 1.7 & 0 \\ 0.05 & 0.6 \end{bmatrix}, A_3^2 = \begin{bmatrix} 1.4 & 0 \\ 0.09 & 0.6 \end{bmatrix}, B_3^1 = B_3^2 = \begin{bmatrix} 1 \\ 0 \end{bmatrix},$$

$$A_{31}^{11} = \begin{bmatrix} 0.02 & 0 \\ 0.02 & 0.04 \end{bmatrix}, A_{31}^{12} = \begin{bmatrix} 0.03 & 0 \\ 0.03 & 0.02 \end{bmatrix}, A_{31}^{21} = \begin{bmatrix} 0.04 & 0 \\ 0.01 & 0.02 \end{bmatrix}, A_{31}^{22} = \begin{bmatrix} 0.03 & 0 \\ 0.02 & 0.03 \end{bmatrix},$$

$$A_{32}^{11} = \begin{bmatrix} 0.03 & 0 \\ 0.02 & 0.04 \end{bmatrix}, A_{32}^{12} = \begin{bmatrix} 0.02 & 0 \\ 0.03 & 0.05 \end{bmatrix}, A_{32}^{21} = \begin{bmatrix} 0.01 & 0 \\ 0.04 & 0.04 \end{bmatrix}, A_{32}^{22} = \begin{bmatrix} 0.04 & 0 \\ 0.01 & 0.03 \end{bmatrix}$$

for the subsystem 3.

The normalized membership functions are shown in Figure 1, where $r_i = 5$. It is noted that the open-loop system is unstable. Here, the objective is to design a decentralized fuzzy controller such that the resulting closed-loop control system is asymptotically stable. by using Theorem 3.2.2, we find a feasible solution to the stability problem for the considered system, and the corresponding controller gains are

$$
K_1^1 = \begin{bmatrix} -1.5092 & -0.1284 \end{bmatrix}, K_1^2 = \begin{bmatrix} -1.8092 & -0.1284 \end{bmatrix},
$$
$$
K_2^1 = \begin{bmatrix} -1.8091 & -0.1272 \end{bmatrix}, K_2^2 = \begin{bmatrix} -1.2091 & -0.1272 \end{bmatrix},
$$
$$
K_3^1 = \begin{bmatrix} -1.7068 & -0.0810 \end{bmatrix}, K_3^2 = \begin{bmatrix} -1.4068 & -0.0810 \end{bmatrix}.
$$

Under the initial conditions $x_1(0) = \begin{bmatrix} 1.1 & -0.8 \end{bmatrix}^T$, $x_2(0) = \begin{bmatrix} 1.4 & -0.6 \end{bmatrix}^T$, and $x_3(0) = \begin{bmatrix} 1.5 & -1.1 \end{bmatrix}^T$, and take the above controller gains, Figures 5, 6, and 7 show the state responses for the
closed-loop large-scale fuzzy interconnected system, respectively. Thus, showing the effectiveness of the decentralized fuzzy controller design methods.

Figure 5. Response of closed-loop subsystem 1

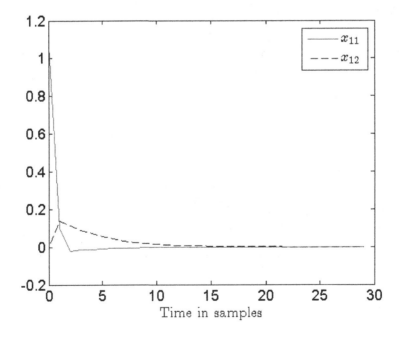

Figure 6. Response of closed-loop subsystem 2

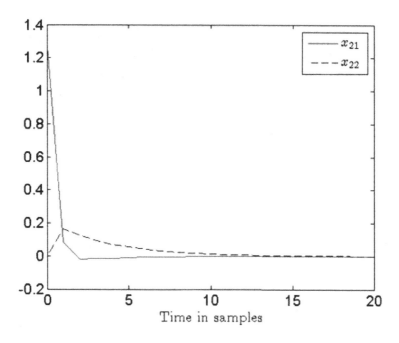

Figure 7. Response of closed-loop subsystem 3

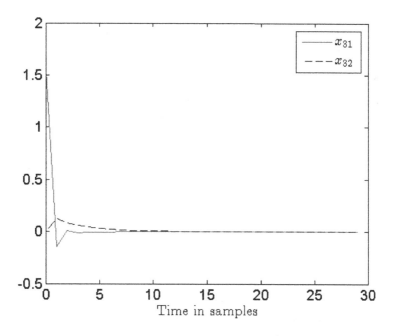

3.5 CONCLUSION

The stabilization problem for large-scale T-S fuzzy interconnected systems has been studied in this chapter. Various LMI-based stabilization conditions have been established for the continuous-time and discrete-time systems, and for the decentralized control and distributed control, respectively. Also, the derived design results on the state feedback control are extended to the case of the SOF control. Several examples have been given to illustrate the proposed methods.

REFERENCES

Chadli, M., & Guerra, T. (2012). LMI solution for robust static output feedback control of discrete Takagi-Sugeno fuzzy models. *IEEE Transactions on Fuzzy Systems*, *20*(6), 1160–1165. doi:10.1109/TFUZZ.2012.2196048

Chang, W., & Wang, W. (2015). Fuzzy control synthesis for a large-scale system with a reduced number of LMIs. *IEEE Transactions on Fuzzy Systems*, *23*(4), 1197–1210. doi:10.1109/TFUZZ.2014.2347995

Dong, J., & Yang, G. (2007). Robust H∞ controller design via static output feedback of uncertain discrete-time T-S fuzzy systems. *Proceedings of the 2007 IEEE Conference on American Control*, New York, NY (pp. 4053-4058). doi:10.1109/ACC.2007.4282398

He, Y., Wu, M., Liu, G., & She, J.-H. (2008). Output feedback stabilization for a discrete-time system with a time-varying delay. *IEEE Transactions on Automatic Control*, *53*(10), 2372–2377. doi:10.1109/TAC.2008.2007522

Kau, S., Lee, H., Yang, C., Lee, C., Hong, L., & Fang, C. (2007). Robust H_∞ fuzzy static output feedback control of T-S fuzzy systems with parametric uncertainties. *Fuzzy Sets and Systems*, *158*(2), 135–146. doi:10.1016/j.fss.2006.09.010

Kazempour, F., & Ghaisari, J. (2013). Stability analysis of model-based networked distributed control systems. *Journal of Process Control*, *23*(3), 444–452. doi:10.1016/j.jprocont.2012.12.010

Lo, J., & Lin, M. (2003). Robust H_∞ nonlinear control via fuzzy static output feedback. *IEEE Transactions on Circuits and Systems. I, Fundamental Theory and Applications*, *50*(11), 1494–1502. doi:10.1109/TCSI.2003.818623

Qiu, J., Ding, S., Gao, H., & Yin, S. (2016). Fuzzy-model-based reliable static output feedback control of nonlinear hyperbolic PDE systems. *IEEE Transactions on Fuzzy Systems*, *24*(2), 388–400. doi:10.1109/TFUZZ.2015.2457934

Qiu, J., Feng, G., & Gao, H. (2010). Fuzzy-model-based piecewise H_∞ static-output-feedback controller design for networked nonlinear systems. *IEEE Transactions on Fuzzy Systems*, *18*(5), 919–934. doi:10.1109/TFUZZ.2010.2052259

Qiu, J., Feng, G., & Gao, H. (2011). Approaches to robust H_∞ static output feedback control of discrete-time piecewise-affine systems with norm-bounded uncertainties. *International Journal of Robust and Nonlinear Control*, *21*(7), 790–814. doi:10.1002/rnc.1627

Chapter 4
Sampled–Data Control of Large–Scale Fuzzy Interconnected Systems

ABSTRACT

This chapter aims to study the sampled-data stabilization for large-scale fuzzy interconnected systems. We use two approaches to design the decentralized fuzzy sampled-data controller: Wirtinger's inequality and scaled small gain (SSG) theorem. Our aim is to derive the co-design consisting of the controller gains and sampled period in terms of a set of LMIs. Also, we consider the distributed sampled-data control problem, where the sampling periods among all subsystems may be different, and the actuator in each subsystem is time-driven. Finally, two simulation examples are provided to validate the advantage of the proposed methods.

4.1 INTRODUCTION

With the development of modern high-speed computers, microelectronics, and communication networks, increasing research efforts have been devoted to sampled-data control systems. It is well-known that the control input in sampled-data systems keeps constant between any two consecutive sampling instants and the feedback signals could only be updated at each sampling instant. In that case, a long sampling period may result in instability, and/or poor performance of sampled-data control systems (Chen & Francis, 2012).

DOI: 10.4018/978-1-5225-2385-7.ch004

However, a short sampling period may also result in high communication channel occupation and signal transmission, and increasing cost on control hardware. An important issue arises here as to how to choose a longer sampling period such that a sampled-data controller to implement the system stability. Until now, three main approaches have been used to analyze and synthesize sampled-data systems (Liu, Fridman, & Johansson, 2015): Discrete model-based approach (Hetel, Kruszewski, Perruquetti, & Richard, 2011), impulsive model-based approach (Naghshtabrizi, Teel, & Hespanha, 2008), and input delay approach in which the sampled-data system is transformed into a continuous-time system with a delayed control input (Fridman, 2010). When taking the uncertainties in system parameters and time-varying sampling periods, and dynamic behavior in the nonlinear systems, the first two approaches fail to avoid difficulties in the complexities of the design procedure. The main advantage of the input delay approach over the other two main approaches is that the sampling holder can be modeled as a delayed control input. In that case, the Lyapunov-Krasovskii functional (LKF) method can be used to establish the stability conditions (Fridman, Seuret, & Richard, 2004).

Recently, there has been relatively some works on using discrete model-based approach to design decentralized sampled-data controller for large-scale fuzzy interconnected systems (Kim et al., 2015; Koo, Park, & Joo, 2016). However, some tuning scalars have to give a prior, while it is not clear that how to find appropriate values of these scalars such that the obtained LMIs have a feasible solution.

This chapter studies the sampled-data control for large-scale nonlinear interconnected systems. Each nonlinear subsystem in the considered large-scale system is represented by a T-S model, and obtains its feedback information through a sampler. First, by using input delay approach, the closed-loop sampled-data fuzzy control system is formulated into a continuous-time system with time-varying delay. Then, based on the new model, we use two approaches to design the decentralized fuzzy sampled-data controller: Wirtinger's inequality and scaled small gain (SSG) theorem. We further introduce a novel Lyapunov-Krasovskii functional (LKF), where not all of the Lyapunov matrices are required to be positive definite. The co-design problem consisting of the controller gains and sampled period can be solved in terms of a set of LMIs. Also, we consider the distributed sampled-data control problem, where the sampling periods among all subsystems may be different, and the actuator in each subsystem is time-driven. Similarly, based on the input delay approach combined with the LKF, sufficient conditions for the existence of the distributed sampled-data controller can be derived in terms of a set of LMIs. Finally, two simulation examples are provided to validate the advantage of the proposed methods.

4.2 DECENTRALIZED SAMPLE-DATA CONTROL

In this section, we study the decentralized sampled-data controller design for large-scale T-S fuzzy interconnected systems, and the co-design problem consisting of the controller gains and sampled period can be solved in terms of a set of LMIs.

4.2.1 Problem Formulation

Consider a class of continuous-time large-scale nonlinear interconnected systems, where each nonlinear subsystem is described by the following T-S fuzzy model:

$$\dot{x}_i(t) = A_i(\mu_i)x_i(t) + B_i(\mu_i)u_i(t) + \sum_{j=1, j \neq i}^{N} \bar{A}_{ij}(\mu_i, \mu_j)x_j(t), \tag{1}$$

where

$$A_i(\mu_i) := \sum_{l=1}^{r_i} \mu_i^l A_i^l, B_i(\mu_i) := \sum_{l=1}^{r_i} \mu_i^l B_i^l, \bar{A}_{ij}(\mu_i, \mu_j) := \sum_{l=1}^{r_i} \sum_{s=1}^{r_j} \mu_i^l \mu_j^s \bar{A}_{ij}^{ls}. \tag{2}$$

Throughout this subsection, we make the following assumptions.

1. The sampler in each subsystem is clock-driven. Let h_i denote the upper bound of sampling intervals, it yields

$$t_i^{k+1} - t_i^k \leq h_i, k \in \mathbb{N} \tag{3}$$

where $h_i > 0$.

2.   The zero-order-hold (ZOH) is event-driven, and it uses the latest sampled-data signals and holds them until the next transmitted data come.

In the following, we will focus on the decentralized sampled-data controller design for large-scale fuzzy interconnected systems. Now, consider a decentralized sampled-data fuzzy controller as below.

Controller Rule R_i^l: IF $\varsigma_{i1}\left(\mathrm{t}_i^k\right)$ is F_{i1}^l and $\varsigma_{i2}\left(\mathrm{t}_i^k\right)$ is F_{i2}^l and $\cdots$ and $\varsigma_{ig}\left(\mathrm{t}_i^k\right)$ is F_{ig}^l, THEN

$$u_i\left(t\right) = K_i^f x_i\left(\mathrm{t}_i^k\right), t \in \left[t_i^k, t_i^{k+1}\right), f \in \mathcal{L}_i, i \in \mathcal{N} \tag{4}$$

where K_i^f is the controller gain to be determined.

Similarly, the overall fuzzy controller can be rewritten as

$$u_i\left(t\right) = K_i\left(\hat{\mu}_i\right) x_i\left(\mathrm{t}_i^k\right), t \in \left[t_i^k, t_i^{k+1}\right), i \in \mathcal{N} \tag{5}$$

with

$$\mu_i^f\left[\varsigma_i\left(t_i^k\right)\right] := \frac{\Pi_{\varnothing=1}^g \mu_{i\varnothing}^f\left[\varsigma_{i\varnothing}\left(t_i^k\right)\right]}{\sum_{\varsigma=1}^{r_i} \Pi_{\varnothing=1}^g \mu_{i\varnothing}^\varsigma\left[\varsigma_{i\varnothing}\left(t_i^k\right)\right]} \geq 0, \sum_{f=1}^{r_i} \mu_i^f\left[\varsigma_i\left(t_i^k\right)\right] := 1, \tag{6}$$

where $\mu_{i\varnothing}^f\left[\varsigma_{i\varnothing}\left(t_i^k\right)\right]$ is the grade of membership of $\varsigma_{i\varnothing}\left(t_i^k\right)$ in $\mathrm{F}_{i\varnothing}^f$. In the following we will denote $\hat{\mu}_i^f := \mu_i^f\left[\varsigma_i\left(t_i^k\right)\right]$ for brevity.

NOTE: It is noted that the decentralized sampled-data fuzzy controller reduces to an PDC one when $\hat{\mu}_i^l = \mu_i^l$. However, the premise variables of the fuzzy controller (5) undergo sampled-data measurement. In such circumstances the asynchronous variables between $\hat{\mu}_i^l$ and μ_i^l are more realistic.

4.2.2 Wirtinger's Inequality to Decentralized Sampled-Data Controller Design

In this subsystem, our aim is to design the decentralized sampled-data fuzzy controller in the form of (5) by using Wirtinger's inequality. Before start it, we define

$$x_i(v) = x_i\left(t_i^k\right) - x_i(t). \tag{7}$$

Substituting (7) into (5) and combined with the fuzzy system in (1), then the closed-loop fuzzy control system can be given by

$$\dot{x}_i(t) = A_i(\mu_i) x_i(t) + B_i(\mu_i) K_i(\hat{\mu}_i)\left[x_i(t) + x_i(v)\right] + \sum_{j=1, j \neq i}^{N} \overline{A}_{ij}(\mu_i, \mu_j) x_j(t). \tag{8}$$

Inspired from (Liu & Fridman 2012), we consider the Lyapunov-Krasovskii functional (LKF) with virtue of Wirtinger's inequality as below:

$$V\left(x(t)\right) = \sum_{i=1}^{N} V_i\left(x_i(t)\right), \tag{9}$$

with

$$
\begin{aligned}
V_i\left(x_i(t)\right) &= x_i^T(t) P_i x_i(t) + h_i^2 \int_{t_i^k}^{t} \dot{x}_i^T(\alpha) Q_i \dot{x}_i(\alpha) d\alpha \\
&\quad - \frac{\pi^2}{4} \int_{t_i^k}^{t} \left[x_i(\alpha) - x_i\left(t_i^k\right)\right]^T Q_i \left[x_i(\alpha) - x_i\left(t_i^k\right)\right] d\alpha
\end{aligned} \tag{10}
$$

where $\{P_i, Q_i\} \in \Re^{n_{xi} \times n_{xi}}$ are symmetric positive definite matrices.

It follows from Wirtinger's inequality in Appendent C that the inequality $V\left(x(t)\right) > 0$ holds. Based on the closed-loop fuzzy control system in (8) and the LKF in (9), a sufficient condition for the existence of the decentralized sampled-data controller is derived as below.

Lemma 4.2.1 Given the large-scale T-S fuzzy interconnected system in (1) and the decentralized sampled-data fuzzy controller in (5), then the resulting closed-loop fuzzy control system is asymptotically stable, if there exist symmetric positive definite matrices $\left\{P_i, Q_i, M_{ij}\right\} \in \mathfrak{R}^{n_{zi} \times n_{zi}}$, matrix multipliers $\mathcal{G}_i \in \mathfrak{R}^{3n_{zi} \times n_{zi}}$, such that for all $\left\{i, j\right\} \in \mathcal{N}, j \neq i,$ the following matrix inequalities hold:

$$\begin{bmatrix} \Theta_i + \mathrm{Sym}\left\{\mathcal{G}_i \mathbb{A}_i\left(\mu_i, \hat{\mu}_i\right)\right\} & \mathbb{G}_i\left(\mu_i\right) \\ \star & -\mathbb{M}_i \end{bmatrix} < 0, \tag{11}$$

where

$$\begin{cases} \mathbb{A}_i\left(\mu_i, \hat{\mu}_i\right) = \begin{bmatrix} -I & A_i\left(\mu_i\right) + B_i\left(\mu_i\right)K_i\left(\hat{\mu}_i\right) & B_i\left(\mu_i\right)K_i\left(\hat{\mu}_i\right) \end{bmatrix} \\ \Theta_i = \begin{bmatrix} h_i^2 Q_i & P_i & 0 \\ \star & \sum\limits_{j=1, j \neq i}^{N} M_{ji} & 0 \\ \star & \star & -\dfrac{\pi^2}{4} Q_i \end{bmatrix}, \mathbb{I} = \underbrace{\begin{bmatrix} I \cdots I \cdots I \end{bmatrix}}_{N-1} \\ \mathbb{M}_i = \mathrm{diag}\underbrace{\left\{M_{i1} \cdots M_{ij, j \neq i} \cdots M_{iN}\right\}}_{N-1} \\ \mathbb{G}_i\left(\mu_i\right) = \underbrace{\left\{\mathcal{G}_i \bar{A}_{i1}\left(\mu_i, \mu_1\right) \cdots \mathcal{G}_i \bar{A}_{ij, j \neq i}\left(\mu_i, \mu_j\right) \cdots \mathcal{G}_i \bar{A}_{iN}\left(\mu_i, \mu_N\right)\right\}}_{N-1} \end{cases} \tag{12}$$

Proof. By taking the time derivative of $V\left(x(t)\right)$ along the trajectory of the closed-loop system in (8), one has

$$\dot{V}_i\left(x_i(t)\right) = 2x_i^T(t)P_i\dot{x}_i(t) + h_i^2\dot{x}_i^T(t)Q_i\dot{x}_i(t) - \frac{\pi^2}{4}x_i^T(v)Q_i x(v). \tag{13}$$

In addition, define the matrix multipliers $\mathcal{G}_i \in \mathfrak{R}^{3n_{zi} \times n_{zi}}$ and the matrix $0 < M_{ij} = M_{ij}^T \in \mathfrak{R}^{n_{zi} \times n_{zi}}$, and follows from (8) that

$$0 =$$

$$2\chi_i^T(t)\mathcal{G}_i\left[-\dot{x}_i(t) + A_i(\mu_i)x_i(t) + B_i(\mu_i)K_i(\hat{\mu}_i)[x_i(t) + x_i(v)] + \sum_{j=1,j\neq i}^{N} \bar{A}_{ij}(\mu_i,\mu_j)x_j(t)\right]$$

$$\leq 2\chi_i^T(t)\mathcal{G}_i\left[-\dot{x}_i(t) + A_i(\mu_i)x_i(t) + B_i(\mu_i)K_i(\hat{\mu}_i)[x_i(t) + x_i(v)]\right]$$

$$+ \sum_{j=1,j\neq i}^{N} \chi_i^T(t)\left[\mathcal{G}_i\bar{A}_{ij}(\mu_i,\mu_j)\right]M_{ij}\left[\mathcal{G}_i\bar{A}_{ij}(\mu_i,\mu_j)\right]^T \chi_i(t) + \sum_{j=1,j\neq i}^{N} x_i^T(t)M_{ji}x_i(t),$$

$$(14)$$

where $\chi_i(t) = \begin{bmatrix} \dot{x}_i^T(t) & x_i^T(t) & x_i^T(v) \end{bmatrix}^T$.

It follows from (13) and (14) that

$$V(x(t)) \leq \sum_{i=1}^{N}\left[2x_i^T(t)P_i\dot{x}_i(t) + h_i^2\dot{x}_i^T(t)Q_i\dot{x}_i(t) - \frac{\pi^2}{4}x_i^T(v)Q_ix(v)\right]$$

$$+ \sum_{i=1}^{N} 2\chi_i^T(t)\mathcal{G}_i\mathbb{A}_i(\mu_i,\hat{\mu}_i)\chi_i(t)$$

$$+ \sum_{i=1}^{N}\sum_{j=1,j\neq i}^{N} \chi_i^T(t)\left[\mathcal{G}_i\bar{A}_{ij}(\mu_i,\mu_j)\right]M_{ij}^{-1}\left[\mathcal{G}_i\bar{A}_{ij}(\mu_i,\mu_j)\right]^T \chi_i(t) \qquad (15)$$

$$+ \sum_{i=1}^{N}\sum_{j=1,j\neq i}^{N} \left\{x_i^T(t)M_{ji}x_i(t)\right\}$$

$$= \sum_{i=1}^{N}\chi_i^T(t)\Sigma_i(\mu_i,\mu_j,\hat{\mu}_i)\chi_i(t)$$

Where

$$\left[\begin{array}{l} \Sigma_i\left(\mu_i,\mu_j,\hat{\mu}_i\right) = \Theta_i + \mathrm{Sym}\left\{\mathcal{G}_i\mathbb{A}_i\left(\mu_i,\hat{\mu}_i\right)\right\} + \sum_{j=1,j\neq i}^{N}\left[\mathcal{G}_i\overline{A}_{ij}\left(\mu_i,\mu_j\right)\right]M_{ij}^{-1}\left[\mathcal{G}_i\overline{A}_{ij}\left(\mu_i,\mu_j\right)\right]^T \\ \mathbb{A}_i\left(\mu_i,\hat{\mu}_i\right) = \left[\begin{array}{ccc} -I & A_i\left(\mu_i\right)+B_i\left(\mu_i\right)K_i\left(\hat{\mu}_i\right) & B_i\left(\mu_i\right)K_i\left(\hat{\mu}_i\right) \end{array}\right] \\ \Theta_i = \left[\begin{array}{ccc} h_i^2 Q_i & P_i & 0 \\ \star & \displaystyle\sum_{j=1,j\neq i}^{N}M_{ji} & 0 \\ \star & \star & -\dfrac{\pi^2}{4}Q_i \end{array}\right] \end{array}\right.$$

$$(16)$$

Now, by using Schur complement to (11), it is easy to see that the inequality in (11) implies $V\left(x\left(t\right)\right) < 0$. Thus, the proof is completed.

It is noted that the conditions given in (11) are nonlinear matrix inequalities when the controller gains are unknown. It is also noted that when the knowledge between μ_i^l and $\hat{\mu}_i^l$ is unavailable, the condition $\mu_i \neq \hat{\mu}_i$ generally leads to a linear controller instead of a fuzzy one, which induces the design conservatism (Ario & Sala 2008). From a practical perspective, it is possible to obtain a prior knowledge between μ_i^l and $\hat{\mu}_i^l$. Thus, we assume

$$\underline{\rho}_i^l \leq \frac{\mu_i^l}{\hat{\mu}_i^l} \leq \overline{\rho}_i^l,$$

$$(17)$$

where $\underline{\rho}_i^l$ and $\overline{\rho}_i^l$ are known positive scalars.

Based on Lemma 4.2.1 and (17), we will present the co-design result consisting of the fuzzy controller gains and sampled period in terms of a set of LMIs, the result is summarized as follows.

Theorem 4.2.1 Given the large-scale T-S fuzzy interconnected system in (1) and the decentralized sampled-data fuzzy controller in (5), then the resulting closed-loop fuzzy control system with the assumption (17) is asymptotically stable, if there exist symmetric positive definite matrices $\left\{\overline{P}_i,\overline{Q}_i,W_{ij}\right\} \in \mathfrak{R}^{n_{zi}\times n_{zi}}$, and the matrices $G_i \in \mathfrak{R}^{n_{zi}\times n_{zi}}, \overline{K}_i^l \in \mathfrak{R}^{n_{ui}\times n_{zi}}$, and scalar h_i, such that for all $l \in \mathcal{L}_i, j \neq i, \{i,j\} \in \mathcal{N}$, the following LMIs hold:

$$\overline{\rho}_i^l \, \Phi_i^{ll} + X_i^{ll} < 0, \tag{18}$$

$$\underline{\rho}_i^l \Phi_i^{ll} + X_i^{ll} < 0, \tag{19}$$

$$\overline{\rho}_i^f \, \Phi_i^{lf} + \overline{\rho}_i^l \, \Phi_i^{fl} + X_i^{lf} + X_i^{fl} < 0, \tag{20}$$

$$\underline{\rho}_i^f \, \Phi_i^{lf} + \underline{\rho}_i^l \, \Phi_i^{fl} + X_i^{lf} + X_i^{fl} < 0, \tag{21}$$

$$\underline{\rho}_i^f \, \Phi_i^{lf} + \overline{\rho}_i^l \, \Phi_i^{fl} + X_i^{lf} + X_i^{fl} < 0, \tag{22}$$

$$\overline{\rho}_i^f \, \Phi_i^{lf} + \underline{\rho}_i^l \, \Phi_i^{fl} + X_i^{lf} + X_i^{fl} < 0, \tag{23}$$

$$\begin{bmatrix} X_i^{11} & \cdots & X_i^{1r_i} \\ \vdots & \ddots & \vdots \\ X_i^{r_i 1} & \cdots & X_i^{r_i r_i} \end{bmatrix} > 0, \tag{24}$$

where

$$\begin{cases} \Phi_i^{lf} = \begin{bmatrix} \Phi_{i(1)}^{lf} & \Phi_{i(2)} \\ \star & -\mathbb{W}_i \end{bmatrix}, \Phi_{i(2)} = \begin{bmatrix} 0 \\ G_i \mathbb{I} \\ 0 \end{bmatrix} \\ \mathbb{W}_i = \text{diag} \underbrace{\left\{ W_{1i} \cdots W_{ji, j \neq i} \cdots W_{Ni} \right\}}_{N-1}, \mathbb{I} = \underbrace{\begin{bmatrix} \mathrm{I} \cdots \mathrm{I} \cdots \mathrm{I} \end{bmatrix}}_{N-1}, \\ \Phi_{i(1)}^{lf} = \begin{bmatrix} h_i^2 \overline{Q}_i & \overline{P}_i & 0 \\ \star & 0 & 0 \\ \star & \star & -\dfrac{\pi^2}{4} \overline{Q}_i \end{bmatrix} + \text{Sym} \left\{ \begin{bmatrix} -G_i^T & A_i^l G_i^T + B_i^l \overline{K}_i^f & B_i^l \overline{K}_i^f \\ -G_i^T & A_i^l G_i^T + B_i^l \overline{K}_i^f & B_i^l \overline{K}_i^f \\ 0 & 0 & 0 \end{bmatrix} \right\} \\ + \sum_{j=1, j \neq i}^N R \left[\sum_{s=1}^{r_j} \overline{A}_{ij}^{ls} W_{ij} \left[\overline{A}_{ij}^{ls} \right]^T \right] R^T, R = \begin{bmatrix} \mathrm{I} \\ \mathrm{I} \\ 0 \end{bmatrix} \end{cases} \tag{25}$$

In that case, the decentralized sampled-data fuzzy controller gains in (5) can be obtained as

$$K_i^f = \bar{K}_i^f G_i^{-T}, f \in \mathcal{L}_i. \tag{26}$$

Proof. Recalling the results on (11) and by using Schur complement in Appendix A, it yields,

$$\begin{bmatrix} \bar{\Theta}_i + \mathrm{Sym}\left\{\mathcal{G}_i \mathbb{A}_i\left(\mu_i, \hat{\mu}_i\right)\right\} + \displaystyle\sum_{j=1, j \neq i}^{N}\left[\mathcal{G}_i \bar{A}_{ij}\left(\mu_i, \mu_j\right)\right] W_{ij}\left[\mathcal{G}_i \bar{A}_{ij}\left(\mu_i, \mu_j\right)\right]^T & \begin{bmatrix} 0 \\ \mathbb{I} \\ 0 \end{bmatrix} \\ \star & -\mathbb{W}_i \end{bmatrix} < 0, \tag{27}$$

where

$$\begin{cases} \bar{\Theta}_i = \begin{bmatrix} h_i^2 Q_i & P_i & 0 \\ \star & 0 & 0 \\ \star & \star & -\dfrac{\pi^2}{4} Q_i \end{bmatrix}, \mathbb{W}_i = \mathrm{diag}\underbrace{\left\{W_{1i} \cdots W_{ji, j \neq i} \cdots W_{Ni}\right\}}_{N-1}, \\ \mathbb{I} = \underbrace{\left[\mathrm{I} \cdots \mathrm{I} \cdots \mathrm{I}\right]}_{N-1}, \mathbb{A}_i\left(\mu_i, \hat{\mu}_i\right) = \begin{bmatrix} -I & A_i\left(\mu_i\right) + B_i\left(\mu_i\right) K_i\left(\hat{\mu}_i\right) & B_i\left(\mu_i\right) K_i\left(\hat{\mu}_i\right) \end{bmatrix}. \end{cases} \tag{28}$$

Now, in order to cast the inequality (27) into LMI-based condition, we define

$$\begin{aligned} \mathcal{G}_i &= \begin{bmatrix} G_i^{-1} \\ G_i^{-1} \\ 0 \end{bmatrix}, \Gamma_i \doteq \mathrm{diag}\left\{G_i\, G_i\, G_i\, \underbrace{\mathrm{I} \cdots \mathrm{I} \cdots \mathrm{I}}_{N-1}\right\}, \\ \bar{P}_i &= G_i P_i G_i^T, \bar{Q}_i = G_i Q_i G_i^T, \bar{K}_i^l = K_i^l G_i^T. \end{aligned} \tag{29}$$

By performing a congruence transformation to (27) by Γ_i, and considering the relation in (29) and Lemma 2.3.1, one has

$$\sum_{l=1}^{r_i}\sum_{f=1}^{r_i}\mu_i^l\hat{\mu}_i^f\left\{\Phi_i^{lf}\right\}<0,\tag{30}$$

where Φ_i^{lf} is defined in (25).

Now, by using virtue of Appendix E, the LMI-based results on (18)-(24) can be obtained. Thus completing this proof.

It is noted that when the knowledge between μ_i^l and $\hat{\mu}_i^f$ is unavailable, the design result on decentralized sampled-data linear controller can be obtained as below.

Theorem 4.2.2 Given the large-scale T-S fuzzy interconnected system in (1) and a decentralized sampled-data linear controller, then the resulting closed-loop control system is asymptotically stable, if there exist symmetric positive definite matrices $\left\{\bar{P}_i,\bar{Q}_i,W_{ij}\right\}\in\mathfrak{R}^{n_{xi}\times n_{xi}}$, and the matrix $G_i\in\mathfrak{R}^{n_{xi}\times n_{xi}},\bar{K}_i^l\in\mathfrak{R}^{n_{ui}\times n_{xi}}$, and scalar h_i, such that for all $l\in\mathcal{L}_i,j\neq i,\left\{i,j\right\}\in\mathcal{N}$, the following LMIs hold:

$$\begin{bmatrix}\Phi_{i(1)}^{ls} & \Phi_{i(2)}\\ \star & -\mathbb{W}_i\end{bmatrix}<0,\tag{31}$$

where

$$\begin{cases}\Phi_{i(1)}^{ls}=\begin{bmatrix}h_i^2\bar{Q}_i & \bar{P}_i & 0\\ \star & 0 & 0\\ \star & \star & -\dfrac{\pi^2}{4}\bar{Q}_i\end{bmatrix}+\text{Sym}\left\{\begin{bmatrix}-G_i^T & A_i^lG_i^T+B_i^l\bar{K}_i & B_i^l\bar{K}_i\\ -G_i^T & A_i^lG_i^T+B_i^l\bar{K}_i & B_i^l\bar{K}_i\\ 0 & 0 & 0\end{bmatrix}\right\}\\ \quad +\sum_{j=1,j\neq i}^N R\left[\sum_{s=1}^{r_j}\bar{A}_{ij}^{ls}W_{ij}\left[\bar{A}_{ij}^{ls}\right]^T\right]R^T,R=\begin{bmatrix}\mathrm{I}\\ \mathrm{I}\\ 0\end{bmatrix}\\ \Phi_{i(2)}=\begin{bmatrix}0\\ G_i\mathbb{I}\\ 0\end{bmatrix},\mathbb{W}_i=\text{diag}\underbrace{\left\{W_{1i}\cdots W_{ji,j\neq i}\cdots W_{Ni}\right\}}_{N-1},\mathbb{I}=\underbrace{\left[\mathrm{I}\cdots\mathrm{I}\cdots\mathrm{I}\right]}_{N-1}\end{cases}\tag{32}$$

In that case, the decentralized sampled-data linear controller gains can be obtained as

$$K_i = \bar{K}_i G_i^{-T}, i \in \mathcal{N}. \tag{33}$$

4.2.3 SSG Method to Decentralized Sampled-Data Controller Design

This subsection will propose a model transformation that reformulates the resulting closed-loop fuzzy control system as several feedback interconnections with extra inputs and outputs. The problem of sampled-data controller design is thus subject to the input-output (IO) stability. It can be referred to (Zhang, Knopse, & Tsiotras, 2001) in detail.

First, based on the input delay approach, the sampled-data fuzzy controller in (5) is reformulated as (Fridman, 2010),

$$u_i\left(t\right) = K_i\left(\hat{\mu}_i\right)x_i\left(t - \eta_i\left(t\right)\right), t \in \left[t_i^k, t_i^{k+1}\right), i \in \mathcal{N} \tag{34}$$

where $\eta_i\left(t\right) = t - t_i^k$.

It follows from (3) that

$$0 \leq \eta_i\left(t\right) < h_i, t \in \left[t_i^k, t_i^{k+1}\right), k \in \mathbb{N} \tag{35}$$

Combined with the system in (1) and the controller in (34), we obtain the closed-loop fuzzy control system as below,

$$\dot{x}_i\left(t\right) = A_i\left(\mu_i\right)x_i\left(t\right) + B_i\left(\mu_i\right)K_i\left(\hat{\mu}_i\right)x_i\left(t - \eta_i\left(t\right)\right) + \sum_{j=1, j \neq i}^{N} \bar{A}_{ij}\left(\mu_i, \mu_j\right)x_j\left(t\right). \tag{36}$$

Before moving on, we define (Gu, Zhang, & Xu, 2011)

$$\frac{h_i}{2}\omega_i\left(t\right) = x_i\left(t-\eta_i\left(t\right)\right) - \frac{1}{2}\left[x_i\left(t\right) + x_i\left(t-h_i\right)\right]$$

$$= \frac{1}{2}\int_{-h_i}^{-\eta_i(t)}\dot{x}_i\left(t+\alpha\right)d\alpha - \frac{1}{2}\int_{-\eta_i(t)}^{0}\dot{x}_i\left(t+\alpha\right)d\alpha \tag{37}$$

$$= \frac{1}{2}\int_{-h_i}^{0}\rho_i\left(\alpha\right)\dot{x}_i\left(t+\alpha\right)d\alpha,$$

where

$$\rho_i\left(\alpha\right) = \begin{cases} 1, & \text{if } \alpha \leq \eta_i\left(t\right), \\ -1, & \text{if } \alpha > \eta_i\left(t\right). \end{cases} \tag{38}$$

Submitted (37) into (36), it yields

$$S_{i1}: \begin{cases} \dot{x}_i\left(t\right) = A_i\left(\mu_i\right)x_i\left(t\right) + B_i\left(\mu_i\right)K_i\left(\hat{\mu}_i\right)\left[\frac{1}{2}x_i\left(t\right) + \frac{1}{2}x_i\left(t-h_i\right) + \frac{h_i}{2}\omega_i\left(t\right)\right] \\ \qquad\qquad + \sum\limits_{j=1, j\neq i}^{N}\bar{A}_{ij}\left(\mu_i, \mu_j\right)x_j\left(t\right), \\ y_i\left(t\right) = \dot{x}_i\left(t\right), \end{cases}$$

$$S_{i2}: \omega_i\left(t\right) = \Delta_i y_i\left(t\right), \tag{39}$$

where Δ_i denotes an operator with uncertainties.

In that case, the fuzzy control system in (36) is transformed into a feedback interconnection with extra input and output. In order to apply the SSG method, we give the following lemma.

Lemma 4.2.2 Consider the interconnected system in (39), the operator $\Delta_i: y_i\left(t\right) \rightarrow \omega_i\left(t\right)$ satisfies the property $\left\|\Delta_i\right\| \leq 1$.

Proof. Consider the zero-initial conditions, define symmetric positive definite matrix $H_i \in \Re^{n_{zi} \times n_{zi}}$, and by using Jensen's inequality (Gu, 2000) in Appendix B, one has

$$
\begin{aligned}
\int_0^t \omega_i^T(\beta) H_i \omega_i(\beta) d\beta \quad &= \frac{1}{h_i^2} \int_0^t \left[\int_{-h_i}^0 \rho_i(\alpha) \dot{x}_i(\beta+\alpha) d\alpha \right]^T H_i \left[\int_{-h_i}^0 \rho_i(\alpha) \dot{x}_i(\beta+\alpha) d\alpha \right] d\beta \\
&\leq \frac{1}{h_i} \int_0^t \left\{ \int_{-h_i}^0 \left[\dot{x}_i(\beta+\alpha) \right]^T H_i \left[\dot{x}_i(\beta+\alpha) \right] d\alpha \right\} d\beta \\
&= \frac{1}{h_i} \int_{-h_i}^0 \left\{ \int_0^t \left[\dot{x}_i(\alpha+\beta) \right]^T H_i \left[\dot{x}_i(\alpha+\beta) \right] d\beta \right\} d\alpha \\
&= \frac{1}{h_i} \int_{-h_i}^0 \left\{ \int_\alpha^{t+\alpha} \dot{x}_i^T(\beta) H_i \dot{x}_i(\beta) d\beta \right\} d\alpha \\
&\leq \frac{1}{h_i} \int_{-h_i}^0 \left\{ \int_0^t \dot{x}_i^T(\beta) H_i \dot{x}_i(\beta) d\beta \right\} d\alpha \\
&= \int_0^t y_i^T(\beta) H_i y_i(\beta) d\beta.
\end{aligned}
$$

$$(40)$$

It is easy to see that the inequality in (40) implies $\lVert \Delta_i \rVert \leq 1$. Thus completing this proof.

Based on the new model in (39), we choose the Lyapunov-Krasovskii functional (LKF) as below,

$$
V(x(t)) = \sum_{i=1}^N V_i(x_i(t)), \tag{41}
$$

with

$$
V_i(x_i(t)) = x_i^T(t) P_i x_i(t) + \int_{t-h_i}^t x_i^T(\alpha) Q_i x_i(\alpha) d\alpha +
$$

$$
h_i \int_{-h_i}^0 \int_{t+\beta}^t \dot{x}_i^T(\alpha) Z_i \dot{x}_i(\alpha) d\alpha d\beta, \tag{42}
$$

where $\{P_i, Q_i, Z_i\} \in \mathfrak{R}^{n_{xi} \times n_{xi}}$ are symmetric matrices, and $P_i > 0, Z_i > 0$.

Inspired by (Xu, Lam, Zhang, & Zou, 2015), we do not require that the matrix Q_i in (42) is necessarily positive definite. To ensure the positive property of $V\left(x(t)\right)$, we give the following lemma.

Lemma 4.2.3 Consider the Lyapunov–Krasovskii functional (LKF) in (41), then $V\left(x(t)\right) \geq \epsilon x(t)^2$, where $\epsilon > 0, x(t) = \left[x_1^T(t) \ x_2^T(t) \cdots x_N^T(t)\right]^T$, if there exist symmetric positive definite matrices $\{P_i, Z_i\} \in \mathfrak{R}^{n_{xi} \times n_{xi}}$ and symmetric matrix $Q_i \in \mathfrak{R}^{n_{xi} \times n_{xi}}$, such that for all $i \in \mathcal{N}$ the following inequalities hold:

$$\begin{bmatrix} \dfrac{1}{h_i} P_i + Z_i & -Z_i \\[2mm] \star & Q_i + Z_i \end{bmatrix} > 0. \tag{43}$$

Proof. Firstly, by using Jensen's inequality (Gu, 2000) in Appendix B, we have

$$
\begin{aligned}
h_i \int_{-h_i}^{0}\int_{t+\beta}^{t} \dot{x}_i^T(\alpha) Z_i \dot{x}_i(\alpha)\, d\alpha\, d\beta \ &\geq h_i \int_{-h_i}^{0} \frac{-1}{\beta}\left[\int_{t+\beta}^{t} \dot{x}_i(\alpha)\, d\alpha\right]^T Z_i \left[\int_{t+\beta}^{t} \dot{x}_i(\alpha)\, d\alpha\right] d\beta \\
&= h_i \int_{-h_i}^{0} \frac{-1}{\beta}\left[x_i(t) - x_i(t+\beta)\right]^T Z_i \left[x_i(t) - x_i(t+\beta)\right] d\beta \\
&= h_i \int_{0}^{h_i} \frac{1}{\beta}\left[x_i(t) - x_i(t-\beta)\right]^T Z_i \left[x_i(t) - x_i(t-\beta)\right] d\beta \\
&\geq \int_{0}^{h_i} \left[x_i(t) - x_i(t-\beta)\right]^T Z_i \left[x_i(t) - x_i(t-\beta)\right] d\beta \\
&= \int_{t-h_i}^{t} \left[x_i(t) - x_i(\alpha)\right]^T Z_i \left[x_i(t) - x_i(\alpha)\right] d\alpha
\end{aligned}
$$

$$\tag{44}$$

It follows from (42) and (44) that

$$V_i\big(x_i(t)\big) \geq \int_{t-h_i}^{t} \begin{bmatrix} x_i(t) \\ x_i(\alpha) \end{bmatrix}^T \begin{bmatrix} \dfrac{1}{h_i}P_i + Z_i & -Z_i \\ \star & Q_i + Z_i \end{bmatrix} \begin{bmatrix} x_i(t) \\ x_i(\alpha) \end{bmatrix} d\pm. \tag{45}$$

Therefore, there always exists a positive scalar ϵ such that the inequality $V\big(x(t)\big) \geq \epsilon\, x(t)^2$ holds if the inequality in (43) holds. Thus, completing this proof.

Based on the new model in (39), and the LKF in (41), a sufficient condition for the existence of the decentralized sampled-data fuzzy controller is derived as below.

Lemma 4.2.4 Given the large-scale T-S fuzzy interconnected system in (1) and the decentralized sampled-data fuzzy controller in (5), then the resulting closed-loop fuzzy control system with the assumption (36) is asymptotically stable, if there exist symmetric positive definite matrices $\{P_i, H_i, M_{ij}, Z_i\} \in \Re^{n_{xi} \times n_{xi}}$ and symmetric matrix $Q_i \in \Re^{n_{xi} \times n_{xi}}$, and scalar h_i, such that for all $l \in \mathcal{L}_i, j \neq i, \{i, j\} \in \mathcal{N}$, the following LMIs hold:

$$\begin{bmatrix} \dfrac{1}{h_i}P_i + Z_i & -Z_i \\ \star & Q_i + Z_i \end{bmatrix} > 0, \tag{46}$$

$$\begin{bmatrix} \Theta_i + \mathrm{Sym}\big\{\mathcal{G}_i \mathbb{A}_i\big(\mu_i, \hat{\mu}_i\big)\big\} & \mathbb{G}_i \\ \star & -\mathbb{M}_i \end{bmatrix} < 0, \tag{47}$$

where

$$
\begin{cases}
\mathbb{G}_i = \Big[\underbrace{\mathcal{G}_i \overline{A}_{i1}(\mu_i,\mu_1) \cdots \mathcal{G}_i \overline{A}_{ij,j\neq i}(\mu_i,\mu_j) \cdots \mathcal{G}_i \overline{A}_{iN}(\mu_i,\mu_N)}_{N-1}\Big] \\[2mm]
\mathbb{M}_i = \mathrm{diag}\Big\{\underbrace{M_{i1} \cdots M_{ij,j\neq i} \cdots M_{iN}}_{N-1}\Big\} \\[2mm]
\Theta_i = \begin{bmatrix}
h_i^2 Z_i + H_i & P_i & 0 & 0 \\[2mm]
\star & Q_i - Z_i + \displaystyle\sum_{j=1,j\neq i}^{N} M_{ji} & Z_i & 0 \\[2mm]
\star & \star & -Q_i - Z_i & 0 \\[2mm]
\star & \star & \star & -H_i
\end{bmatrix}
\end{cases}
\tag{48}
$$

Proof. By taking the time derivative of $V(x(t))$, one has

$$
\begin{aligned}
\dot{V}_i\big(x_i(t)\big) = {} & 2x_i^T(t)P_i\dot{x}_i(t) + x_i^T(t)Q_i x(t) - x_i^T(t-h_i)Q_i x(t-h_i) \\
& + h_i^2 \dot{x}_i^T(t)Z_i\dot{x}(t) - h_i \int_{t-h_i}^{t} \dot{x}_i^T(\alpha)Z_i\dot{x}_i(\alpha)\,d\alpha.
\end{aligned}
\tag{49}
$$

By using Jensen's inequality in Appendix B, we have

$$
\begin{aligned}
-h_i \int_{t-h_i}^{t} \dot{x}_i^T(\alpha)Z_i\dot{x}_i(\alpha)\,d\alpha \;\le\; & -\left[\int_{t-h_i}^{t}\dot{x}_i(\alpha)\,d\alpha\right]^T Z_i\left[\int_{t-h_i}^{t}\dot{x}_i(\alpha)\,d\alpha\right] \\
= {} & -\big[x_i(t)-x_i(t-h_i)\big]^T Z_i\big[x_i(t)-x_i(t-h_i)\big]
\end{aligned}
\tag{50}
$$

Define the matrix $\mathcal{G}_i \in \Re^{4n_{xi} \times n_{xi}}$ and symmetric positive definite matrices $M_{ij} \in \Re^{n_{xi} \times n_{xi}}$, it yields

$$
\begin{aligned}
0 = & \sum_{i=1}^{N} 2\chi_i^T(t)\mathcal{G}_i \mathbb{A}_i(\mu_i,\hat{\mu}_i)\chi_i(t) + \sum_{i=1}^{N} 2\chi_i^T(t)\mathcal{G}_i \sum_{j=1,j\neq i}^{N} \bar{A}_{ij}(\mu_i,\mu_j)x_j(t) \\
\leq & \sum_{i=1}^{N} 2\chi_i^T(t)\mathcal{G}_i \mathbb{A}_i(\mu_i,\hat{\mu}_i)\chi_i(t) \\
& + \sum_{i=1}^{N}\sum_{j=1,j\neq i}^{N} \chi_i^T(t)\mathcal{G}_i\left\{\left[\bar{A}_{ij}(\mu_i,\mu_j)\right]M_{ij}^{-1}\left[\bar{A}_{ij}(\mu_i,\mu_j)\right]^T\right\}\mathcal{G}_i^T\chi_i(t) \\
& + \sum_{i=1}^{N}\sum_{j=1,j\neq i}^{N} \left\{x_i^T(t)M_{ji}x_i(t)\right\},
\end{aligned}
\tag{51}
$$

where

$$
\begin{cases}
\chi_i(t) = \left[\dot{x}_i^T(t) \quad x_i^T(t) \quad x_i^T(t-h_i) \quad \omega_i^T(t)\right]^T, \\[2mm]
\mathbb{A}_i(\mu_i,\hat{\mu}_i) = \left[-I \quad A_i(\mu_i) \quad \dfrac{1}{2}B_i(\mu_i)K_i(\hat{\mu}_i) \quad \dfrac{1}{2}B_i(\mu_i)K_i(\hat{\mu}_i) \quad \dfrac{h_i}{2}B_i(\mu_i)K_i(\hat{\mu}_i)\right]
\end{cases}
\tag{52}
$$

Define symmetric positive definite matrices $H_i \in \mathfrak{R}^{n_{xi} \times n_{xi}}$, and consider the following index,

$$
\begin{aligned}
\mathcal{J}(t) &= \sum_{i=1}^{N} \mathcal{J}_i(t) \\
&= \sum_{i=1}^{N} \int_0^{\infty} \left[y_i^T(t)H_i y_i(t) - \omega_i^T(t)H_i\omega_i(t)\right]dt
\end{aligned}
\tag{53}
$$

In addition, it can be known that $V(x(0)) = 0$ and $V(x(\infty)) \geq 0$ under zero-initial condition. Then, it follows from (49)-(53) that

$$
\begin{aligned}
\mathcal{J}(t) &\leq \sum_{i=1}^{N} \mathcal{J}_i(t) + V_i(x_i(\infty)) - V_i(x_i(0)) \\
&= \sum_{i=1}^{N} \int_0^{\infty} \left[\dot{V}_i(x_i(t)) + y_i^T(t)H_i y_i(t) - \omega_i^T(t)H_i\omega_i(t)\right]dt \\
&\leq \sum_{i=1}^{N} \int_0^{\infty} \chi_i^T(t)\Pi_i(\mu_i,\hat{\mu}_i)\chi_i(t)dt
\end{aligned}
\tag{54}
$$

where

$$
\left[
\begin{aligned}
&\Pi_i\left(\mu_i,\hat{\mu}_i\right) = \tilde{}\,_i + \mathrm{Sym}\left\{\mathcal{G}_i\mathbb{A}_i\left(\mu_i,\hat{\mu}_i\right)\right\} + \mathcal{G}_i\left\{\sum_{j=1,j\neq i}^{N}\left[\overline{A}_{ij}\left(\mu_i,\mu_j\right)\right]M_{ij}^{-1}\left[\overline{A}_{ij}\left(\mu_i,\mu_j\right)\right]^T\right\}\mathcal{G}_i^T \\
&\mathbb{A}_i\left(\mu_i,\hat{\mu}_i\right) = \left[-I \quad A_i\left(\mu_i\right) \quad \frac{1}{2}B_i\left(\mu_i\right)K_i\left(\hat{\mu}_i\right) \quad \frac{1}{2}B_i\left(\mu_i\right)K_i\left(\hat{\mu}_i\right) \quad \frac{h_i}{2}B_i\left(\mu_i\right)K_i\left(\hat{\mu}_i\right)\right] \\
&\Theta_i = \begin{bmatrix} h_i^2 Z_i + H_i & P_i & 0 & 0 \\ \star & Q_i - Z_i + \displaystyle\sum_{j=1,j\neq i}^{N} M_{ji} & Z_i & 0 \\ \star & \star & -Q_i - Z_i & 0 \\ \star & \star & \star & -H_i \end{bmatrix}
\end{aligned}
\right.
$$

$$(55)$$

By using Schur lemma to (47), it is easy to see that the inequality in (54) implies $\dot{V}\left(x(t)\right) < 0$. In addition, it can be known that $V\left(x(0)\right) = 0$ and $V\left(x(\infty)\right) \geq 0$, which implies $\mathcal{J}(t) < 0$. By using virtue of SSG theorem in Appendix D, the stability of the closed-loop system in (36) can be verified. Thus, the proof is completed.

It is noted that the conditions given in (47) are nonlinear matrix inequalities when the controller gains are unknown. In the following, by using some matrix linearizing techniques, we will present the design results on decentralized sampled-data controller as below.

Theorem 4.2.3 Given the large-scale T-S fuzzy interconnected system in (1) and the decentralized sampled-data fuzzy controller in (5), then the resulting closed-loop fuzzy control system with the assumption (36) is asymptotically stable, if there exist symmetric positive definite matrices $\left\{\overline{P}_i,\overline{Z}_i,\overline{H}_i,W_{ij}\right\} \in \mathfrak{R}^{n_{xi}\times n_{xi}}$, and the matrices $\overline{Q}_i \in \mathfrak{R}^{n_{xi}\times n_{xi}}$, $\overline{K}_i^l \in \mathfrak{R}^{n_{xi}\times n_{xi}}$, and scalar h_i, such that for all $l \in \mathcal{L}_i, j \neq i, \{i,j\} \in \mathcal{N}$, the following LMIs hold:

$$
\begin{bmatrix} \dfrac{1}{h_i}\overline{P}_i + \overline{Z}_i & -\overline{Z}_i \\ \star & \overline{Q}_i + \overline{Z}_i \end{bmatrix} > 0,
$$

$$(56)$$

$$\bar{\rho}_i^l \Sigma_i^{ll} + \mathrm{X}_i^{ll} < 0, \tag{57}$$

$$\underline{\rho}_i^l \Sigma_i^{ll} + \mathrm{X}_i^{ll} < 0, \tag{58}$$

$$\bar{\rho}_i^s \Sigma_i^{ls} + \bar{\rho}_i^l \Sigma_i^{sl} + \mathrm{X}_i^{ls} + \mathrm{X}_i^{sl} < 0, \tag{59}$$

$$\underline{\rho}_i^s \Sigma_i^{ls} + \underline{\rho}_i^l \Sigma_i^{sl} + \mathrm{X}_i^{ls} + \mathrm{X}_i^{sl} < 0, \tag{60}$$

$$\underline{\rho}_i^s \Sigma_i^{ls} + \bar{\rho}_i^l \Sigma_i^{sl} + \mathrm{X}_i^{ls} + \mathrm{X}_i^{sl} < 0, \tag{61}$$

$$\bar{\rho}_i^s \Sigma_i^{ls} + \underline{\rho}_i^l \Sigma_i^{sl} + \mathrm{X}_i^{ls} + \mathrm{X}_i^{sl} < 0, \tag{62}$$

$$\begin{bmatrix} \mathrm{X}_i^{11} & \cdots & \mathrm{X}_i^{1r_i} \\ \vdots & \ddots & \vdots \\ \mathrm{X}_i^{r_i 1} & \cdots & \mathrm{X}_i^{r_i r_i} \end{bmatrix} > 0, \tag{63}$$

where

$$\begin{cases} \Sigma_i^{lf} = \begin{bmatrix} \bar{\Pi}_i^{lf} & \bar{\mathbb{T}}_i \\ \star & -\mathbb{W}_i \end{bmatrix} \\[2mm] \bar{\Pi}_i^{lf} = \bar{\Theta}_i + \mathrm{Sym}\left\{ \mathcal{T}_{(2)} \bar{\mathbb{A}}_i^{lf} \right\} + \mathcal{T}_{(2)} \left\{ \sum_{j=1,j\neq i}^{N} \sum_{s=1}^{r_j} \bar{A}_{ij}^{ls} W_{ij} \left[\bar{A}_{ij}^{ls} \right]^T \right\} \mathcal{T}_{(2)}^{\mathbf{T}} \\[3mm] \bar{\Theta}_i = \begin{bmatrix} h_i^2 \bar{Z}_i + \bar{H}_i & \bar{P}_i & 0 & 0 \\ \star & \bar{Q}_i - \bar{Z}_i & \bar{Z}_i & 0 \\ \star & \star & -\bar{Q}_i - \bar{Z}_i & 0 \\ \star & \star & \star & -\bar{H}_i \end{bmatrix}, \; \mathcal{T}_{(1)} = \begin{bmatrix} 0 \\ I \\ 0 \\ 0 \end{bmatrix}, \mathcal{T}_{(2)} = \begin{bmatrix} I \\ I \\ 0 \\ 0 \end{bmatrix} \\[3mm] \bar{\mathbb{A}}_i^{lf} = \begin{bmatrix} -G_i & A_i^l G_i + \frac{1}{2} B_i^l \bar{K}_i^f & \frac{1}{2} B_i^l \bar{K}_i^f & \frac{h_i}{2} B_i^l \bar{K}_i^f \end{bmatrix} \\[3mm] \bar{\mathbb{T}}_i = \underbrace{\begin{bmatrix} \mathcal{T}_{(1)} G_i \cdots \mathcal{T}_{(1)} G_i \cdots \mathcal{T}_{(1)} G_i \end{bmatrix}}_{N-1}, \mathbb{W}_i = \mathrm{diag}\underbrace{\left\{ W_{1i} \cdots W_{ji,j\neq i} \cdots W_{Ni} \right\}}_{N-1} \end{cases} \tag{64}$$

In that case, a decentralized sampled-data fuzzy controller gains can be obtained as

$$K_i^s = \bar{K}_i^s G_i^{-1}, s \in \mathcal{L}_i. \tag{65}$$

Proof: Recalling the inequality in (47), and define $W_{ij} = M_{ij}^{-1}$, one has

$$\begin{bmatrix} \Theta_i + \mathrm{Sym}\left\{ \mathcal{G}_i \mathbb{A}_i\left(\mu_i, \hat{\mu}_i\right)\right\} + \mathcal{G}_i \left\{ \displaystyle\sum_{j=1, j \neq i}^{N} \left[\bar{A}_{ij}\left(\mu_i, \mu_j\right)\right] W_{ij} \left[\bar{A}_{ij}\left(\mu_i, \mu_j\right)\right]^T \right\} \mathcal{G}_i^T & \mathcal{T}_{(1)} \\ \star & -\mathbb{W}_i \end{bmatrix} < 0, \tag{66}$$

where $\mathcal{T}_{(1)}$ is defined in (64), and

$$\begin{bmatrix} \mathbb{A}_i\left(\mu_i, \hat{\mu}_i\right) = \begin{bmatrix} -I & A_i\left(\mu_i\right) & \dfrac{1}{2}B_i\left(\mu_i\right)K_i\left(\hat{\mu}_i\right) & \dfrac{1}{2}B_i\left(\mu_i\right)K_i\left(\hat{\mu}_i\right) & \dfrac{h_i}{2}B_i\left(\mu_i\right)K_i\left(\hat{\mu}_i\right) \end{bmatrix} \\ \Theta_i = \begin{bmatrix} h_i^2 Z_i + H_i & P_i & 0 & 0 \\ \star & Q_i - Z_i & Z_i & 0 \\ \star & \star & -Q_i - Z_i & 0 \\ \star & \star & \star & -H_i \end{bmatrix}, \mathbb{W}_i = \mathrm{diag}\underbrace{\left\{ W_{1i} \cdots W_{ji, j\neq i} \cdots W_{Ni}\right\}}_{N-1} \end{bmatrix} \tag{67}$$

It follows from (59) that

$$h_i^2 \bar{Z}_i + \bar{H}_i - \mathrm{Sym}\left\{G_i\right\} < 0, \tag{68}$$

which implies that the matrix G_i is nonsingular.

For matrix inequality linearization purpose, we can specify the matrix multipliers $\mathcal{G}_i \in \mathfrak{R}^{4n_{zi} \times n_{zi}}$ as

$$\mathcal{G}_i = \begin{bmatrix} G_i^{-T} \\ G_i^{-T} \\ 0_{2n_{zi} \times n_{zi}} \end{bmatrix}, \tag{69}$$

where $G_i \in \Re^{n_{zi} \times n_{zi}}$.

Define

$$
\begin{cases}
\Gamma_{i1} := \text{diag}\left\{G_i\, G_i\, G_i\, G_i\ I_{(N-1)n_{xi} \times (N-1)n_{xi}}\right\}, \\
\Gamma_{i2} := \text{diag}\left\{G_i\, G_i\right\}, \\
\bar{P}_i = G_i^T P_i G_i, \bar{Q}_i = G_i^T Q_i G_i, \bar{H}_i = G_i^T H_i G_i, \\
\bar{Z}_i = G_i^T Z_i G_i, \bar{K}_i^l = K_i^l G_i.
\end{cases}
\tag{70}
$$

Now, by performing a congruence transformation to (46) by Γ_{i2}, the inequality in (56) can be obtained. Then, by substituting (69) into (66) and performing a congruence transformation to (66) by Γ_{i1}, and considering the relations in (70) and Lemma 2.3.1, and extracting the premise variables, one has

$$
\sum_{l=1}^{r_i}\sum_{f=1}^{r_i} \mu_i^l \hat{\mu}_i^f \Sigma_i^{lf} < 0,
\tag{71}
$$

where Σ_i^{lf} is defined in (64).

By using the result in Appendix E, the inequalities in (57)-(63) can be obtained. Thus completing this proof.

It is noted that the when the knowledge between μ_i^l and $\hat{\mu}_i^f$ is unavailable, the result on decentralized sampled-data linear controller can be obtained as below.

Theorem 4.2.4 Given the large-scale T-S fuzzy interconnected system in (1) and a decentralized sampled-data linear controller, then the resulting closed-loop control system is asymptotically stable, if there exist symmetric positive definite matrices $\left\{\bar{P}_i, \bar{Q}_i, W_{ij}\right\} \in \Re^{n_{zi} \times n_{zi}}$, and the matrix $G_i \in \Re^{n_{zi} \times n_{zi}}, \bar{K}_i^l \in \Re^{n_{ui} \times n_{zi}}$, and scalar h_i, such that for all $l \in \mathcal{L}, j \neq i, \{i, j\} \in \mathcal{N}$, the following LMIs hold:

$$
\begin{bmatrix} \bar{\Pi}_i^l & \bar{\mathbb{T}}_i \\ \star & -\mathbb{W}_i \end{bmatrix} < 0,
\tag{72}
$$

where

$$
\left[
\begin{aligned}
&\overline{\Pi}_i^l = \overline{\Theta}_i + \mathrm{Sym}\left\{\mathcal{T}_{(2)}\overline{\mathbb{A}}_i^l\right\} + \mathcal{T}_{(2)}\left\{\sum_{j=1,j\neq i}^{N}\sum_{s=1}^{r_j}\overline{A}_{ij}^{ls}W_{ij}\left[\overline{A}_{ij}^{ls}\right]^T\right\}\mathcal{T}_{(2)}^{\mathbf{T}}\\
&\overline{\Theta}_i = \begin{bmatrix} h_i^2\overline{Z}_i + \overline{H}_i & \overline{P}_i & 0 & 0 \\ \star & \overline{Q}_i - \overline{Z}_i & \overline{Z}_i & 0 \\ \star & \star & -\overline{Q}_i - \overline{Z}_i & 0 \\ \star & \star & \star & -\overline{H}_i \end{bmatrix}, \ \mathcal{T}_{(1)} = \begin{bmatrix} 0 \\ I \\ 0 \\ 0 \end{bmatrix}, \mathcal{T}_{(2)} = \begin{bmatrix} I \\ I \\ 0 \\ 0 \end{bmatrix} \\
&\overline{\mathbb{A}}_i^l = \begin{bmatrix} -G_i & A_i^l G_i + \dfrac{1}{2}B_i^l\overline{K}_i & \dfrac{1}{2}B_i^l\overline{K}_i & \dfrac{h_i}{2}B_i^l\overline{K}_i \end{bmatrix} \\
&\overline{\mathbb{T}}_i = \underbrace{\begin{bmatrix} \mathcal{T}_{(1)}G_i \cdots \mathcal{T}_{(1)}G_i \cdots \mathcal{T}_{(1)}G_i \end{bmatrix}}_{N-1}, \ \mathbb{W}_i = \mathrm{diag}\underbrace{\left\{W_{1i}\cdots W_{ji,j\neq i}\cdots W_{Ni}\right\}}_{N-1}
\end{aligned}
\right.
\tag{73}
$$

In that case, the decentralized sampled-data linear controller gains can be obtained as

$$
K_i = \overline{K}_i G_i^{-T}, i \in \mathcal{N}. \tag{74}
$$

4.3 DISTRIBUTED SAMPLE-DATA CONTROL

In this section, we will study the problem of distributed sampled-data control for large-scale T-S fuzzy interconnected system. Due to the fact that the sampling instants among subsystems may be different, the updating intervals may tend to zero, which leads to a difficult implication. In this subsystem, we will propose the ZOHs with time-driven, which avoids such condition that the minimal updating time is zero.

4.3.1 Problem Formulation

Before start it, we make the following assumptions (Moarref & Rodrigues, 2014):

1. Sensors are time-driven, and satisfy the set,

$$
\underline{s}_i \leq s_i^{k+1} - s_i^k \leq \overline{s}_i, k \in \mathbb{N}. \tag{75}
$$

2. ZOHs are time-driven, and satisfy the set,

$$\underline{z}_i \leq z_i^{k+1} - z_i^k \leq \overline{z}_i, k \in \mathbb{N}. \tag{76}$$

Based on the assumptions in a) and b), it can be known that the controller sends new values to the ZOHs as soon as it receives new data from the sensor. However, the ZOHs are time-driven and are not updated instantly. Figure 1 gives an example to show a distributed sampled-data control scheme with time-driven ZOH. One can see that all of sampling periods may be different, and the ZOH in every subsystem updates all of the sampled signals in a time-driven form. For example, the ZOH at the instant z_i^5 updates the signals sampled at the instants s_1^4, s_2^3, and s_i^4. Here, we define the time elapsed as $\rho_i^z(t)$, then it yields (Moarref & Rodrigues, 2014):

$$0 \leq \rho_i^z(t) < \overline{z}_i \tag{77}$$

Thus, it is easy to see that

$$\begin{aligned} \rho_{ij}^{zs}(t) &= \rho_i^z(t) + t - s_j^k \\ &= \rho_i^z(t) + \rho_j^s(t), t \in \left[z_i^k, z_i^{k+1}\right) \end{aligned} \tag{78}$$

where $0 \leq \rho_j^s(t) < \overline{s}_j, 0 \leq \rho_{ij}^{zs}(t) < \overline{z}_i + \overline{s}_j$.

Figure 1. Example of signal sampling and holding

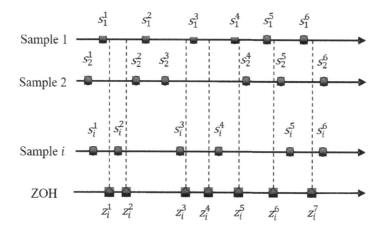

Now, consider the following distributed sampled-data fuzzy controller:

Controller Rule R_i^f: IF $\varsigma_{i1}\left(z_i^k\right)$ is F_{i1}^f and $\varsigma_{i2}\left(z_i^k\right)$ is F_{i2}^f and $\cdots$ and $\varsigma_{ig}\left(z_i^k\right)$ is F_{ig}^f, THEN

$$u_i\left(t\right) = K_i^f x_i\left(z_i^k\right) + \sum_{j=1,j\neq i}^{N} K_{ij}^f x_j\left(z_i^k\right), t \in \left[z_i^k, z_i^{k+1}\right), i \in \mathcal{N} \tag{79}$$

where K_i^f is the controller gains to be determined.

Similarly, the overall fuzzy controller can be rewritten as

$$u_i\left(t\right) = K_i\left(\hat{\mu}_i\right)x_i\left(z_i^k\right) + \sum_{j=1,j\neq i}^{N} K_{ij}\left(\hat{\mu}_i\right)x_j\left(z_i^k\right), t \in \left[z_i^k, z_i^{k+1}\right), i \in \mathcal{N} \tag{80}$$

with

$$\mu_i^f\left[\varsigma_i\left(z_i^k\right)\right] := \frac{\Pi_{\varnothing=1}^{g}\mu_{i\varnothing}^f\left[\varsigma_{i\varnothing}\left(z_i^k\right)\right]}{\sum_{\varsigma=1}^{r_i}\Pi_{\varnothing=1}^{g}\mu_{i\varnothing}^{\varsigma}\left[\varsigma_{i\varnothing}\left(z_i^k\right)\right]} \geq 0, \sum_{l=1}^{r_i}\mu_i^f\left[\varsigma_i\left(z_i^k\right)\right] := 1, \tag{81}$$

where $\mu_{i\varnothing}^f\left[\varsigma_{i\varnothing}\left(z_i^k\right)\right]$ is the grade of membership of $\varsigma_{i\varnothing}\left(z_i^k\right)$ in $F_{i\varnothing}^f$. In this subsection we will denote $\hat{\mu}_i^l := \mu_i^f\left[\varsigma_i\left(z_i^k\right)\right]$ for brevity.

Here, we further define

$$x_j\left(v_i\right) = x_j\left(z_i^k\right) - x_j\left(t\right), j \neq i, \{i,j\} \in \mathcal{N}. \tag{82}$$

Based on the system in (1) and controller in (80), we have

$$\dot{x}_i\left(t\right) = A_i\left(\mu_i\right)x_i\left(t\right) + B_i\left(\mu_i\right)\left[K_i\left(\hat{\mu}_i\right)\left(x_i\left(t\right) + x_i\left(v_i\right)\right) + \sum_{j=1,j\neq i}^{N} K_{ij}\left(\hat{\mu}_i\right)\left(x_j\left(t\right) + x_j\left(v_i\right)\right)\right]$$
$$+ \sum_{j=1,j\neq i}^{N} \overline{A}_{ij}\left(\mu_i\right)x_j\left(t\right),$$

$$\tag{83}$$

4.3.2 Distributed Sampled-Data Controller Design

Inspired from Liu and Fridman (2012), we choose the Lyapunov-Krasovskii functional (LKF) with virtue of Wirtinger's inequality as below:

$$V\left(x\left(t\right)\right) = \sum_{i=1}^{N} V_i\left(x_i\left(t\right)\right), \tag{84}$$

with

$$
\begin{aligned}
V_i\left(x_i\left(t\right)\right) = \ & x_i^T\left(t\right) P_i x_i\left(t\right) + \left[\overline{z}_i + \overline{s}_i\right]^2 \int_{z_i^k}^{t} \dot{x}_i^T\left(\alpha\right) Q_i \dot{x}_i\left(\alpha\right) d\alpha \\
& - \frac{\pi^2}{4} \int_{z_i^k}^{t} \left[x_i\left(\alpha\right) - x_i\left(z_i^k\right)\right]^T Q_i \left[x_i\left(\alpha\right) - x_i\left(z_i^k\right)\right] d\alpha \\
& + \sum_{j=1, j\neq i}^{N} \left\{\left[\overline{z}_i + \overline{s}_i\right]^2 \int_{z_i^k}^{t} \dot{x}_j^T\left(\alpha\right) Z_{ij} \dot{x}_j\left(\alpha\right) d\alpha\right\} \\
& - \sum_{j=1, j\neq i}^{N} \left\{\frac{\pi^2}{4} \int_{z_i^k}^{t} \left[x_j\left(\alpha\right) - x_j\left(z_i^k\right)\right]^T Z_{ij} \left[x_j\left(\alpha\right) - x_j\left(z_i^k\right)\right] d\alpha\right\},
\end{aligned}
\tag{85}
$$

where $\left\{P_i, Q_i, Z_{ij}\right\} \in \mathfrak{R}^{n_{xi} \times n_{xi}}$ are symmetric positive matrices.

Based on the new model in (83) and the LKF in (84), a sufficient condition for the existence of the distributed sampled-data fuzzy controller can be given as below.

Theorem 4.3.1 Given the large-scale T-S fuzzy interconnected system in (1) and a distributed sampled-data fuzzy controller in (80), then the resulting closed-loop control system with the assumption (17) is asymptotically stable, if there exist symmetric positive definite matrices $\left\{\overline{P}_i, \overline{Q}_i, M_{ij}, M_{0i}, H_{ij}, H_{0i}\right\} \in \mathfrak{R}^{n_{xi} \times n_{xi}}$, $H_{0i} \leq H_{ji}, M_{0i} \leq M_{ji}$ and matrices $G_i \in \mathfrak{R}^{n_{xi} \times n_{xi}}, \left\{\overline{K}_i^l, \overline{K}_{ij}^l\right\} \in \mathfrak{R}^{n_{ui} \times n_{xi}}$, and scalars $\left\{\overline{z}_i, \overline{s}_i\right\}$, such that for all $\left\{l, f\right\} \in \mathcal{L}_i, j \neq i, \left\{i, j\right\} \in \mathcal{N}$, the following LMIs hold:

$$\overline{\rho}_i^l \sum_i^{ll} + \mathrm{X}_i^{ll} < 0, \tag{86}$$

$$\underline{\rho}_i^l \sum_i^{ll} + \mathrm{X}_i^{ll} < 0, \tag{87}$$

$$\overline{\rho}_i^f \sum_i^{lf} + \overline{\rho}_i^l \sum_i^{fl} + \mathrm{X}_i^{lf} + \mathrm{X}_i^{fl} < 0, \tag{88}$$

$$\underline{\rho}_i^f \sum_i^{lf} + \underline{\rho}_i^l \sum_i^{fl} + \mathrm{X}_i^{lf} + \mathrm{X}_i^{fl} < 0, \tag{89}$$

$$\underline{\rho}_i^f \sum_i^{lf} + \overline{\rho}_i^l \sum_i^{fl} + \mathrm{X}_i^{lf} + \mathrm{X}_i^{fl} < 0, \tag{90}$$

$$\overline{\rho}_i^f \sum_i^{lf} + \underline{\rho}_i^l \sum_i^{fl} + \mathrm{X}_i^{lf} + \mathrm{X}_i^{fl} < 0, \tag{91}$$

$$\begin{bmatrix} \mathrm{X}_i^{11} & \cdots & \mathrm{X}_i^{1r_i} \\ \vdots & \ddots & \vdots \\ \mathrm{X}_i^{r_i 1} & \cdots & \mathrm{X}_i^{r_i r_i} \end{bmatrix} > 0, \tag{92}$$

where

$$\sum_i^{lf} = \begin{bmatrix} \overline{\Pi}_i^{lf} & \mathbb{B}_i^{lf} & \mathbb{A}_i^{lf} & \mathcal{T}_{(1)} G_i^T & \mathcal{T}_{(2)} G_i^T \\ \star & \mathbb{H}_i - \mathbb{G}_i - \mathbb{G}_i^T & 0 & 0 & 0 \\ \star & \star & \mathbb{M}_i - \mathbb{G}_i - \mathbb{G}_i^T & 0 & 0 \\ \star & \star & \star & -\dfrac{H_{0i}}{\sum_{j=1,j\neq i}^{N} \left\{ \left[\overline{z}_j + \overline{s}_i \right]^2 \right\}} & 0 \\ \star & \star & \star & \star & -\dfrac{M_{0i}}{N-1} \end{bmatrix}, \tag{93}$$

and

$$
\left[
\begin{aligned}
\overline{\Pi}_i^{lf} &= \overline{\Theta}_i + \mathrm{Sym}\left\{ \mathcal{T}_{(3)} \mathcal{A}_i^{lf} \right\} \\
\overline{\Theta}_i &= \begin{bmatrix} \left[\overline{z}_i + \overline{s}_i \right]^2 \overline{Q}_i & \overline{P}_i & 0 \\ \star & 0 & 0 \\ \star & \star & -\dfrac{\pi^2}{4} \overline{Q}_i \end{bmatrix} \\
\mathcal{A}_i^{lf} &= \begin{bmatrix} -G_i & A_i^l G_i + B_i^l \overline{K}_i^f & B_i^l \overline{K}_i^f \end{bmatrix} \\
\mathbb{B}_i^{lf} &= \begin{bmatrix} \mathcal{T}_{(3)} B_i^l \overline{K}_{i1}^f \cdots \mathcal{T}_{(3)} B_i^l \overline{K}_{ij,j\neq i}^f \cdots \mathcal{T}_{(3)} B_i^l \overline{K}_{iN}^f \end{bmatrix} \\
\mathbb{H}_i &= \mathrm{diag}\left\{ \dfrac{4}{\pi^2} H_{i1} \cdots \dfrac{4}{\pi^2} H_{ij,j\neq i} \cdots \dfrac{4}{\pi^2} H_{iN} \right\} \\
\mathcal{T}_{(1)} &= \begin{bmatrix} I \\ 0 \\ 0 \end{bmatrix}, \mathcal{T}_{(2)} = \begin{bmatrix} 0 \\ I \\ 0 \end{bmatrix}, \mathcal{T}_{(3)} = \begin{bmatrix} I \\ I \\ 0 \end{bmatrix} \\
\mathbb{M}_i &= \mathrm{diag}\left\{ M_{i1} \cdots M_{ij,j\neq i} \cdots M_{iN} \right\} \\
\mathbb{A}_i^{lf} &= \begin{bmatrix} \mathcal{A}_{i1} \cdots \mathcal{A}_{ij,j\neq i} \cdots \mathcal{A}_{iN} \end{bmatrix}, \mathcal{A}_{ij} = \mathcal{T}_{(3)}\left(B_i^l \overline{K}_{ij}^f + \overline{A}_{ij}^l G_i \right)
\end{aligned}
\right. \tag{94}
$$

In that case, the distributed sampled-data fuzzy controller gains can be obtained as

$$
K_i^l = \overline{K}_i^l G_i^{-1}, K_{ij}^l = \overline{K}_{ij}^l G_i^{-1}, l \in \mathcal{L}_i. \tag{95}
$$

Proof. By taking the time derivative of $V\left(x(t)\right)$ in (84), one has

$$
\begin{aligned}
\dot{V}_i\left(x_i(t)\right) &= 2x_i^T(t) P_i \dot{x}_i(t) + \left[\overline{z}_i + \overline{s}_i \right]^2 \dot{x}_i^T(t) Q_i \dot{x}_i(t) - \frac{\pi^2}{4} x_i^T(v_i) Q_i x_i(v_i) \\
&\quad + \sum_{j=1,j\neq i}^{N} \left\{ \left[\overline{z}_i + \overline{s}_j \right]^2 \dot{x}_j^T(t) Z_{ij} \dot{x}_j(t) - \frac{\pi^2}{4} x_j^T(v_i) Z_{ij} x_j(v_i) \right\}
\end{aligned} \tag{96}
$$

Define the matrix $\mathcal{G}_i \in \mathfrak{R}^{4n_{zi}\times n_{zi}}$ and symmetric positive definite matrices $M_{ij} \in \mathfrak{R}^{n_{zi}\times n_{zi}}$ it yields

$$0 = \sum_{i=1}^{N} 2\chi_i^T(t)\mathcal{G}_i \left\{ -\dot{x}_i(t) + A_i(\mu_i)x_i(t) + B_i(\mu_i)K_i(\hat{\mu}_i)(x_i(t) + x_i(v_i)) \right\}$$

$$+ \sum_{i=1}^{N} \sum_{j=1,j\neq i}^{N} 2\chi_i^T(t)\mathcal{G}_i B_i(\mu_i)K_{ij}(\hat{\mu}_i)x_j(v_i)$$

$$+ \sum_{i=1}^{N} \sum_{j=1,j\neq i}^{N} 2\chi_i^T(t)\mathcal{G}_i \left[B_i(\mu_i)K_{ij}(\hat{\mu}_i) + \overline{A}_{ij}(\mu_i) \right] x_j(t)$$

$$\leq \sum_{i=1}^{N} 2\chi_i^T(t)\mathcal{G}_i \left\{ -\dot{x}_i(t) + A_i(\mu_i)x_i(t) + B_i(\mu_i)K_i(\hat{\mu}_i)(x_i(t) + x_i(v_i)) \right\}$$

$$+ \sum_{i=1}^{N} \sum_{j=1,j\neq i}^{N} 2\chi_i^T(t)\mathcal{G}_i B_i(\mu_i)K_{ij}(\hat{\mu}_i)x_j(v_i)$$

$$+ \sum_{i=1}^{N} \sum_{j=1,j\neq i}^{N} \chi_i^T(t)\mathcal{G}_i \left[B_i(\mu_i)K_{ij}(\hat{\mu}_i) + \overline{A}_{ij}(\mu_i) \right] M_{ij}(\star)\mathcal{G}_i^T \chi_i(t)$$

$$+ \sum_{i=1}^{N} \sum_{j=1,j\neq i}^{N} x_j^T(t)M_{ij}^{-1}x_j(t) \tag{97}$$

where $\chi_i(t) = \begin{bmatrix} \dot{x}_i^T(t) & x_i^T(t) & x_i^T(v_i) \end{bmatrix}^T$.

In addition, we have

$$\sum_{i=1}^{N} \sum_{j=1,j\neq i}^{N} \left[\overline{z}_i + \overline{s}_j \right]^2 \dot{x}_j^T(t)Z_{ij}\dot{x}_j(t) = \sum_{i=1}^{N} \sum_{j=1,j\neq i}^{N} \left[\overline{z}_j + \overline{s}_i \right]^2 \dot{x}_i^T(t)Z_{ji}\dot{x}_i(t), \tag{98}$$

$$\sum_{i=1}^{N} \sum_{j=1,j\neq i}^{N} x_j^T(t)M_{ij}^{-1}x_j(t) = \sum_{i=1}^{N} \sum_{j=1,j\neq i}^{N} x_i^T(t)M_{ji}^{-1}x_i(t). \tag{99}$$

It follows from (96)-(99) that

$$
\begin{aligned}
\dot{V}\left(x\left(t\right)\right) \leq & \sum_{i=1}^{N}\left[2x_i^T\left(t\right)P_i\dot{x}_i\left(t\right)+\left[\bar{z}_i+\bar{s}_i\right]^2\dot{x}_i^T\left(t\right)Q_i\dot{x}\left(t\right)-\frac{\pi^2}{4}x_i^T\left(v_i\right)Q_ix_i\left(v_i\right)\right] \\
& +\sum_{j=1,j\neq i}^{N}\left\{\left[\bar{z}_j+\bar{s}_i\right]^2\dot{x}_i^T\left(t\right)Z_{ji}\dot{x}_i\left(t\right)-\frac{\pi^2}{4}x_j^T\left(v_i\right)Z_{ij}x_j\left(v_i\right)\right\} \\
& +\sum_{i=1}^{N}2\chi_i^T\left(t\right)\mathcal{G}_i\left\{-\dot{x}_i\left(t\right)+A_i\left(\mu_i\right)x_i\left(t\right)+B_i\left(\mu_i\right)K_i\left(\hat{\mu}_i\right)\left(x_i\left(t\right)+x_i\left(v_i\right)\right)\right\} \\
& +\sum_{i=1}^{N}\sum_{j=1,j\neq i}^{N}2\chi_i^T\left(t\right)\mathcal{G}_iB_i\left(\mu_i\right)K_{ij}\left(\hat{\mu}_i\right)x_j\left(v_i\right) \\
& +\sum_{i=1}^{N}\sum_{j=1,j\neq i}^{N}\chi_i^T\left(t\right)\mathcal{G}_i\left[B_i\left(\mu_i\right)K_{ij}\left(\hat{\mu}_i\right)+\bar{A}_{ij}\left(\mu_i\right)\right]M_{ij}\left(\star\right)\mathcal{G}_i^T\chi_i\left(t\right) \\
& +\sum_{i=1}^{N}\sum_{j=1,j\neq i}^{N}x_i^T\left(t\right)M_{ji}^{-1}x_i\left(t\right) \\
= & \bar{\chi}_i^T\left(t\right)\left[\begin{matrix}\Pi_i\left(\mu_i,\hat{\mu}_i\right) & \mathbb{B}_i\left(\mu_i,\hat{\mu}_i\right) \\ \star & -\dfrac{\pi^2}{4}\mathbb{Z}_i\end{matrix}\right]\bar{\chi}_i\left(t\right)
\end{aligned}
$$

(100)

where

$$
\left\{
\begin{aligned}
\Pi_i&\left(\mu_i,\hat{\mu}_i\right)=\Theta_i+\mathrm{Sym}\left\{\mathcal{G}_i\mathcal{A}_i\left(\tfrac{1}{4},\hat{\mu}_i\right)\right\} \\
&+\sum_{j=1,j\neq i}^{N}\mathcal{G}_i\left[B_i\left(\mu_i\right)K_{ij}\left(\hat{\mu}_i\right)+\bar{A}_{ij}\left(\mu_i\right)\right]M_{ij}\left[B_i\left(\mu_i\right)K_{ij}\left(\hat{\mu}_i\right)+\bar{A}_{ij}\left(\mu_i\right)\right]^T\mathcal{G}_i^T \\
\Theta_i&=\left[\begin{matrix}\left[\bar{z}_i+\bar{s}_i\right]^2Q_i+\displaystyle\sum_{j=1,j\neq i}^{N}\left\{\left[\bar{z}_j+\bar{s}_i\right]^2Z_{ji}\right\} & P_i & 0 \\[4mm] \star & \displaystyle\sum_{j=1,j\neq i}^{N}M_{ji}^{-1} & 0 \\[4mm] \star & \star & -\dfrac{\pi^2}{4}Q_i\end{matrix}\right] \\
\mathcal{A}_i&\left(\mu_i,\hat{\mu}_i\right)=\left[-I \quad A_i\left(\mu_i\right)+B_i\left(\mu_i\right)K_i\left(\hat{\mu}_i\right) \quad B_i\left(\mu_i\right)K_i\left(\hat{\mu}_i\right)\right] \\
\mathbb{B}_i&\left(\mu_i,\hat{\mu}_i\right)=\left[\mathcal{G}_iB_i\left(\mu_i\right)K_{i1}\left(\hat{\mu}_i\right)\cdots\mathcal{G}_iB_i\left(\mu_i\right)K_{ij,j\neq i}\left(\hat{\mu}_i\right)\cdots\mathcal{G}_iB_i\left(\mu_i\right)K_{iN}\left(\hat{\mu}_i\right)\right] \\
\mathbb{Z}_i&=\mathrm{diag}\left\{Z_{i1}\cdots Z_{ij,j\neq i}\cdots Z_{iN}\right\}, \\
\bar{\chi}_i&\left(t\right)=\left[\dot{x}_i^T\left(t\right) \quad x_i^T\left(t\right) \quad x_i^T\left(v_i\right) \quad \underbrace{x_1^T\left(v_i\right)\cdots x_{j,j\neq i}^T\left(v_i\right)\cdots x_N^T\left(v_i\right)}_{N-1}\right]^T
\end{aligned}
\right.
$$

(101)

113

Define $Z_{ij} = H_{ij}^{-1}, H_{0i} \leq H_{ji}, M_{0i} \leq M_{ji}$, and by using Schur complement, the following inequality implies $\dot{V}\left(x(t)\right) < 0$,

$$
\begin{bmatrix}
\overline{\Pi}_i\left(\mu_i, \hat{\mu}_i\right) & \mathbb{B}_i\left(\mu_i, \hat{\mu}_i\right) & \mathbb{A}_i\left(\mu_i, \hat{\mu}_i\right) & \boldsymbol{T}_{(1)} & \boldsymbol{T}_{(2)} \\
\star & -\mathbb{H}_i^{-1} & 0 & 0 & 0 \\
\star & \star & -\mathbb{M}_i^{-1} & 0 & 0 \\
\star & \star & \star & -\dfrac{H_{0i}}{\sum_{j=1, j\neq i}^{N}\left\{\left[\overline{z}_j + \overline{s}_i\right]^2\right\}} & 0 \\
\star & \star & \star & \star & -\dfrac{M_{0i}}{N-1}
\end{bmatrix} < 0,
$$

(102)

where

$$
\begin{cases}
\overline{\Pi}_i\left(\mu_i, \hat{\mu}_i\right) = \overline{\Theta}_i + \text{Sym}\left\{\mathcal{G}_i \mathcal{A}_i\left(\mu_i, \hat{\mu}_i\right)\right\} \\[2mm]
\overline{\Theta}_i = \begin{bmatrix}
\left[\overline{z}_i + \overline{s}_i\right]^2 Q_i & P_i & 0 \\
\star & 0 & 0 \\
\star & \star & -\dfrac{\pi^2}{4} Q_i
\end{bmatrix} \\[6mm]
\mathcal{A}_i\left(\mu_i, \hat{\mu}_i\right) = \begin{bmatrix} -I & A_i\left(\mu_i\right) + B_i\left(\mu_i\right) K_i\left(\hat{\mu}_i\right) & B_i\left(\mu_i\right) K_i\left(\hat{\mu}_i\right) \end{bmatrix} \\[2mm]
\mathbb{B}_i\left(\mu_i, \hat{\mu}_i\right) = \begin{bmatrix} \mathcal{G}_i B_i\left(\mu_i\right) K_{i1}\left(\hat{\mu}_i\right) \cdots \mathcal{G}_i B_i\left(\mu_i\right) K_{ij, j\neq i}\left(\hat{\mu}_i\right) \cdots \mathcal{G}_i B_i\left(\mu_i\right) K_{iN}\left(\hat{\mu}_i\right) \end{bmatrix} \\[2mm]
\mathbb{H}_i = \text{diag}\left\{\dfrac{4}{\pi^2} H_{i1} \cdots \dfrac{4}{\pi^2} H_{ij, j\neq i} \cdots \dfrac{4}{\pi^2} H_{iN}\right\}, \boldsymbol{T}_{(1)} = \begin{bmatrix} I \\ 0 \\ 0 \end{bmatrix}, \boldsymbol{T}_{(2)} = \begin{bmatrix} 0 \\ I \\ 0 \end{bmatrix}, \\[4mm]
\mathbb{M}_i = \text{diag}\left\{M_{i1} \cdots M_{ij, j\neq i} \cdots M_{iN}\right\} \\[2mm]
\mathbb{A}_i\left(\mu_i, \hat{\mu}_i\right) = \begin{bmatrix} \mathcal{A}_{i1} \cdots \mathcal{A}_{ij, j\neq i} \cdots \mathcal{A}_{iN} \end{bmatrix}, \mathcal{A}_{ij} = \mathcal{G}_i B_i\left(\mu_i\right) K_{ij}\left(\hat{\mu}_i\right) + \mathcal{G}_i \overline{A}_{ij}\left(\mu_i\right)
\end{cases}
$$

(103)

Here, we further define

$$\begin{cases} \mathcal{G}_i = \begin{bmatrix} G_i^{-T} \\ G_i^{-T} \\ I \end{bmatrix}, \Gamma_i \doteq \mathrm{diag}\left\{ \mathbb{G}_i \ G_i \ G_i \ \mathbb{G}_i \ \mathbb{G}_i \ \mathbb{I} \ \mathbb{I} \right\}, \\ \mathbb{G}_i = \mathrm{diag}\underbrace{\left\{ G_i \cdots G_i \cdots G_i \right\}}_{N-1}, \mathbb{I} = \mathrm{diag}\underbrace{\left\{ I \cdots I \cdots I \right\}}_{N-1} \\ \bar{P}_i = G_i^T P_i G_i, \bar{Q}_i = G_i^T Q_i G_i, \ K_i^l = \bar{K}_i^l G_i^{-1} \\ K_{ij}^l = \bar{K}_{ij}^l G_i^{-1}, j \neq i, \{i,j\} \in \mathcal{N} \end{cases} \tag{104}$$

Note that

$$M_i - G_i - G_i^T + G_i^T M_i^{-1} G_i = \left[M_i - G_i \right]^T M_i^{-1} \left[M_i - G_i \right] \geq 0, \tag{105}$$

which implies that

$$-G_i^T M_i^{-1} G_i \leq M_i - G_i - G_i^T. \tag{106}$$

Now, by performing a congruence transformation to (102) by Γ_i, and considering the relation in (105), and extracting the premise variables, we have

$$\sum_{l=1}^{r_i} \sum_{s=1}^{r_i} \mu^l \mu^s \sum_i^{ls} < 0 \tag{107}$$

where $\sum_i^{ls}$ is defined in (93).

By using the result in Appendix E, the inequalities in (86)-(92) can be obtained. Thus, the proof is completed.

It is noted that the when the knowledge between μ_i^l and $\hat{\mu}_i^f$ is unavailable, the result on decentralized sampled-data linear controller can be obtained as below.

Theorem 4.3.2 Given the large-scale T-S fuzzy interconnected system in (1) and a decentralized sampled-data linear controller, then the resulting closed-loop control system in (10) is asymptotically stable, if there exist symmetric positive definite matrices $\left\{ \bar{P}_i, \bar{Q}_i, M_{ij}, M_{0i}, H_{ij}, H_{0i} \right\} \in \mathfrak{R}^{n_{zi} \times n_{zi}}$,

$H_{0i} \leq H_{ji}, M_{0i} \leq M_{ji}$, and the matrix $G_i \in \mathfrak{R}^{n_{zi} \times n_{zi}}, \bar{K}_i^l \in \mathfrak{R}^{n_{ui} \times n_{zi}}$, such that for all $l \in \mathcal{L}_i, j \neq i, \{i, j\} \in \mathcal{N}$, the following LMIs hold:

$$
\begin{bmatrix}
\bar{\Pi}_i^l & \mathbb{B}_i^l & \mathbb{A}_i^l & \mathcal{T}_{(1)} G_i^T & \mathcal{T}_{(2)} G_i^T \\
\star & \mathbb{H}_i - \mathbb{G}_i - \mathbb{G}_i^T & 0 & 0 & 0 \\
\star & \star & \mathbb{M}_i - \mathbb{G}_i - \mathbb{G}_i^T & 0 & 0 \\
\star & \star & \star & -\dfrac{H_{0i}}{\sum_{j=1,j\neq i}^{N} \left\{ \left[\bar{z}_j + \bar{s}_i \right]^2 \right\}} & 0 \\
\star & \star & \star & \star & -\dfrac{M_{0i}}{N-1}
\end{bmatrix} < 0,
$$

(108)

where

$$
\begin{cases}
\bar{\Pi}_i^l = \bar{\Theta}_i + \mathrm{Sym}\left\{ \mathcal{T}_{(3)} \mathcal{A}_i^l \right\}, \bar{\Theta}_i = \begin{bmatrix} \left[\bar{z}_i + \bar{s}_i \right]^2 \bar{Q}_i & \bar{P}_i & 0 \\ \star & 0 & 0 \\ \star & \star & -\dfrac{\pi^2}{4} \bar{Q}_i \end{bmatrix} \\
\mathcal{A}_i^l = \begin{bmatrix} -G_i & A_i^l G_i + B_i^l \bar{K}_i & B_i^l \bar{K}_i \end{bmatrix} \\
\mathbb{B}_i^l = \begin{bmatrix} \mathcal{T}_{(3)} B_i^l \bar{K}_{i1} \cdots \mathcal{T}_{(3)} B_i^l \bar{K}_{ij,j\neq i} \cdots \mathcal{T}_{(3)} B_i^l \bar{K}_{iN} \end{bmatrix} \\
\mathbb{H}_i = \mathrm{diag}\left\{ \dfrac{4}{\pi^2} H_{i1} \cdots \dfrac{4}{\pi^2} H_{ij,j\neq i} \cdots \dfrac{4}{\pi^2} H_{iN} \right\} \\
\mathcal{T}_{(1)} = \begin{bmatrix} I \\ 0 \\ 0 \end{bmatrix}, \mathcal{T}_{(2)} = \begin{bmatrix} 0 \\ I \\ 0 \end{bmatrix}, \mathcal{T}_{(3)} = \begin{bmatrix} I \\ I \\ 0 \end{bmatrix} \\
\mathbb{M}_i = \mathrm{diag}\left\{ M_{i1} \cdots M_{ij,j\neq i} \cdots M_{iN} \right\} \\
\mathbb{A}_i^l = \begin{bmatrix} \mathcal{A}_{i1} \cdots \mathcal{A}_{ij,j\neq i} \cdots \mathcal{A}_{iN} \end{bmatrix}, \mathcal{A}_{ij} = \mathcal{T}_{(3)} \left(B_i^l \bar{K}_{ij} + \bar{A}_{ij}^l G_i \right)
\end{cases}
$$

(103)

In that case, the distributed sampled-data linear controller gains can be obtained as

$$K_i = \bar{K}_i G_i^{-1}, K_{ij} = \bar{K}_{ij} G_i^{-1}, \left\{ i, j_{j \neq i} \right\} \in \mathcal{N}. \qquad (110)$$

4.4 ILLUSTRATIVE EXAMPLES

This chapter has shown theoretically some design results on the decentralized and distributed sampled-data controls for large-scale T-S fuzzy interconnected systems. In this section, we use two numerical examples to further verify the derived results.

Example 1

Consider a continuous-time large-scale interconnected system with three fuzzy subsystems as below.

Plant Rule R_i^{11}: IF $\varsigma_{i1}(t)$ is F_{i1}^1 and $\varsigma_{j2}(t)$ is F_{j2}^1 and $\varsigma_{k3}(t)$ is F_{k3}^1, THEN

$$\dot{x}_i(t) = A_i^1 x_i(t) + \bar{A}_{ij, j \neq i}^{11} x_j(t) + \bar{A}_{ik, k \neq i, k \neq j}^{11} x_k(t), i \in \{1, 2, 3\}$$

Plant Rule R_i^{12}: IF $\varsigma_{i1}(t)$ is F_{i1}^1 and $\varsigma_{j2}(t)$ is F_{j2}^2 and $\varsigma_{k3}(t)$ is F_{k3}^1, THEN

$$\dot{x}_i(t) = A_i^1 x_i(t) + \bar{A}_{ij, j \neq i}^{12} x_j(t) + \bar{A}_{ik, k \neq i, k \neq j}^{11} x_k(t), i \in \{1, 2, 3\}$$

Plant Rule R_i^{13}: IF $\varsigma_{i1}(t)$ is F_{i1}^1 and $\varsigma_{j2}(t)$ is F_{j2}^1 and $\varsigma_{k3}(t)$ is F_{k3}^2, THEN

$$\dot{x}_i(t) = A_i^1 x_i(t) + \bar{A}_{ij, j \neq i}^{11} x_j(t) + \bar{A}_{ik, k \neq i, k \neq j}^{12} x_k(t), i \in \{1, 2, 3\}$$

Plant Rule R_i^{14}: IF $\varsigma_{i1}(t)$ is F_{i1}^1 and $\varsigma_{j2}(t)$ is F_{j2}^2 and $\varsigma_{k3}(t)$ is F_{k3}^2, THEN

$$\dot{x}_i(t) = A_i^1 x_i(t) + \bar{A}_{ij, j \neq i}^{12} x_j(t) + \bar{A}_{ik, k \neq i, k \neq j}^{12} x_k(t), i \in \{1, 2, 3\}$$

Plant Rule R_i^{21}: IF $\varsigma_{i1}(t)$ is F_{i1}^2 and $\varsigma_{j2}(t)$ is F_{j2}^1 and $\varsigma_{k3}(t)$ is F_{k3}^1, THEN

$$\dot{x}_i(t) = A_i^2 x_i(t) + \bar{A}_{ij, j \neq i}^{11} x_j(t) + \bar{A}_{ik, k \neq i, k \neq j}^{11} x_k(t), i \in \{1, 2, 3\}$$

Plant Rule R_i^{22} : IF $\varsigma_{i1}(t)$ is F_{i1}^2 and $\varsigma_{j2}(t)$ is F_{j2}^2 and $\varsigma_{k3}(t)$ is F_{k3}^1 , THEN

$$\dot{x}_i(t) = A_i^2 x_i(t) + \bar{A}_{ij,j\neq i}^{12} x_j(t) + \bar{A}_{ik,k\neq i,k\neq j}^{11} x_k(t), i \in \{1,2,3\}$$

Plant Rule R_i^{23} : IF $\varsigma_{i1}(t)$ is F_{i1}^2 and $\varsigma_{j2}(t)$ is F_{j2}^1 and $\varsigma_{k3}(t)$ is F_{k3}^2 , THEN

$$\dot{x}_i(t) = A_i^2 x_i(t) + \bar{A}_{ij,j\neq i}^{11} x_j(t) + \bar{A}_{ik,k\neq i,k\neq j}^{12} x_k(t), i \in \{1,2,3\}$$

Plant Rule R_i^{24} : IF $\varsigma_{i1}(t)$ is F_{i1}^2 and $\varsigma_{j2}(t)$ is F_{j2}^2 and $\varsigma_{k3}(t)$ is F_{k3}^2 , THEN

$$\dot{x}_i(t) = A_i^2 x_i(t) + \bar{A}_{ij,j\neq i}^{12} x_j(t) + \bar{A}_{ik,k\neq i,k\neq j}^{12} x_k(t), i \in \{1,2,3\}$$

where

$$A_1^1 = \begin{bmatrix} -2.1 & 0.4 \\ 0 & -3.3 \end{bmatrix}, A_1^2 = \begin{bmatrix} -2.5 & 0.2 \\ 0 & -2.8 \end{bmatrix},$$

$$A_{12}^{11} = \begin{bmatrix} 0.7 & 0 \\ 0 & 0.2 \end{bmatrix}, A_{12}^{12} = \begin{bmatrix} 0.6 & 0 \\ 0 & 0.2 \end{bmatrix}, A_{12}^{21} = \begin{bmatrix} 0.7 & 0 \\ 0 & 0.1 \end{bmatrix}, A_{12}^{22} = \begin{bmatrix} 0.6 & 0 \\ 0 & 0.3 \end{bmatrix},$$

$$A_{13}^{11} = \begin{bmatrix} 0.1 & 0 \\ 0 & 0.4 \end{bmatrix}, A_{13}^{12} = \begin{bmatrix} 0.2 & 0 \\ 0 & 0.4 \end{bmatrix}, A_{13}^{21} = \begin{bmatrix} 0.1 & 0 \\ 0 & 0.5 \end{bmatrix}, A_{13}^{22} = \begin{bmatrix} 0.2 & 0 \\ 0 & 0.5 \end{bmatrix},$$

for the subsystem 1, and

$$A_2^1 = \begin{bmatrix} -2.6 & 0.6 \\ 0 & -2.2 \end{bmatrix}, A_2^2 = \begin{bmatrix} -2.8 & 0.3 \\ 0 & -2.2 \end{bmatrix},$$

$$A_{21}^{11} = \begin{bmatrix} 0.4 & 0 \\ 0 & 0.1 \end{bmatrix}, A_{21}^{12} = \begin{bmatrix} 0.6 & 0 \\ 0 & 0.3 \end{bmatrix}, A_{21}^{21} = \begin{bmatrix} 0.5 & 0 \\ 0 & 0.2 \end{bmatrix}, A_{21}^{22} = \begin{bmatrix} 0.6 & 0 \\ 0 & 0.4 \end{bmatrix},$$

$$A_{23}^{11} = \begin{bmatrix} 0.1 & 0 \\ 0 & 0.3 \end{bmatrix}, A_{23}^{12} = \begin{bmatrix} 0.3 & 0 \\ 0 & 0.4 \end{bmatrix}, A_{23}^{21} = \begin{bmatrix} 0.2 & 0 \\ 0 & 0.5 \end{bmatrix}, A_{23}^{22} = \begin{bmatrix} 0.2 & 0 \\ 0 & 0.4 \end{bmatrix},$$

for the subsystem 2, and

$$A_3^1 = \begin{bmatrix} -1.9 & 0.5 \\ 0 & -2.6 \end{bmatrix}, A_3^2 = \begin{bmatrix} -2.1 & 0.1 \\ 0 & -2.3 \end{bmatrix},$$

$$A_{31}^{11} = \begin{bmatrix} 0.4 & 0 \\ 0 & 0.5 \end{bmatrix}, A_{31}^{12} = \begin{bmatrix} 0.2 & 0 \\ 0 & 0.6 \end{bmatrix}, A_{31}^{21} = \begin{bmatrix} 0.3 & 0 \\ 0 & 0.7 \end{bmatrix}, A_{31}^{22} = \begin{bmatrix} 0.2 & 0 \\ 0 & 0.8 \end{bmatrix},$$

$$A_{32}^{11} = \begin{bmatrix} 0.2 & 0 \\ 0 & 0.3 \end{bmatrix}, A_{32}^{12} = \begin{bmatrix} 0.4 & 0 \\ 0 & 0.2 \end{bmatrix}, A_{32}^{21} = \begin{bmatrix} 0.1 & 0 \\ 0 & 0.4 \end{bmatrix}, A_{32}^{22} = \begin{bmatrix} 0.3 & 0 \\ 0 & 0.5 \end{bmatrix},$$

for the subsystem 3.

The normalized membership functions are shown in Figure 1, Chapter 3, where $r_i = 5$. It is noted that the open-loop system is unstable. Here, the objective is to design a sampled-data controller such that the resulting closed-loop control system is asymptotically stable. Here, by using Theorem 4.2.2, we find a feasible solution to the decentralized sampled-data controller design for the considered system. The maximum sampling interval is $h_i = 0.15$, and the corresponding controller gains are

$$K_1 = \begin{bmatrix} -0.2424 & -0.0254 \end{bmatrix}, K_2 = \begin{bmatrix} -0.2490 & -0.0164 \end{bmatrix},$$
$$K_3 = \begin{bmatrix} -0.2479 & -0.0279 \end{bmatrix}.$$

When using Theorem 4.2.4, the maximum sampling interval $h_i = 0.10$ is obtained, and the corresponding controller gains are

$$K_1 = \begin{bmatrix} -6.1494 & -1.0612 \end{bmatrix}, K_2 = \begin{bmatrix} -5.8737 & -0.5516 \end{bmatrix},$$
$$K_3 = \begin{bmatrix} -5.7009 & -1.2153 \end{bmatrix}.$$

The detail comparison can be shown in Table 1. It is easy to see that the results based on Wirtinger's inequality are less conservative than the results based on the SSG ones. Under the initial conditions $x_1(0) = \begin{bmatrix} 1.5 & -2 \end{bmatrix}^T$,

Table 1. Comparison results of maximum updating interval for different methods

Methods	Theorem 4.2.2	Theorem 4.2.4
Maximum updating interval	0.15	0.10

$x_2(0) = \begin{bmatrix} 1.8 & -2.2 \end{bmatrix}^T$, and $x_3(0) = \begin{bmatrix} 1.2 & -1.7 \end{bmatrix}^T$, and take the above controller gains, Figures 2, 3, and 4 show the state responses for the closed-loop large-scale fuzzy interconnected system, respectively. Thus, showing the effectiveness of the decentralized sampled-data controller design methods.

Example 2

Consider a continuous-time large-scale interconnected system with three fuzzy subsystems, its parameters are given as below:

$$A_1^1 = \begin{bmatrix} -2.1 & 0.4 \\ 0 & -3.3 \end{bmatrix}, A_1^2 = \begin{bmatrix} -2.5 & 0.2 \\ 0 & -2.8 \end{bmatrix},$$

$$A_{12}^1 = \begin{bmatrix} 0.7 & 0 \\ 0 & 0.2 \end{bmatrix}, A_{12}^2 = \begin{bmatrix} 0.6 & 0 \\ 0 & 0.2 \end{bmatrix},$$

Figure 2. Response of closed-loop subsystem 1

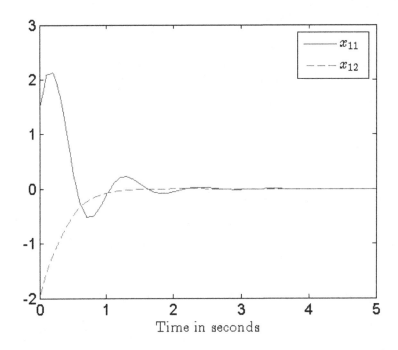

Figure 3. Response of closed-loop subsystem 2

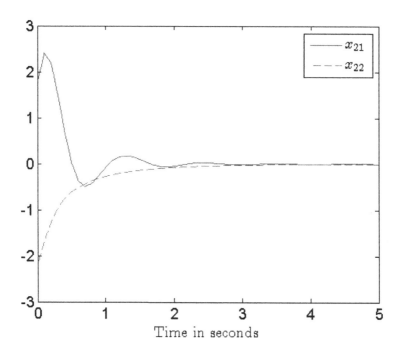

Figure 4. Response of closed-loop subsystem 2

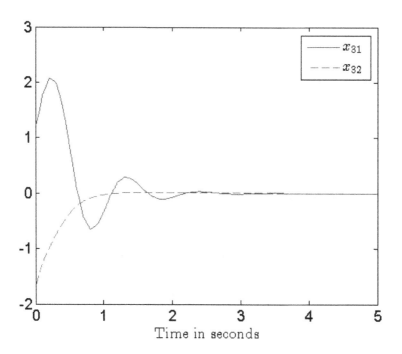

for the subsystem 1, and

$$A_2^1 = \begin{bmatrix} -2.6 & 0.6 \\ 0 & -2.2 \end{bmatrix}, A_2^2 = \begin{bmatrix} -2.8 & 0.3 \\ 0 & -2.2 \end{bmatrix},$$

$$A_{21}^1 = \begin{bmatrix} 0.4 & 0 \\ 0 & 0.1 \end{bmatrix}, A_{21}^2 = \begin{bmatrix} 0.6 & 0 \\ 0 & 0.3 \end{bmatrix},$$

for the subsystem 2, and

$$A_3^1 = \begin{bmatrix} -1.9 & 0.5 \\ 0 & -2.6 \end{bmatrix}, A_3^2 = \begin{bmatrix} -2.1 & 0.1 \\ 0 & -2.3 \end{bmatrix},$$

$$A_{31}^1 = \begin{bmatrix} 0.4 & 0 \\ 0 & 0.5 \end{bmatrix}, A_{31}^2 = \begin{bmatrix} 0.2 & 0 \\ 0 & 0.6 \end{bmatrix},$$

for the subsystems 3.

Now, the objective is to design a distributed sampled-data controller such that the resulting closed-loop control system is asymptotically stable. Here, by using Theorem 4.3.2, we find a feasible solution to the distributed sampled-data control problem for the considered system, and the sampling period and updating period are $\bar{s}_i = 0.13, \bar{z}_i = 0.1$. The corresponding controller gains can be obtained as

$$K_1 = \begin{bmatrix} -4.5818 & -0.6515 \end{bmatrix}, K_{12} = \begin{bmatrix} -0.3790 & -0.0188 \end{bmatrix}, K_{13} = \begin{bmatrix} -0.3242 & 0.0255 \end{bmatrix},$$

$$K_2 = \begin{bmatrix} -4.5240 & -0.1856 \end{bmatrix}, K_{21} = \begin{bmatrix} -0.5059 & -0.0010 \end{bmatrix}, K_{23} = \begin{bmatrix} -0.3460 & 0.0045 \end{bmatrix},$$

$$K_3 = \begin{bmatrix} -4.3076 & -0.3046 \end{bmatrix}, K_{31} = \begin{bmatrix} -0.3576 & -0.0297 \end{bmatrix}, K_{32} = \begin{bmatrix} -0.3061 & 0.0325 \end{bmatrix}.$$

Under the initial conditions $x_1(0) = \begin{bmatrix} 1.5 & -2 \end{bmatrix}^T$, $x_2(0) = \begin{bmatrix} 1.8 & -2.2 \end{bmatrix}^T$, and $x_3(0) = \begin{bmatrix} 1.2 & -1.7 \end{bmatrix}^T$, and take the above controller gains, Figures 5, 6, and 7 show the state responses for the closed-loop large-scale fuzzy interconnected system, respectively. Thus, these show the effectiveness of the design methods of distributed sampled-data control.

Figure 5. Response of closed-loop subsystem 1

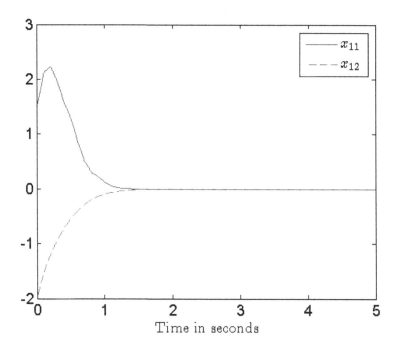

Figure 6. Response of closed-loop subsystem 2

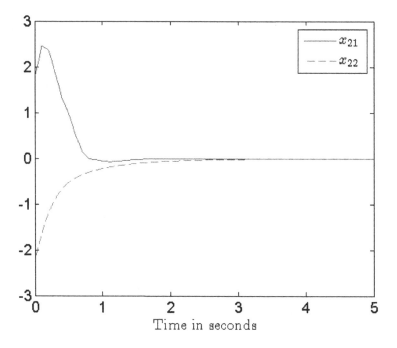

Figure 7. Response of closed-loop subsystem 3

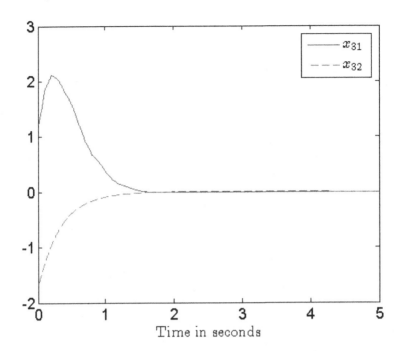

4.5 CONCLUSION

The sampled-data control problem for large-scale T-S fuzzy interconnected systems has been studied in this chapter. Various LMI-based sampled-data stabilization conditions have been established for both the decentralized and distributed controls. Two numerical examples have been given to illustrate the proposed methods.

REFERENCES

Ario, C., & Sala, A. (2008). Extensions to "stability analysis of fuzzy control systems subject to uncertain grades of membership." *IEEE Transactions on Systems, Man, and Cybernetics. Part B, Cybernetics*, *38*(2), 558–563. doi:10.1109/TSMCB.2007.913596 PMID:18348938

Chen, T., & Francis, B. (2012). *Optimal Sampled-Data Control Systems* (1st ed.). New York: Springer Science & Business Media.

Fridman, E. (2010). A refined input delay approach to sampled-data control. *Automatica*, *46*(2), 421–427. doi:10.1016/j.automatica.2009.11.017

Fridman, E., Seuret, A., & Richard, J. (2004). Robust sampled-data stabilization of linear systems: An input delay approach. *Automatica*, *40*(8), 1441–1446. doi:10.1016/j.automatica.2004.03.003

Gu, K. (2000). An integral inequality in the stability problem of time-delay systems. *Proceedings of the 2000 IEEE Conference on Decision and Control* (pp. 2805-2810). doi:10.1109/CDC.2000.914233

Gu, K., Zhang, Y., & Xu, S. (2011). 2011, Small gain problem in coupled differential-difference equations, time-varying delays, and direct Lyapunov method. *International Journal of Robust and Nonlinear Control*, *21*(4), 429–451. doi:10.1002/rnc.1604

Hetel, L., Kruszewski, A., Perruquetti, W., & Richard, J. (2011). Discrete and intersample analysis of systems with aperiodic sampling. *IEEE Transactions on Automatic Control*, *56*(7), 1696–1701. doi:10.1109/TAC.2011.2122690

Kim, H., Koo, G., & Park, J., & Joo, Y.H. (2015). Decentralized sampled-data $\mathcal{H}_\infty$ fuzzy filter for nonlinear large-scale systems. *Fuzzy Sets and Systems*, *273*, 68–86. doi:10.1016/j.fss.2014.11.024

Koo, G., Park, J., & Joo, Y. (2016). Decentralised sampled-data control for large-scale systems with nonlinear interconnections. *International Journal of Control*.

Liu, K., & Fridman, E. (2012). Wirtingers inequality and Lyapunov-based sampled-data stabilization. *Automatica*, *48*(1), 102–108. doi:10.1016/j.automatica.2011.09.029

Liu, K., Fridman, E., & Johansson, K. (2015). Dynamic quantization of uncertain linear networked control systems. *Automatica*, *59*, 248–255. doi:10.1016/j.automatica.2015.06.041

Moarref, M., & Rodrigues, L. (2014). Stability and stabilization of linear sampled-data systems with multi-rate samplers and time driven zero order holds. *Automatica*, *50*(10), 2685–2691. doi:10.1016/j.automatica.2014.08.037

Naghshtabrizi, P., Teel, A., & Hespanha, J. (2008). Exponential stability of impulsive systems with application to uncertain sampled-data systems. *Systems & Control Letters*, *57*(5), 378–385. doi:10.1016/j.sysconle.2007.10.009

Xu, S., Lam, J., Zhang, B., & Zou, Y. (2015). New insight into delay-dependent stability of time-delay systems. *International Journal of Robust and Nonlinear Control, 25*(7), 961–970. doi:10.1002/rnc.3120

Zhang, J., Knopse, C., & Tsiotras, P. (2001). Stability of time-delay systems: Equivalence between Lyapunov and scaled small-gain conditions. *IEEE Transactions on Automatic Control, 46*(3), 482–486. doi:10.1109/9.911428

Chapter 5
Event–Triggered Control of Large–Scale Fuzzy Interconnected Systems

ABSTRACT

This chapter studies the event-triggered control problem for large-scale networked fuzzy systems with transmission delays and nonlinear interconnections. Our considered scheme is decentralized event-triggered control in the sense that each subsystem is able to make broadcast decisions by using its locally sampled data when a prescribed event is triggered. We propose two different approaches to solve the co-design problem consisting of the controller gains, sampled period, network delay, and event-triggered parameter in terms of a set of LMIs. Also, we consider a self-triggered control scheme in which the next triggered time is precomputed. Finally, two simulation examples are provided to validate the advantage of the proposed methods.

5.1 INTRODUCTION

With the rapid development of digital technology, in the feedback loops communication networks are often applied instead of point-to-point connections due to their great advantages, such as low cost, simple installation and maintenance, reduced weight and power requirements (Zhang, Gao, & Kaynak, 2013). Unfortunately, the network-induced imperfections, such as quantization errors, packet dropouts, and time delays, can degrade significantly

DOI: 10.4018/978-1-5225-2385-7.ch005

the performance of the closed-loop control system and may even lead to instability (Yang, 2006). Recently, networked control systems (NCSs) have received considerable attention, and lots of results on studying combinations of these imperfections are available in the open literature, see (Zhang, Han, & Yu, 2015; Hespanha, Naghshtabrizi, & Xu, 2007), and references therein. It is worth mentioning that the design of an NCS often requires tradeoffs among the network-induced imperfections. More specifically, these features of sending larger control-packets and requiring time-stamping of messages will reduce quantization errors and packet dropouts but typically result in transmitting larger or more packets and inducing larger transmission delays (Heemels, Donkers, Teel, Wouw, & Nesic, 2010). In that case, an important issue arises in the implementation of NCSs as to how to identify methods such that the limited network bandwidth can be more effectively utilized.

In many digital implementations of networked control systems (NCSs), computers are often required to execute control tasks comprising of sampling, quantizing, transmitting the output of the plant, and computing, implementing the control input. In the execution of control tasks, the conventional principle is based on time-triggered control in the sense that the control task is executed in a periodic manner, and it will bring collision or channel congestion or larger time delays in the network due to the limited communication bandwidth. Recently, interest is shown in the event-triggered control aiming at reduction in data transmissions. The working principle based on event-triggered control is to decide whether or not to transmit control signals in term of a given threshold. In other words, the control signals are not always implemented in every sampling period x. The idea of event-based control has appeared under a variety of names, such as event-triggered feedback (Heemels & Donkers, 2013; Donkers & Heemels, 2012; Yue, Tian, & Han, 2013), interrupt-based feedback (Hristu & Kumar, 2002), self-triggered feedback (Wang & Lemmon, 2011), state-triggered feedback (Tabuada & Wang, 2006).

This chapter studies the event-triggered control problem for large-scale networked nonlinear systems with transmission delays and nonlinear interconnections. Each nonlinear subsystem in the considered large-scale system is represented by a T-S model, and exchanges its information through a digital channel. Our considered scheme is decentralized event-triggered control in the sense that each subsystem is able to make broadcast decisions by using its locally sampled data when a prescribed event is triggered. We propose two different approaches to solve the co-design problem consisting of the controller gains, sampled period, network delay, and event-triggered parameter in terms of a set of LMIs. Also, we consider a self-triggered control scheme in which the next triggered time is precomputed. Finally, two simulation examples are provided to validate the advantage of the proposed methods.

5.2 DECENTRALIZED EVENT-TRIGGERED CONTROL

In this section, our aim is to design a decentralized event-triggered fuzzy controller, such that the resulting closed-loop fuzzy control system is asymptotically stable, while the sampled data are updated as few as possible.

5.2.1 Problem Formulation

Before start it, we given some assumptions as below,

1. The sampler in each subsystem is clock-driven. Let h_i denote the upper bound of sampling intervals, we have

$$t_i^{k+1} - t_i^k \leq h_i, k \in \mathbb{N} \tag{1}$$

where $h_i > 0$.

2. Each subsystem in the large-scale system is closed by a communication channel with constant time delay τ_i. The sampled signals at the instant t_i^k are transmitted over the communication network.
3. The zero-order-hold (ZOH) is event-driven, and it uses the latest sampled-data signals and holds them until the next transmitted data come.

Recalling the large-scale T-S fuzzy interconnected system as below,

$$x_i(t) = A_i(\mu_i) x_i(t) + B_i(\mu_i) u_i(t) + \sum_{j=1, j \neq i}^{N} \bar{A}_{ij}(\mu_i, \mu_j) x_j(t), \tag{2}$$

Based the above assumptions, we consider the decentralized event-triggered fuzzy controller

Controller Rule R_i^f : IF $\hat{\varsigma}_{i1}\left(t_i^k - \tau_i\right)$ is F_{i1}^f and $\hat{\varsigma}_{i2}\left(t_i^k - \tau_i\right)$ is F_{i2}^f and $\cdots$ and $\hat{\varsigma}_{ig}\left(t_i^k - \tau_i\right)$ is F_{ig}^f, THEN

$$u_i\left(t\right) = K_i^f \hat{x}_i\left(t_i^k - \tau_i\right), t \in \left[t_i^k, t_i^{k+1}\right), i \in \mathcal{N} \tag{3}$$

where $K_i^f \in \mathfrak{R}^{n_{ui} \times n_{yi}}, f \in \mathcal{L}_i, i \in \mathcal{N}$ is the controller gains to be determined. $\hat{\varsigma}_i\left(t_i^k - \tau_i\right) = \left[\hat{\varsigma}_{i1}\left(t_i^k - \tau_i\right), \hat{\varsigma}_{i2}\left(t_i^k - \tau_i\right), \cdots, \hat{\varsigma}_{ig}\left(t_i^k - \tau_i\right)\right];$ $\hat{x}_i\left(t_i^k - \tau_i\right)$ and $\hat{x}_i\left(t_i^k - \tau_i\right)$ denote the updating signals in the fuzzy controller.

Thus, the overall fuzzy controller can be rewritten as

$$u_i\left(t\right) = K_i\left(\hat{\mu}_i\right)\hat{x}_i\left(t_i^k - \tau_i\right), t \in \left[t_i^k, t_i^{k+1}\right), i \in \mathcal{N} \tag{4}$$

with

$$\left[\begin{array}{l} K_i\left(\hat{\mu}_i\right) := \sum_{l=1}^{r_i} \hat{\mu}_i^f \left[\hat{\varsigma}_i\left(t_i^k - \tau_i\right)\right] K_i^f, \sum_{l=1}^{r_i} \hat{\mu}_i^f \left[\hat{\varsigma}_i\left(t_i^k - \tau_i\right)\right] := 1 \\[4mm] \hat{\mu}_i^f \left[\hat{\varsigma}_i\left(t_i^k - \tau_i\right)\right] := \dfrac{\Pi_{\varnothing=1}^g \hat{\mu}_{i\varnothing}^f \left[\hat{\varsigma}_{i\varnothing}\left(t_i^k - \tau_i\right)\right]}{\sum_{\varsigma=1}^{r_i} \Pi_{\varnothing=1}^g \hat{\mu}_{i\varnothing}^\varsigma \left[\hat{\varsigma}_{i\varnothing}\left(t_i^k - \tau_i\right)\right]} \geq 0 \end{array} \right. \tag{5}$$

where $\hat{\mu}_{i\varnothing}^f \left[\hat{\varsigma}_{i\varnothing}\left(t_i^k - \tau_i\right)\right]$ is the grade of membership of $\hat{\varsigma}_{i\varnothing}\left(t_i^k - \tau_i\right)$ in $F_{i\varnothing}^f$; In this chapter we will denote $\hat{\mu}_i^f = \hat{\mu}_i^f \left[\hat{\varsigma}_i\left(t_i^k - \tau_i\right)\right]$ for brevity.

NOTE: It is noted that the decentralized event-triggered fuzzy controller reduces to an PDC one when $\hat{\mu}_i^l = \mu_i^l$. However, the premise variables of the fuzzy controller (4) undergo sampled-data measurement, event-triggered control, and network-induced delay. In such circumstances the asynchronous variables between $\hat{\mu}_i^l$ and μ_i^l are more realistic. As pointed out in (Ario & Sala, 2008), when the knowledge between $\hat{\mu}_i^l$ and μ_i^l is unavailable, the condition $\hat{\mu}_i^l = \mu_i^l$ generally leads to a linear controller instead of a fuzzy one, which degrades the stabilization ability of the controller. When the knowledge on $\hat{\mu}_i^l$ and μ_i^l is available, the design conservatism can be improved, and obtaining the corresponding fuzzy controller.

In order to implement the event-triggered fuzzy controller given by (4), we assume that each subsystem transmits its measurements through a networked channel, and propose a solution in Figure 1, where SP, BF and ETM are the sampler, buffer and event-triggering mechanism, respectively. For each subsystem, a smart sensor consists of an BF that is to store $\hat{x}_i\left(t_i^k - \tau_i\right)$, which represents the latest measurement datum transmitted successfully to the controller, and an ETM that determines whether or not to transmit both $x_i\left(t_i^k\right)$ and $\varsigma_i\left(t_i^k\right)$ to the controller. Hence, in every sample period both $x_i\left(t\right)$ and $\varsigma_i\left(t\right)$ are firstly sampled by the SP. Then, they are transmitted to the controller and are executed, only when a prescribed event is violated. This leads to a reduction of data transmissions.

To formalize the described solution, the ETM in the sensor can operate as

$$\text{ETM}: \text{Both } x_i\left(t_i^k\right) \text{ and } \varsigma_i\left(t_i^k\right) \text{ are sent} \Leftrightarrow x_i\left(t_i^k\right) - \hat{x}_i\left(t_i^{k-1}\right) > \sigma_i x_i\left(t_i^k\right),$$

(6)

where $\sigma_i \geq 0$ is a suitably chosen design parameter.

Figure 1. An event-triggered state-feedback fuzzy controller

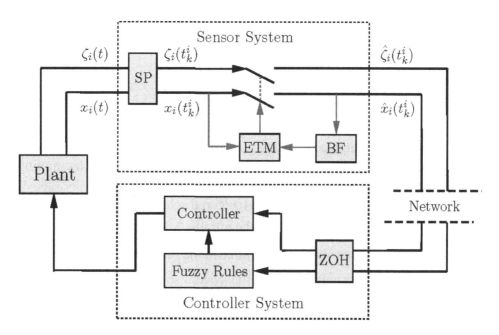

Based on the operating condition given in (6), an event-triggered strategy is formulated as follows:

$$\hat{x}_i\left(t_i^k\right) = \begin{cases} x_i\left(t_i^k\right), & \text{when } x_i\left(t_i^k\right) - \hat{x}_i\left(t_i^{k-1}\right) > \sigma_i x_i\left(t_i^k\right), \\ \hat{x}_i\left(t_i^{k-1}\right), & \text{when } x_i\left(t_i^k\right) - \hat{x}_i\left(t_i^{k-1}\right) \le \sigma_i x_i\left(t_i^k\right), \end{cases} \tag{7}$$

$$\hat{\varsigma}_i\left(t_i^k\right) = \begin{cases} \varsigma_i\left(t_i^k\right), & \text{when } x_i\left(t_i^k\right) \text{is sent}, \\ \hat{\varsigma}_i\left(t_i^{k-1}\right), & \text{when } x_i\left(t_i^k\right) \text{is not sent}, \end{cases} \tag{8}$$

In that case, the i-th closed-loop fuzzy control system is given by

$$\dot{x}_i\left(t\right) = A_i\left(\mu_i\right)x_i\left(t\right) + B_i\left(\mu_i\right)K_i\left(\hat{\mu}_i\right)\hat{x}_i\left(t_i^k - \tau_i\right)$$
$$+ \sum_{j=1, j\ne i}^{N} \overline{A}_{ij}\left(\mu_i, \mu_j\right)x_j\left(t\right), \tag{9}$$

where

$$A_i\left(\mu_i\right) := \sum_{l=1}^{r_i}\mu_i^l A_i^l, B_i\left(\mu_i\right) := \sum_{l=1}^{r_i}\mu_i^l B_i^l, K_i\left(\hat{\mu}_i\right) \doteq$$
$$\sum_{f=1}^{r_i}\hat{\mu}_i^f K_i^f, \overline{A}_{ij}\left(\mu_i, \mu_j\right) := \sum_{l=1}^{r_i}\sum_{s=1}^{r_j}\mu_i^l \mu_j^s \overline{A}_{ij}^{ls}. \tag{10}$$

NOTE: It is noted that the event-triggered strategy $x_i\left(t_i^k\right) - \hat{x}_i\left(t_i^{k-1}\right) > \sigma_i x_i\left(t_i^k\right)$ proposed in (Wang & Lemmonm, 2011) is required to examine the triggered condition, continuously. However, the event-triggered scheme given in (7) and (8) only verifies the triggered condition at each sampling instant.

NOTE: It is also noted that the event-triggered scheme given in (7) and (8) shows that at the instant t_i^k both the premise variable $\varsigma_i\left(t_i^k\right)$ and system state $x_i\left(t_i^k\right)$ are not always transmitted to the fuzzy controller only when a prescribed threshold based on the system state is violated. Thus, the proposed triggered scheme significantly reduces data transmissions.

5.2.2 Wirtinger's Inequality to Decentralized Sampled-Data Controller Design

Based on the input delay approach (Fridman, 2010), the event-triggered controller in (4) is reformulated as a delayed controller as follows:

$$u_i\left(t\right) = K_i\left(\hat{\mu}_i\right)\hat{x}_i\left(t - \eta_i\left(t\right)\right), t \in \left[t_i^k, t_i^{k+1}\right) \tag{11}$$

where $\eta_i\left(t\right) = t - t_i^k + \tau_i$. It follows from (1) and the assumptions a)-c) that

$$\tau_i \leq \eta_i\left(t\right) < \overline{\eta}_i, \overline{\eta}_i = \tau_i + h_i, t \in \left[t_i^k, t_i^{k+1}\right), k \in \mathbb{N}. \tag{12}$$

Based on the delayed controller in (11), the closed-loop event-triggered fuzzy control system in (9) can be rewritten as

$$\dot{x}_i\left(t\right) = A_i\left(\mu_i\right)x_i\left(t\right) + B_i\left(\mu_i\right)K_i\left(\hat{\mu}_i\right)\hat{x}_i\left(t - \eta_i\left(t\right)\right) + \\ \sum_{j=1, j \neq i}^{N} \overline{A}_{ij}\left(\mu_i, \mu_j\right)x_j\left(t\right). \tag{13}$$

Here, we model the event-triggered counterpart as a disturbance, it yields

$$\begin{cases} e_i\left(t\right) = \hat{x}_i\left(t - \eta_i\left(t\right)\right) - x_i\left(t - \eta_i\left(t\right)\right), \\ x_i\left(v\right) = x_i\left(t - \eta_i\left(t\right)\right) - x_i\left(t - \tau_i\right), t \in \left[t_i^k, t_i^{k+1}\right). \end{cases} \tag{14}$$

Then, by substituting (14) into (13), the closed-loop fuzzy control system in (13) can be further rewritten as

$$\dot{x}_i\left(t\right) = A_i\left(\mu_i\right)x_i\left(t\right) + B_i\left(\mu_i\right)K_i\left(\hat{\mu}_i\right)x_i\left(t - \tau_i\right) + \\ x_i\left(v\right) + e_i\left(t\right) + \sum_{j=1, j \neq i}^{N} \overline{A}_{ij}\left(\mu_i, \mu_j\right)x_j\left(t\right). \tag{15}$$

Inspired by (Liu & Fridman 2012), we introduce the following LKF with virtue of Wirtinger's inequality:

$$V(t) = \sum_{i=1}^{N} \left[V_{i1}(t) + V_{i2}(t) \right], t \in \left[t_i^k, t_i^{k+1} \right) \tag{16}$$

with

$$
\begin{cases}
V_{i1}(t) = x_i^T(t) P_i x_i(t) + \int\limits_{t-\tau_i}^{t} x_i^T(\alpha) Q_i x_i(\alpha) d\alpha + \tau_i \int\limits_{-\tau_i}^{0} \int\limits_{t+\beta}^{t} \dot{x}_i^T(\alpha) Z_i \dot{x}_i(\alpha) d\alpha d\beta \\[2ex]
V_{i2}(t) = \left(\overline{\eta}_i - \tau_i \right)^2 \int\limits_{t_i^k - \tau_i}^{t} \dot{x}_i^T(\alpha) W_i \dot{x}_i(\alpha) d\alpha \\[2ex]
\qquad - \dfrac{\pi^2}{4} \int\limits_{t_i^k - \tau_i}^{t-\tau_i} \left[x_i(\alpha) - x_i\left(t_i^k - \tau_i \right) \right]^T W_i \left[x_i(\alpha) - x_i\left(t_i^k - \tau_i \right) \right] d\alpha,
\end{cases}
\tag{17}
$$

where $\left\{ P_i, Q_i, Z_i, W_i \right\} t \in \mathfrak{R}^{n_{zi} \times n_{zi}}$, are symmetric matrices, and $P_i > 0, Z_i > 0, W_i > 0$.

Inspired by (Xu & Lam & Zhang & Zou 2015), we do not require the matrix Q_i in (17) is necessarily positive definite. To ensure the positive property of $V(t)$, we give the following lemma.

Lemma 5.2.1 Consider the Lyapunov-Krasovskii functional (LKF) in (16), then $V(t) \geq \epsilon x(t)$, where $\epsilon > 0$, $x(t) = \left[x_1^T(t), x_2^T(t), \cdots, x_N^T(t) \right]^T$, if there exist symmetric positive definite matrices $\left\{ P_i, Z_i, W_i \right\} \in \mathfrak{R}^{n_{zi} \times n_{zi}}$, and symmetric matrix $Q_i \in \mathfrak{R}^{n_{zi} \times n_{zi}}$, such that for all $i \in \mathcal{N}$ the following inequalities hold:

$$
\begin{bmatrix} \dfrac{1}{\tau_i} P_i + Z_i & -Z_i \\[2ex] \star & Q_i + Z_i \end{bmatrix} > 0.
\tag{18}
$$

Proof: Firstly, by using Jensen's inequality in Append B, we have

$$\tau_i \int_{-\tau_i}^{0} \int_{t+\beta}^{t} \dot{x}_i^T(\alpha) Z_i \dot{x}_i(\alpha) d\alpha d\beta \ge \tau_i \int_{-\tau_i}^{0} \frac{-1}{\beta} \left[\int_{t+\beta}^{t} \dot{x}_i^T(\alpha) d\alpha \right] Z_i \left[\int_{t+\beta}^{t} \dot{x}_i(\alpha) d\alpha \right] d\beta$$

$$= \tau_i \int_{-\tau_i}^{0} \frac{-1}{\beta} \left[x_i(t) - x_i(t+\beta) \right]^T Z_i \left[x_i(t) - x_i(t+\beta) \right] d\beta$$

$$= \tau_i \int_{0}^{\tau_i} \frac{1}{\beta} \left[x_i(t) - x_i(t-\beta) \right]^T Z_i \left[x_i(t) - x_i(t-\beta) \right] d\beta$$

$$\ge \int_{0}^{\tau_i} \left[x_i(t) - x_i(t-\beta) \right]^T Z_i \left[x_i(t) - x_i(t-\beta) \right] d\beta$$

$$= \int_{t-\tau_i}^{t} \left[x_i(t) - x_i(\alpha) \right]^T Z_i \left[x_i(t) - x_i(\alpha) \right] d\alpha$$

$$(19)$$

It follows from (17) and (19) that

$$V_{i1}(t) = x_i^T(t) P_i x_i(t) + \int_{t-\tau_i}^{t} x_i^T(\alpha) Q_i x_i(\alpha) d\alpha + \tau_i \int_{-\tau_i}^{0} \int_{t+\beta}^{t} \dot{x}_i^T(\alpha) Z_i \dot{x}_i(\alpha) d\alpha d\beta$$

$$\ge \int_{t-\tau_i}^{t} \begin{bmatrix} x_i(t) \\ x_i(\alpha) \end{bmatrix}^T \begin{bmatrix} \dfrac{1}{\tau_i} P_i + Z_i & -Z_i \\ \star & Q_i + Z_i \end{bmatrix} \begin{bmatrix} x_i(t) \\ x_i(\alpha) \end{bmatrix} d\alpha.$$

$$(20)$$

For $V_{i2}(t)$ given in (17), we have $x_i(\alpha) - x_i(t_i^k - \tau_i) = 0$ when $\alpha = t_i^k - \tau_i$. By using Wirtinger's inequality given in Appendix C, it is easy to see that $V_{i2}(t) \ge 0$. Therefore, there always exists a positive scalar ϵ such that the inequality $V(t) \ge \epsilon x(t)$ holds if the inequality in (18) holds.

Based on the LKF in (16), a sufficient condition for the existence of the event-triggered controller which guarantees the stability of the closed-loop fuzzy control system in (13) is derived as below.

Lemma 5.2.2 Given the large-scale T-S fuzzy interconnected system in (1) and an event-triggered fuzzy controller in the form of (4), then the resulting closed-loop fuzzy control system is asymptotically stable, if there exist symmetric positive definite matrices $\{P_i, Z_i, W_i, M_{ij}\} \in \mathfrak{R}^{n_{zi} \times n_{zi}}$, and symmetric matrix $Q_i \in \mathfrak{R}^{n_{zi} \times n_{zi}}$, matrix multipliers $\mathcal{G}_i \in \mathfrak{R}^{5n_{zi} \times n_{zi}}$, such that for all $l \in \mathcal{L}_i, j \neq i, \{i, j\} \in \mathcal{N}$, the following LMIs hold:

$$
\begin{bmatrix}
\dfrac{1}{\tau_i} P_i + Z_i & -Z_i \\[2mm]
\star & Q_i + Z_i
\end{bmatrix} > 0,
\tag{21}
$$

$$
\begin{bmatrix}
\Theta_i + \mathrm{Sym}\left\{ \mathcal{G}_i \mathbb{A}_i\left(\mu_i, \hat{\mu}_i\right)\right\} & \mathcal{G}_i \mathcal{A}_{ij}\left(\mu_i\right) \\[2mm]
\star & -\mathbb{M}_i
\end{bmatrix} < 0,
\tag{22}
$$

where

$$
\begin{aligned}
&\Theta_i = \begin{bmatrix}
\Theta_i^{(1)} & P_i & 0 & 0 & 0 \\[2mm]
\star & Q_i - Z_i + \displaystyle\sum_{j=1, j\neq i}^{N} M_{ji} & Z_i & 0 & 0 \\[2mm]
\star & \star & -Q_i - Z_i + \sigma_i^2 U_i & \sigma_i^2 U_i & 0 \\[2mm]
\star & \star & \star & -\dfrac{\pi^2}{4} W_i + \sigma_i^2 U_i & 0 \\[2mm]
\star & \star & \star & \star & -U_i
\end{bmatrix} \\[2mm]
&\Theta_i^{(1)} = \pi^2 Z_i + \left(\overline{\eta}_i - \tau_i\right)^2 W_i, \mathbb{M}_i = \mathrm{diag}\underbrace{\left\{ M_{i1} \cdots M_{ij, j\neq i} \cdots M_{iN}\right\}}_{N-1} \\[2mm]
&\mathbb{A}_i\left(\mu_i, \hat{\mu}_i\right) = \begin{bmatrix} -I & A_i\left(\mu_i\right) & B_i\left(\mu_i\right) K_i\left(\hat{\mu}_i\right) & B_i\left(\mu_i\right) K_i\left(\hat{\mu}_i\right) & B_i\left(\mu_i\right) K_i\left(\hat{\mu}_i\right)\end{bmatrix} \\[2mm]
&\mathcal{A}_{ij}\left(\mu_i\right) = \underbrace{\begin{bmatrix} \overline{A}_{i1}\left(\mu_i, \mu_j\right) \cdots \overline{A}_{ij, j\neq i}\left(\mu_i, \mu_j\right) \cdots \overline{A}_{iN}\left(\mu_i, \mu_j\right)\end{bmatrix}}_{N-1}
\end{aligned}
\tag{23}
$$

Proof: By taking the time derivative of $V\left(t\right)$, one has

$$
\begin{aligned}
\dot{V}_{i1}\left(t\right) \leq\ & 2x_i^T\left(t\right) P_i \dot{x}_i\left(t\right) + x_i^T\left(t\right) Q_i x_i\left(t\right) - x_i^T\left(t - \tau_i\right) Q_i x_i\left(t - \tau_i\right) \\
& + \tau_i^2 \dot{x}_i^T\left(t\right) Z_i \dot{x}_i\left(t\right) - \tau_i \int_{t-\tau_i}^{t} \dot{x}_i^T\left(\alpha\right) Z_i \dot{x}_i\left(\alpha\right) d\alpha,
\end{aligned}
\tag{24}
$$

$$
\dot{V}_{i2}\left(t\right) \leq \left(\overline{\eta}_i - \tau_i\right)^2 \dot{x}_i^T\left(t\right) W_i \dot{x}_i\left(t\right) - \dfrac{\pi^2}{4} x_i^T\left(v\right) W_i x_i\left(v\right).
\tag{25}
$$

Based on Jensen's inequality in Appendix B, we have

$$-\tau_i \int_{t-\tau_i}^{t} \dot{x}_i^T(\alpha) Z_i \dot{x}_i(\alpha) d\alpha \qquad \leq -\left[\int_{t-\tau_i}^{t} \dot{x}_i^T(\alpha) d\alpha\right] Z_i \left[\int_{t-\tau_i}^{t} \dot{x}_i(\alpha) d\alpha\right]$$

$$= -\left[x_i(t) - x_i(t-\tau_i)\right]^T Z_i \left[x_i(t) - x_i(t-\tau_i)\right]. \tag{26}$$

Define the matrix multipliers $\mathcal{G}_i \in \mathfrak{R}^{5n_{zi} \times 5n_{zi}}$ and it follows from (15) that

$$0 = \sum_{i=1}^{N} 2\chi_i^T(t) \mathcal{G}_i \mathbb{A}_i(\mu_i, \hat{\mu}_i) \chi_i(t) + \sum_{i=1}^{N} 2\chi_i^T(t) \mathcal{G}_i \sum_{j=1, j \neq i}^{N} \overline{A}_{ij}(\mu_i, \mu_j) x_j(t), \tag{27}$$

where

$$\begin{cases} \chi_i(t) = \begin{bmatrix} \dot{x}_i^T(t) & x_i^T(t) & x_i^T(t-\tau_i) & x_i^T(v) & e_i^T(t) \end{bmatrix} \\ \mathbb{A}_i(\mu_i, \hat{\mu}_i) = \begin{bmatrix} -I & A_i(\mu_i) & B_i(\mu_i)K_i(\hat{\mu}_i) & B_i(\mu_i)K_i(\hat{\mu}_i) & B_i(\mu_i)K_i(\hat{\mu}_i) \end{bmatrix} \end{cases} \tag{28}$$

Define $M_i \in \mathfrak{R}^{n_{zi} \times n_{zi}}$ and based on Young's inequality $2\overline{x}^T\overline{y} \leq \overline{x}^T M^{-1}\overline{x} + \overline{y}^T M\overline{y}$ for symmetric positive definite matrix $M_{ij} \in \mathfrak{R}^{n_{zi} \times n_{zi}}$, it yields

$$\sum_{i=1}^{N} 2\chi_i^T(t) \mathcal{G}_i \sum_{j=1, j \neq i}^{N} \overline{A}_{ij}(\mu_i, \mu_j) x_j(t)$$

$$\leq \sum_{i=1}^{N} \sum_{j=1, j \neq i}^{N} \chi_i^T(t) \mathcal{G}_i \left\{ \left[\overline{A}_{ij}(\mu_i, \mu_j)\right] M_{ij} \left[\overline{A}_{ij}(\mu_i, \mu_j)\right]^T \right\} \mathcal{G}_i^T \chi_i(t) \tag{29}$$

$$+ \sum_{i=1}^{N} \sum_{j=1, j \neq i}^{N} \left\{ x_i^T(t) M_{ji}^{-1} x_i(t) \right\}$$

In addition, it follows from (7) that

$$e_i(t) = \hat{x}_i(t - \eta_i(t)) - x_i(t - \eta_i(t))$$

$$\leq \sigma_i x_i(t - \eta_i(t)) \tag{30}$$

$$= \sigma_i x_i(t - \tau_i) + x_i(v).$$

Based on the relation in (30), and define symmetric positive definite matrix $U_i \in \mathfrak{R}^{n_{zi} \times n_{zi}}$, we have

$$e_i^T(t) U_i e_i(t) \leq \sigma_i^2 \begin{bmatrix} x_i(t - \tau_i) \\ x_i(v) \end{bmatrix}^T \begin{bmatrix} U_i & U_i \\ * & U_i \end{bmatrix} \begin{bmatrix} x_i(t - \tau_i) \\ x_i(v) \end{bmatrix}. \tag{31}$$

It follows from (24)-(31) that

$$\dot{V}(t) \leq \sum_{i=1}^{N} \left[2x_i^T(t) P_i \dot{x}_i(t) + x_i^T(t) Q_i x_i(t) - x_i^T(t - \tau_i) Q_i x_i(t - \tau_i) \right]$$

$$+ \sum_{i=1}^{N} \left\{ \tau_i^2 \dot{x}_i^T(t) Z_i \dot{x}_i(t) - \left[x_i(t) - x_i(t - \tau_i) \right]^T Z_i \left[x_i(t) - x_i(t - \tau_i) \right] \right\}$$

$$+ \sum_{i=1}^{N} \left\{ (\bar{\eta}_i - \tau_i)^2 \dot{x}_i^T(t) W_i \dot{x}_i(t) - \frac{\pi^2}{4} x_i^T(v) W_i x_i(v) \right\}$$

$$+ \sum_{i=1}^{N} \sum_{j=1, j \neq i}^{N} \chi_i^T(t) \mathcal{G}_i \left\{ \sum_{l=1}^{r_i} \mu^l \left[\bar{A}_{ij}^l \right] M_{ij} \left[\bar{A}_{ij}^l \right]^T \right\} \mathcal{G}_i^T \chi_i(t) + \sum_{i=1}^{N} \sum_{j=1, j \neq i}^{N} \left\{ x_i^T(t) M_{ji}^{-1} x_i(t) \right\}$$

$$+ \sum_{i=1}^{N} \left\{ \sigma_i^2 \begin{bmatrix} x_i(t - \tau_i) \\ x_i(v) \end{bmatrix}^T \begin{bmatrix} U_i & U_i \\ * & U_i \end{bmatrix} \begin{bmatrix} x_i(t - \tau_i) \\ x_i(v) \end{bmatrix} - e_i^T(t) U_i e_i(t) \right\}$$

$$= \sum_{i=1}^{N} \chi_i^T(t) \left[\Theta_i + \text{Sym} \left\{ \mathcal{G}_i \mathbb{A}_i(\mu_i, \hat{\mu}_i) \right\} + \sum_{j=1, j \neq i}^{N} \mathcal{G}_i \bar{A}_{ij}(\mu_i, \mu_j) M_{ij}^{-1} \bar{A}_{ij}^T(\mu_i, \mu_j) \mathcal{G}_i^T \right] \chi_i(t) \tag{32}$$

where Θ_i and $\mathbb{A}_i(\mu_i, \hat{\mu}_i)$ are defined in (23).

NOTE: It is noted that the conditions given in (22) are nonlinear matrix inequalities when the controller gains are unknown. It is also noted that when the knowledge between μ_i^l and $\hat{\mu}_i^l$ is unavailable, the condition $\mu_i \neq \hat{\mu}_i$ generally leads to a linear controller instead of a fuzzy one, which induces the design conservatism (Ario & Sala, 2008).

Based on Lemma 5.2.2, we will present the co-design result consisting of the fuzzy controller gains, sampled period, and network delay in terms of a set of LMIs, the result is summarized as follows.

Theorem 5.2.1 Given the large-scale T-S fuzzy interconnected system in (1) and an event-triggered fuzzy controller in the form of (4), then the resulting closed-loop fuzzy control system is asymptotically stable, if there exist symmetric positive definite matrices $\left\{ \bar{P}_i, \bar{Z}_i, \bar{W}_i, \bar{U}_i, H_{ij} \right\} \in \Re^{n_{zi} \times n_{zi}}$, and symmetric matrix $\bar{Q}_i \in \Re^{n_{zi} \times n_{zi}}$, and $\bar{K}_i^f \in \Re^{n_{ui} \times n_{zi}}$, and positive scalars $\left\{ \sigma_i, \tau_i, \bar{\eta}_i \right\}$, such that for all $l \in \mathcal{L}_i, j \neq i, \{i, j\} \in \mathcal{N}$, the following LMIs hold:

$$\begin{bmatrix} \dfrac{1}{\tau_i} P_i + Z_i & -Z_i \\ * & Q_i + Z_i \end{bmatrix} > 0, \tag{33}$$

$$\bar{\rho}_i^l \Sigma_i^{ll} + \mathrm{X}_i^{ll} < 0, \tag{34}$$

$$\underline{\rho}_i^l \Sigma_i^{ll} + \mathrm{X}_i^{ll} < 0, \tag{35}$$

$$\bar{\rho}_i^f \Sigma_i^{lf} + \bar{\rho}_i^l \Sigma_i^{fl} + \mathrm{X}_i^{lf} + \mathrm{X}_i^{fl} < 0, \tag{36}$$

$$\underline{\rho}_i^f \Sigma_i^{lf} + \underline{\rho}_i^l \Sigma_i^{fl} + \mathrm{X}_i^{lf} + \mathrm{X}_i^{fl} < 0, \tag{37}$$

$$\underline{\rho}_i^f \Sigma_i^{lf} + \bar{\rho}_i^l \Sigma_i^{fl} + \mathrm{X}_i^{lf} + \mathrm{X}_i^{fl} < 0, \tag{38}$$

$$\bar{\rho}_i^f \Sigma_i^{lf} + \underline{\rho}_i^l \Sigma_i^{fl} + \mathrm{X}_i^{lf} + \mathrm{X}_i^{fl} < 0, \tag{39}$$

$$\begin{bmatrix} \mathrm{X}_i^{11} & \cdots & \mathrm{X}_i^{1r_i} \\ \vdots & \ddots & \vdots \\ \mathrm{X}_i^{r_i 1} & \cdots & \mathrm{X}_i^{r_i r_i} \end{bmatrix} > 0, \tag{40}$$

where

$$
\left\{
\begin{aligned}
\Sigma_i^{lf} &= \begin{bmatrix} \tilde{\Theta}_i + \mathrm{Sym}\left\{\boldsymbol{\mathcal{T}}_{(2)}\mathbb{A}_i^{lf}\right\} + \boldsymbol{\mathcal{T}}_{(2)}\left\{ \displaystyle\sum_{j=1,j\neq i}^{N}\sum_{s=1}^{r_j}\overline{A}_{ij}^{ls}H_{ij}\left[\overline{A}_{ij}^{ls}\right]^T \right\}\boldsymbol{\mathcal{T}}_{(2)}^T & \overline{\mathbb{T}}_i \\ \star & -\mathbb{H}_i \end{bmatrix} \\
\tilde{\Theta}_i &= \begin{bmatrix} \overline{\Theta}_i^{(1)} & \overline{P}_i & 0 & 0 & 0 \\ \star & \overline{Q}_i - \overline{Z}_i & \overline{Z}_i & 0 & 0 \\ \star & \star & -\overline{Q}_i - \overline{Z}_i + \sigma_i^2\overline{U}_i & \sigma_i^2\overline{U}_i & 0 \\ \star & \star & \star & -\dfrac{\pi^2}{4}\overline{W}_i + \sigma_i^2\overline{U}_i & 0 \\ \star & \star & \star & \star & -\overline{U}_i \end{bmatrix} \\
\overline{\Theta}_i^{(1)} &= \tau_i^2\overline{Z}_i + \left(\overline{\eta}_i - \tau_i\right)^2\overline{W}_i, \overline{\mathbb{T}}_i = \underbrace{\begin{bmatrix} \boldsymbol{\mathcal{T}}_{(1)}G_i^T & \cdots & \boldsymbol{\mathcal{T}}_{(1)}G_i^T & \cdots & \boldsymbol{\mathcal{T}}_{(1)}G_i^T \end{bmatrix}}_{N-1} \\
\boldsymbol{\mathcal{T}}_{(2)} &= \begin{bmatrix} I \\ I \\ 0 \\ 0 \\ 0 \end{bmatrix}, \boldsymbol{\mathcal{T}}_{(1)} = \begin{bmatrix} 0 \\ I \\ 0 \\ 0 \\ 0 \end{bmatrix}, \mathbb{H}_i = \mathrm{diag}\underbrace{\left\{ H_{i1} \cdots H_{ij,j\neq i} \cdots H_{iN} \right\}}_{N-1} \\
\mathbb{A}_i^{lf} &= \begin{bmatrix} -G_i & A_i^lG_i & B_i^l\overline{K}_i^f & B_i^l\overline{K}_i^f & B_i^l\overline{K}_i^f \end{bmatrix}
\end{aligned}
\right. \tag{41}
$$

In that case, a decentralized event-triggered fuzzy controller gains can be obtained as

$$
K_i^l = \overline{K}_i^l G_i^{-1}, l \in \mathcal{L}_i. \tag{42}
$$

Proof: Recalling the result in (32),

$$
\Theta_i + \mathrm{Sym}\left\{\mathcal{G}_i\mathbb{A}_i\left(\mu_i,\hat{\mu}_i\right)\right\} + \sum_{j=1,j\neq i}^{N}\mathcal{G}_i\overline{A}_{ij}\left(\mu_i,\mu_j\right)M_{ij}^{-1}\overline{A}_{ij}^T\left(\mu_i,\mu_j\right)\mathcal{G}_i^T < 0. \tag{43}
$$

For simplify, define $H_{ij} = M_{ij}^{-1}$ and by applying Schur complement lemma, the following inequality implies (22),

$$\begin{bmatrix} \overline{\Theta}_i + \mathrm{Sym}\left\{\mathcal{G}_i\mathbb{A}_i\left(\mu_i,\hat{\mu}_i\right)\right\} + \displaystyle\sum_{j=1,j\neq i}^{N} \mathcal{G}_i\overline{A}_{ij}\left(\mu_i,\mu_j\right)H_{ij}\overline{A}_{ij}^T\left(\mu_i,\mu_j\right)\mathcal{G}_i^T & \mathbb{T}_i \\ \star & -\mathbb{H}_i \end{bmatrix} < 0, \tag{44}$$

Where

$$\begin{cases} \overline{\Theta}_i = \begin{bmatrix} \Theta_i^{(1)} & P_i & 0 & 0 & 0 \\ \star & Q_i - Z_i & Z_i & 0 & 0 \\ \star & \star & -Q_i - Z_i + \sigma_i^2 U_i & \sigma_i^2 U_i & 0 \\ \star & \star & \star & -\dfrac{\pi^2}{4}W_i + \sigma_i^2 U_i & 0 \\ \star & \star & \star & \star & -U_i \end{bmatrix} \\ \Theta_i^{(1)} = \tau_i^2 Z_i + \left(\overline{\eta}_i - \tau_i\right)^2 W_i, \mathbb{H}_i = \mathrm{diag}\underbrace{\left\{H_1 \cdots H_{j,j\neq i} \cdots H_N\right\}}_{N-1}, \\ \mathbb{T}_i = \underbrace{\left[\mathcal{T}_{(1)} \cdots \mathcal{T}_{(1)} \cdots \mathcal{T}_{(1)}\right]}_{N-1}, \mathcal{T}_{(1)} = \begin{bmatrix} 0 \\ I \\ 0 \\ 0 \end{bmatrix}, \\ \mathbb{A}_i\left(\mu_i,\hat{\mu}_i\right) = \begin{bmatrix} -I & A_i\left(\mu_i\right) & B_i\left(\mu_i\right)K_i\left(\hat{\mu}_i\right) & B_i\left(\mu_i\right)K_i\left(\hat{\mu}_i\right) & B_i\left(\mu_i\right)K_i\left(\hat{\mu}_i\right) \end{bmatrix} \end{cases} \tag{45}$$

It follows from (34)-(40) that

$$\tau_i^2 Z_i + \left(\overline{\eta}_i - \tau_i\right)^2 W_i - \mathrm{Sym}\left\{G_i\right\} < 0, i \in \mathcal{N} \tag{46}$$

which implies that G_i are nonsingular matrices.

We further define

$$\begin{cases} \mathcal{G}_i = \begin{bmatrix} G_i^{-1} & G_i^{-1} & 0 & 0 & 0 \end{bmatrix}^T, \Gamma_i := \mathrm{diag}\left\{G_i \quad G_i \quad G_i \quad G_i \quad G_i \quad \underbrace{I \cdots I \cdots I}_{N-1}\right\}, \\ \overline{P}_i = G_i^T P_i G_i, \overline{Q}_i = G_i^T Q_i G_i, \overline{Z}_i = G_i^T Z_i G_i, \overline{U}_i = G_i^T U_i G_i, \overline{W}_i = G_i^T W Q_i G_i. \end{cases} \tag{47}$$

By substituting (47) into (45), and performing a congruence transformation by Γ_i, and extracting the fuzzy membership functions, we have

$$\sum_{l=1}^{r_i}\sum_{f=1}^{r_i}\mu_i^l\mu_i^f \sum_i^{lf} < 0, \tag{48}$$

where $\sum_i^{lf}$ is defined in (41).

Then, by using the result in Appendix E, the inequalities in (34)-(40) can be obtained. Thus completing this proof.

When the information between μ_i^l and $\hat{\mu}_i^s$ is unavailable, the corresponding result on decentralized event-triggered linear controller design can be obtained as below.

Theorem 5.2.2 Given the large-scale T-S fuzzy interconnected system in (1) and an event-triggered linear controller in the form of (4), then the resulting closed-loop fuzzy control system is asymptotically stable, if there exist symmetric positive definite matrices $\left\{\bar{P}_i, \bar{Z}_i, \bar{W}_i, \bar{U}_i, H_{ij}\right\} \in \Re^{n_{zi}\times n_{zi}}$, and symmetric matrix $\bar{Q}_i \in \Re^{n_{zi}\times n_{zi}}$, and $\bar{K}_i \in \Re^{n_{ui}\times n_{zi}}$, and positive scalars $\left\{\sigma_i, \tau_i, \bar{\eta}_i\right\}$, such that for all $l \in \mathcal{L}_i, j \neq i, \{i,j\} \in \mathcal{N},$ the following LMIs hold:

$$\begin{bmatrix} \dfrac{1}{h_i}\bar{P}_i + \bar{Z}_i & -\bar{Z}_i \\ \star & \bar{Q}_i + \bar{Z}_i \end{bmatrix} > 0, \tag{49}$$

$$\begin{bmatrix} \tilde{\Theta}_i + \mathrm{Sym}\left\{\boldsymbol{\mathcal{T}}_{(2)}\mathbb{A}_i^l\right\} + \boldsymbol{\mathcal{T}}_{(2)}\left\{\displaystyle\sum_{j=1,j\neq i}^{N}\sum_{s=1}^{r_j}\bar{A}_{ij}^{ls}H_{ij}\left[\bar{A}_{ij}^{ls}\right]^T\right\}\boldsymbol{\mathcal{T}}_{(2)}^T & \mathbb{T}_i \\ \star & -\mathbb{H}_i \end{bmatrix} < 0, \tag{50}$$

Where

$$
\begin{cases}
\tilde{\Theta}_i = \begin{bmatrix}
\bar{\Theta}_i^{(1)} & \bar{P}_i & 0 & 0 & 0 \\
\star & \bar{Q}_i - \bar{Z}_i & \bar{Z}_i & 0 & 0 \\
\star & \star & -\bar{Q}_i - \bar{Z}_i + \sigma_i^2 \bar{U}_i & \sigma_i^2 \bar{U}_i & 0 \\
\star & \star & \star & -\dfrac{\pi^2}{4}\bar{W}_i + \sigma_i^2 \bar{U}_i & 0 \\
\star & \star & \star & \star & -\bar{U}_i
\end{bmatrix} \\[2pt]
\bar{\mathbb{T}}_i = \underbrace{\begin{bmatrix} \boldsymbol{\mathcal{T}}_{(1)} G_i^T \cdots \boldsymbol{\mathcal{T}}_{(1)} G_i^T \cdots \boldsymbol{\mathcal{T}}_{(1)} G_i^T \end{bmatrix}}_{N-1}, \bar{\Theta}_i^{(1)} = \tau_i^2 \bar{Z}_i + \left(\bar{\eta}_i - \tau_i\right)^2 \bar{W}_i \\[2pt]
\boldsymbol{\mathcal{T}}_{(2)} = \begin{bmatrix} I \\ I \\ 0 \\ 0 \\ 0 \end{bmatrix}, \boldsymbol{\mathcal{T}}_{(1)} = \begin{bmatrix} 0 \\ I \\ 0 \\ 0 \\ 0 \end{bmatrix}, \mathbb{H}_i = \operatorname{diag}\underbrace{\left\{ H_{i1} \cdots H_{ij,j\neq i} \cdots H_{iN} \right\}}_{N-1} \\[2pt]
\bar{\mathbb{A}}_i^l = \begin{bmatrix} -G_i & A_i^l G_i & B_i^l \bar{K}_i^f & B_i^l \bar{K}_i^f & B_i^l \bar{K}_i^f \end{bmatrix}
\end{cases} \tag{51}
$$

In that case, the decentralized event-triggered linear controller gains can be obtained as

$$
K_i = \bar{K}_i G_i^{-1}. \tag{52}
$$

NOTE: It is also noted that when designing an event-triggered linear controller in (51), the premise variables are no longer required to transmit through communication networks. Compared with the event-triggered fuzzy controller in (11), the linear one reduces the requirements for extra hardware and software but raising the design conservatism.

5.2.3 SSG Method to Decentralized Event-Triggered Controller Design

Recalling the closed-loop fuzzy control system

$$
\dot{x}_i(t) = A_i(\mu_i) x_i(t) + B_i(\mu_i) K_i(\hat{\mu}_i) \hat{x}_i\left(t - \eta_i(t)\right) + \sum_{j=1,j\neq i}^{N} \bar{A}_{ij}(\mu_i, \mu_j) x_j(t), \tag{53}
$$

where $\eta_i(t) = t - t_i^k + \tau_i$.

Here, we use the approximated method as below,

$$e_i(t) = \hat{x}_i(t - \eta_i(t)) - x_i(t - \eta_i(t)),$$ (54)

and (Gu, Zhang, & Xu, 2011)

$$
\begin{aligned}
\frac{T_i}{2}\omega_i(t) &= x_i(t - \eta_i(t)) - \frac{1}{2}\left[x_i(t - \tau_i) + x_i(t - \bar{\eta}_i)\right] \\
&= \frac{1}{2}\int_{-\bar{\eta}_i}^{-\eta_i(t)}\dot{x}_i(t + \alpha)\,d\alpha - \frac{1}{2}\int_{-\eta_i(t)}^{-\tau_i}\dot{x}_i(t+\alpha)\,d\alpha \\
&= \frac{1}{2}\int_{-\bar{\eta}_i}^{-\tau_i}\rho_i(\alpha)\dot{x}_i(t + \alpha)\,d\alpha,
\end{aligned}
$$ (55)

where $T_i = \bar{\eta}_i - \tau_i$, and

$$\rho_i(\alpha) = \begin{cases} 1, & \text{if } \alpha \leq \eta_i(t), \\ -1, & \text{if } \alpha > \eta_i(t). \end{cases}$$ (56)

Submitted (54) and (55) into (53), it yields

$$
\begin{aligned}
S_{i1} : & \begin{cases}
\dot{x}_i(t) = A_i(\mu_i)x_i(t) + B_i(\mu_i)K_i(\hat{\mu}_i)\left[\frac{1}{2}\left[x_i(t - \tau_i) + x_i(t - \bar{\eta}_i)\right] + \frac{T_i}{2}\omega_i(t) + e_i(t)\right] \\
\quad + \sum_{j=1, j\neq i}^{N}\bar{A}_{ij}(\mu_i, \mu_j)x_j(t), \\
y_{i1}(t) = \dot{x}_i(t) \\
y_{i2}(t) = \sigma_i\left\{\frac{1}{2}\left[x_i(t - \tau_i) + x_i(t - \bar{\eta}_i)\right] + \frac{T_i}{2}\omega_i(t)\right\}
\end{cases} \\
S_{i2} : & \begin{cases}
\omega_i(t) = \Delta_{i1}y_{i1}(t), \\
e_i(t) = \Delta_{i2}y_{i2}(t),
\end{cases}
\end{aligned}
$$ (57)

where Δ_{i1} and Δ_{i2} denotes uncertain operators.

In that case, the fuzzy control system in (53) is transformed into an interconnection system with extra input and output as shown in (57). In order to apply the SSG method, we give the following lemma.

Lemma 5.2.3 Consider the interconnected system in (57), the operator $\Delta_{i1} : y_{i1}(t) \to \omega_i(t)$ and $\Delta_{i2} : y_{i2}(t) \to e_i(t)$ satisfy the property $\left\| \Delta_{i1} \right\| \leq 1$ and $\left\| \Delta_{i2} \right\| \leq 1$.

Proof. Similar to Lemma 4.2.2, we can directly obtain $\left\| \Delta_{i1} \right\| \leq 1$. Recalling the relation in (54), one has

$$
\begin{aligned}
\left\| e_i(t) \right\| &= \left\| \hat{x}_i \left(t - \eta_i(t) \right) - x_i \left(t - \eta_i(t) \right) \right\| \\
&\leq \left\| \sigma_i x_i \left(t - \eta_i(t) \right) \right\| \\
&= \left\| \sigma_i y_{i2}(t) \right\|
\end{aligned}
\tag{58}
$$

Thus, it is easy to see that $\left\| \Delta_{i2} \right\| \leq 1$.

Based on the new model in (57), we consider the Lyapunov-Krasovskii functional (LKF) as below,

$$
V\left(x(t) \right) = \sum_{i=1}^{N} \left\{ V_{i1}\left(x_i(t) \right) + V_{i2}\left(x_{i2}(t) \right) \right\},
\tag{59}
$$

with

$$
\begin{aligned}
V_{i1}\left(x_i(t) \right) &= x_i^T(t) P_{i1} x_i(t) + \int_{t-\tau_i}^{t} x_i^T(\alpha) Q_{i1} x_i(\alpha) d\alpha \\
&+ \overline{\eta}_i \int_{-\tau_i}^{0} \int_{t+\beta}^{t} \dot{x}_i^T(\alpha) Z_{i1} \dot{x}_i(\alpha) d\alpha d\beta,
\end{aligned}
\tag{60}
$$

and

$$
\begin{aligned}
V_{i2}\left(x_i(t) \right) &= x_i^T(t) P_{i2} x_i(t) + \int_{t-\overline{\eta}_i}^{t} x_i^T(\alpha) Q_{i2} x_i(\alpha) d\alpha + \\
&\overline{\eta}_i \int_{-\overline{\eta}_i}^{0} \int_{t+\beta}^{t} \dot{x}_i^T(\alpha) Z_{i2} \dot{x}_i(\alpha) d\alpha d\beta,
\end{aligned}
\tag{61}
$$

where $\left\{ P_{i2}, P_{i2}, Z_{i1}, Z_{i2} \right\} \in \mathfrak{R}^{n_{xi} \times n_{xi}}$ are symmetric positive matrices, $\left\{ Q_{i1}, Q_{i2} \right\} \in \mathfrak{R}^{n_{xi} \times n_{xi}}$ are symmetric matrices.

Similar to Lemma 4.2.3, we do not require that the matrices $\left\{ Q_{i1}, Q_{i2} \right\}$ in (60) and (61) are necessarily positive definite. To ensure the positive property of $V\left(x\left(t \right) \right)$, we give the following lemma.

Lemma 5.2.4 Given the large-scale T-S fuzzy interconnected system in (1) and an event-triggered linear controller in the form of (4), then the resulting closed-loop fuzzy control system is asymptotically stable, if there exist symmetric positive definite matrices $\left\{ P_{i2}, P_{i2}, Z_{i1}, Z_{i2} \right\} \in \mathfrak{R}^{n_{xi} \times n_{xi}}$, and symmetric matrix $\left\{ Q_{i1}, Q_{i2} \right\} \in \mathfrak{R}^{n_{xi} \times n_{xi}}$, such that for all $l \in \mathcal{L}_i, j \neq i, \left\{ i, j \right\} \in \mathcal{N}$, the following LMIs hold:

$$\begin{bmatrix} \dfrac{1}{\tau_i} P_{i1} + Z_{i1} & -Z_{i1} \\ \star & Q_{i1} + Z_{i1} \end{bmatrix} > 0, \tag{62}$$

and

$$\begin{bmatrix} \dfrac{1}{\bar{\eta}_i} P_{i2} + Z_{i2} & -Z_{i2} \\ \star & Q_{i2} + Z_{i2} \end{bmatrix} > 0. \tag{63}$$

Based on the new model in (57), and the LKF in (59), a sufficient condition for the controller design result can be given as below.

Theorem 5.2.3 Given the large-scale T-S fuzzy interconnected system in (1) and an event-triggered linear controller in the form of (4), then the resulting closed-loop fuzzy control system with the assumption (4-17) is asymptotically stable, if there exist symmetric positive definite matrices $\left\{ \bar{P}_{i2}, \bar{P}_{i2}, \bar{Z}_{i1}, \bar{Z}_{i2}, \bar{H}_i, \bar{U}_i, M_{ij} \right\} \in \mathfrak{R}^{n_{xi} \times n_{xi}}$, and symmetric matrix $\left\{ \bar{Q}_{i1}, \bar{Q}_{i2} \right\} \in \mathfrak{R}^{n_{xi} \times n_{xi}}$, and $\bar{K}_i^f \in \mathfrak{R}^{n_{ui} \times n_{xi}}$, and positive scalars $\left\{ \sigma_i, \tau_i, \bar{\eta}_i \right\}$, such that for all $l \in \mathcal{L}_i, j \neq i, \left\{ i, j \right\} \in \mathcal{N}$, the following LMIs hold:

$$\begin{bmatrix} \dfrac{1}{\tau_i} \bar{P}_{i1} + \bar{Z}_{i1} & -\bar{Z}_{i1} \\ \star & \bar{Q}_{i1} + \bar{Z}_{i1} \end{bmatrix} > 0, \tag{64}$$

$$\begin{bmatrix} \dfrac{1}{\bar{\eta}_i} \bar{P}_{i2} + \bar{Z}_{i2} & -\bar{Z}_{i2} \\ \star & \bar{Q}_{i2} + \bar{Z}_{i2} \end{bmatrix} > 0. \tag{65}$$

$$\bar{\rho}_i^l \sum_i^{ll} + \mathrm{X}_i^{ll} < 0, \tag{66}$$

$$\underline{\rho}_i^l \sum_i^{ll} + \mathrm{X}_i^{ll} < 0, \tag{67}$$

$$\bar{\rho}_i^s \sum_i^{ls} + \bar{\rho}_i^l \sum_i^{sl} + \mathrm{X}_i^{ls} + \mathrm{X}_i^{sl} < 0, \tag{68}$$

$$\underline{\rho}_i^s \sum_i^{ls} + \underline{\rho}_j^l \sum_i^{sl} + \mathrm{X}_i^{ls} + \mathrm{X}_i^{sl} < 0, \tag{69}$$

$$\underline{\rho}_j^s \sum_i^{ls} + \bar{\rho}_i^l \sum_i^{sl} + \mathrm{X}_i^{ls} + \mathrm{X}_i^{sl} < 0, \tag{70}$$

$$\bar{\rho}_i^s \sum_i^{ls} + \underline{\rho}_j^l \sum_i^{sl} + \mathrm{X}_i^{ls} + \mathrm{X}_i^{sl} < 0, \tag{71}$$

$$\begin{bmatrix} \mathrm{X}_i^{11} & \cdots & \mathrm{X}_i^{1r_i} \\ \vdots & \ddots & \vdots \\ \mathrm{X}_i^{r_i 1} & \cdots & \mathrm{X}_i^{r_i r_i} \end{bmatrix} > 0, \tag{72}$$

where

$$\Sigma_i^{lf} = \begin{bmatrix} \bar{\Theta}_i + \sigma_i^2 \mathcal{T}_{(1)}^T \bar{U}_i \mathcal{T}_{(1)} + \mathrm{Sym}\left\{ \mathcal{T}_{(2)} \bar{\mathbb{A}}_i^{lf} \right\} + \mathcal{T}_{(2)} \left\{ \sum\limits_{j=1,j\neq i}^{N} \sum\limits_{s=1}^{r_j} \bar{A}_{ij}^{ls} M_{ij} \left[\bar{A}_{ij}^{ls} \right]^T \right\} \mathcal{T}_{(2)}^T & \bar{\mathbb{T}}_i \\ \star & -\mathbb{M}_i \end{bmatrix}$$

$$\bar{\Theta}_i = \begin{bmatrix} \bar{\Theta}_{i(1)} & \bar{P}_{i1} + \bar{P}_{i2} & 0 & 0 & 0 & 0 \\ \star & \bar{\Theta}_{i(2)} & \bar{Z}_{i1} & \bar{Z}_{i2} & 0 & 0 \\ \star & \star & -\bar{Q}_{i1} - \bar{Z}_{i1} & 0 & 0 & 0 \\ \star & \star & \star & -\bar{Q}_{i2} - \bar{Z}_{i2} & 0 & 0 \\ \star & \star & \star & \star & -\bar{H}_i & 0 \\ \star & \star & \star & \star & \star & -\bar{U}_i \end{bmatrix}, \mathcal{T}_{(3)} = \begin{bmatrix} 0 \\ I \\ 0 \\ 0 \\ 0 \\ 0 \end{bmatrix}, \mathcal{T}_{(2)} = \begin{bmatrix} I \\ I \\ 0 \\ 0 \\ 0 \\ 0 \end{bmatrix}$$

$$\bar{\Theta}_{i(1)} = \tau_i^2 \bar{Z}_{i1} + \bar{\eta}_i^2 \bar{Z}_{i2} + \bar{H}_i, \bar{\Theta}_{i(2)} = \bar{Q}_{i1} + \bar{Q}_{i2} - \bar{Z}_{i1} - \bar{Z}_{i2}, \mathcal{T}_{(1)} = \begin{bmatrix} 0 & 0 & \frac{1}{2}I & \frac{1}{2}I & \frac{\mathcal{T}_i}{2}I & 0 \end{bmatrix}$$

$$\bar{\mathbb{A}}_i^{lf} = \begin{bmatrix} -G_i & A_i^l G_i & \frac{1}{2} B_i^l \bar{K}_i^f & \frac{1}{2} B_i^l \bar{K}_i^f & \frac{\mathcal{T}_i}{2} B_i^l \bar{K}_i^f & B_i^l \bar{K}_i^f \end{bmatrix}$$

$$\bar{\mathbb{T}}_i = \underbrace{\begin{bmatrix} \mathcal{T}_{(3)} G_i^T \cdots \mathcal{T}_{(3)} G_i^T \cdots \mathcal{T}_{(3)} G_i^T \end{bmatrix}}_{N-1}, \mathbb{M}_i = \mathrm{diag}\underbrace{\left\{ M_{1i} \cdots M_{ji,j\neq i} \cdots M_{Ni} \right\}}_{N-1}$$

$$(73)$$

In that case, a decentralized event-triggered fuzzy controller gains can be obtained as

$$K_i^f = \bar{K}_i^f G_i^{-1}, f \in \mathcal{L}_i. \tag{74}$$

Proof. By taking the derivative of $V\big(x(t)\big)$ in (59) and using Jensen's inequality in the Appendix B, we have

$$\begin{aligned} \dot{V}_i\big(x_i(t)\big) &= \dot{V}_{i1}\big(x_i(t)\big) + \dot{V}_{i2}\big(x_i(t)\big) \leq 2x_i^T(t)\big(P_{i1} + P_{i2}\big)\dot{x}_i(t) \\ &\quad + x_i^T(t)\big(Q_{i1} + Q_{i2}\big)x_i(t) - x_i^T\big(t-\tau_i\big)Q_{i1}x_i\big(t-\tau_i\big) \\ &\quad - x_i^T\big(t-\bar{\eta}_i\big)Q_{i2}x_i\big(t-\bar{\eta}_i\big) - \dot{x}_i^T(t)\big(\tau_i^2 Z_{i1} + \bar{\eta}_i^2 Z_{i2}\big)\dot{x}_i(t) \\ &\quad - \big[x_i(t) - x_i\big(t-\tau_i\big)\big]^T Z_{i1}\big[x_i(t) - x_i\big(t-\tau_i\big)\big] \\ &\quad - \big[x_i(t) - x_i\big(t-\bar{\eta}_i\big)\big]^T Z_{i2}\big[x_i(t) - x_i\big(t-\bar{\eta}_i\big)\big] \end{aligned} \tag{75}$$

Define symmetric positive definite matrices $M_{ij} \in \mathfrak{R}^{n_{zi} \times n_{zi}}$ and based on Young's inequality $2\bar{x}^T \bar{y} \leq \bar{x}^T M^{-1}\bar{x} + \bar{y}^T M\bar{y}$, it yields

$$
\begin{aligned}
0 \;=\; & 2\chi_i^T\!\left(t\right)\mathcal{G}_i\left\{
\begin{array}{l}
-\dot{x}_i\!\left(t\right)+A_i\!\left(\mu_i\right)x_i\!\left(t\right) \\[4pt]
+B_i\!\left(\mu_i\right)K_i\!\left(\hat{\mu}_i\right)\dfrac{1}{2}\!\left[\begin{array}{l} x_i\!\left(t-\tau_i\right) \\ +x_i\!\left(t-\bar{\eta}_i\right) \end{array}\right]+\dfrac{\mathcal{I}_i}{2}\,\omega_i\!\left(t\right)+e_i\!\left(\mathrm{t}\right)
\end{array}\right\} \\[8pt]
& +2\chi_i^T\!\left(t\right)\mathcal{G}_i\left[\sum_{j=1,j\neq i}^{N}\overline{A}_{ij}\!\left(\mu_i,\mu_j\right)x_j\!\left(t\right)\right] \\[8pt]
\leq\; & 2\chi_i^T\!\left(t\right)\mathcal{G}_i\left\{
\begin{array}{l}
-\dot{x}_i\!\left(t\right)+A_i\!\left(\mu_i\right)x_i\!\left(t\right) \\[4pt]
+B_i\!\left(\mu_i\right)K_i\!\left(\hat{\mu}_i\right)\dfrac{1}{2}\!\left[\begin{array}{l} x_i\!\left(t-\tau_i\right) \\ +x_i\!\left(t-\bar{\eta}_i\right) \end{array}\right]+\dfrac{\mathcal{I}_i}{2}\,\omega_i\!\left(t\right)+e_i\!\left(t\right)
\end{array}\right\} \\[8pt]
& +\sum_{i=1}^{N}\sum_{j=1,j\neq i}^{N}\chi_i^T\!\left(t\right)\mathcal{G}_i\left[\begin{array}{l}\left[\overline{A}_{ij}\!\left(\mu_i,\mu_j\right)\right] \\ M_{ij}\left[\overline{A}_{ij}\!\left(\mu_i,\mu_j\right)\right]^{T}\end{array}\right]\mathcal{G}_i^T\chi_i\!\left(t\right)+\sum_{i=1}^{N}\sum_{j=1,j\neq i}^{N}\left\{x_j^T\!\left(t\right)M_{ji}^{-1}x_i\!\left(t\right)\right\}
\end{aligned}
$$

$$\tag{76}$$

Define symmetric positive definite matrices $\left\{H_i,U_i\right\}\in\mathfrak{R}^{n_{zi}\times n_{zi}}$ and consider the following index,

$$
\mathcal{J}\!\left(t\right)=\sum_{i=1}^{N}\mathcal{J}_i\!\left(t\right)=
$$
$$
\sum_{i=1}^{N}\int_{0}^{\infty}\left[y_{i1}^T\!\left(t\right)H_i y_{i1}\!\left(t\right)-\omega_i^T\!\left(t\right)H_i\omega_i\!\left(t\right)+y_{i2}^T\!\left(t\right)U_i y_{i2}\!\left(t\right)-e_i^T\!\left(t\right)U_i e_i\!\left(t\right)\right]dt
$$

$$\tag{77}$$

It follows from (75)-(77) that

$$
\begin{aligned}
\mathcal{J}\!\left(t\right)\leq\; & \sum_{i=1}^{N}\left\{\mathcal{J}_i\!\left(t\right)+V_i\!\left(\infty\right)+V_i\!\left(0\right)\right\} \\[6pt]
=\; & \sum_{i=1}^{N}\int_{0}^{\infty}\left[\begin{array}{l}\dot{V}_i\!\left(x_i\!\left(t\right)\right)+y_{i1}^T\!\left(t\right)H_i y_{i1}\!\left(t\right)-\omega_i^T\!\left(t\right) \\ H_i\omega_i\!\left(t\right)+y_{i2}^T\!\left(t\right)U_i y_{i2}\!\left(t\right)-e_i^T\!\left(t\right)U_i e_i\!\left(t\right)\end{array}\right]dt \\[6pt]
=\; & \sum_{i=1}^{N}\int_{0}^{\infty}\left[\chi_i^T\!\left(t\right)\Sigma_i\!\left(\mu_i,\hat{\mu}_i\right)\chi_i\!\left(t\right)\right]dt.
\end{aligned}
$$

$$\tag{78}$$

where

$$
\left[
\begin{aligned}
&\Sigma_i\left(\mu_i,\hat{\mu}_i\right)=\Theta_i+\sigma_i^2\boldsymbol{\mathcal{T}}_{(1)}^T U_i\boldsymbol{\mathcal{T}}_{(1)}+\mathrm{Sym}\left\{\mathcal{G}_i\mathbb{A}_i\left(\mu_i,\hat{\mu}_i\right)\right\}+\mathcal{G}_i\left\{\begin{bmatrix}\left[\bar{A}_{ij}\left(\mu_i,\mu_j\right)\right]\\ M_{ij}\left[\bar{A}_{ij}\left(\mu_i,\mu_j\right)\right]^T\end{bmatrix}\right\}\mathcal{G}_i^T\\[2mm]
&\Theta_i=\begin{bmatrix}\Theta_{i(1)} & P_{i1}+P_{i2} & 0 & 0 & 0 & 0\\[1mm] \star & \Theta_{i(2)}+\displaystyle\sum_{j=1,j\neq i}^{N}M_{ji}^{-1} & Z_{i1} & Z_{i2} & 0 & 0\\[1mm] \star & \star & -Q_{i1}-Z_{i1} & 0 & 0 & 0\\[1mm] \star & \star & \star & -Q_{i2}-Z_{i2} & 0 & 0\\[1mm] \star & \star & \star & \star & -H_i & 0\\[1mm] \star & \star & \star & \star & \star & -U_i\end{bmatrix}\\[2mm]
&\Theta_{i(1)}=\tau_i^2 Z_{i1}+\bar{\eta}^2 Z_{i2}+H_i,\ \Theta_{i(2)}=Q_{i1}+Q_{i2}-Z_{i1}-Z_{i2},\ \boldsymbol{\mathcal{T}}_{(1)}=\begin{bmatrix}0 & 0 & \tfrac{1}{2}I & \tfrac{1}{2}I & \tfrac{\mathcal{T}_i}{2}I & 0\end{bmatrix}\\[2mm]
&\mathbb{A}_i\left(\mu_i,\hat{\mu}_i\right)=\begin{bmatrix}-I & A_i\left(\mu_i\right) & \tfrac{1}{2}B_i\left(\mu_i\right)K_i\left(\hat{\mu}_i\right) & \tfrac{1}{2}B_i\left(\mu_i\right)K_i\left(\hat{\mu}_i\right)\\[1mm] \tfrac{\mathcal{T}_i}{2}B_i\left(\mu_i\right)K_i\left(\hat{\mu}_i\right) & B_i\left(\mu_i\right)K_i\left(\hat{\mu}_i\right)\end{bmatrix}
\end{aligned}
\right.
$$

$$(79)$$

Similar to the process in Theorem 5.2.1, the LMI-based results on (66)-(72) can be obtained. Thus completing this proof.

When the information between μ_i^l and $\hat{\mu}_i^s$ is unavailable, the corresponding result on decentralized event-triggered linear controller design can be obtained as below.

Theorem 5.2.4 Given the large-scale T-S fuzzy interconnected system in (1) and an event-triggered linear controller in the form of (4), then the resulting closed-loop fuzzy control system is asymptotically stable, if there exist symmetric positive definite matrices $\left\{\bar{P}_{i2},\bar{P}_{i2},\bar{Z}_{i1},\bar{Z}_{i2},\bar{H}_i,\bar{U}_i,M_{ij}\right\}\in\Re^{n_{xi}\times n_{xi}}$, and symmetric matrix $\left\{\bar{Q}_{i1},\bar{Q}_{i2}\right\}\in\Re^{n_{xi}\times n_{xi}}$, and $\bar{K}_i\in\Re^{n_{ui}\times n_{xi}}$, and positive scalars $\left\{\sigma_i,\tau_i,\bar{\eta}_i\right\}$, such that for all $l\in\mathcal{L}_i, j\neq i,\{i,j\}\in\mathcal{N}$, the following LMIs hold:

$$
\begin{bmatrix}\dfrac{1}{\tau_i}\bar{P}_{i1}+\bar{Z}_{i1} & -\bar{Z}_{i1}\\[2mm] \star & \bar{Q}_{i1}+\bar{Z}_{i1}\end{bmatrix}>0,
\tag{80}
$$

$$\begin{bmatrix} \frac{1}{\overline{\eta}_i} \overline{P}_{i2} + \overline{Z}_{i2} & -\overline{Z}_{i2} \\ \star & \overline{Q}_{i2} + \overline{Z}_{i2} \end{bmatrix} > 0, \tag{81}$$

$$\begin{bmatrix} \overline{\Theta}_i + \sigma_i^2 \boldsymbol{\mathcal{T}}_{(1)}^T \overline{U}_i \boldsymbol{\mathcal{T}}_{(1)} + \mathrm{Sym}\left\{ \boldsymbol{\mathcal{T}}_{(2)} \overline{\mathbb{A}}_i^l \right\} + \boldsymbol{\mathcal{T}}_{(2)} \left\{ \sum_{j=1, j\neq i}^{N} \sum_{s=1}^{r_j} \overline{A}_{ij}^{ls} M_{ij} \left[\overline{A}_{ij}^{ls} \right]^T \right\} \boldsymbol{\mathcal{T}}_{(2)}^T & \overline{\mathbb{T}}_i \\ \star & -\mathbb{M}_i \end{bmatrix} < 0, \tag{82}$$

where

$$\begin{cases} \overline{\Theta}_i = \begin{bmatrix} \overline{\Theta}_{i(1)} & \overline{P}_{i1} + \overline{P}_{i2} & 0 & 0 & 0 & 0 \\ \star & \overline{\Theta}_{i(2)} & \overline{Z}_{i1} & \overline{Z}_{i2} & 0 & 0 \\ \star & \star & -\overline{Q}_{i1} - \overline{Z}_{i1} & 0 & 0 & 0 \\ \star & \star & \star & -\overline{Q}_{i2} - \overline{Z}_{i2} & 0 & 0 \\ \star & \star & \star & \star & -\overline{H}_i & 0 \\ \star & \star & \star & \star & \star & -\overline{U}_i \end{bmatrix}, \boldsymbol{\mathcal{T}}_{(3)} = \begin{bmatrix} 0 \\ I \\ 0 \\ 0 \\ 0 \\ 0 \end{bmatrix}, \boldsymbol{\mathcal{T}}_{(2)} = \begin{bmatrix} I \\ I \\ 0 \\ 0 \\ 0 \\ 0 \end{bmatrix} \\ \overline{\Theta}_{i(1)} = \tau_i^2 \overline{Z}_{i1} + \overline{\eta}^2 \overline{Z}_{i2} + \overline{H}_i, \overline{\Theta}_{i(2)} = \overline{Q}_{i1} + \overline{Q}_{i2} - \overline{Z}_{i1} - \overline{Z}_{i2}, \boldsymbol{\mathcal{T}}_{(1)} = \begin{bmatrix} 0 & 0 & \frac{1}{2}I & \frac{1}{2}I & \frac{\mathcal{T}_i}{2}I & 0 \end{bmatrix} \\ \overline{\mathbb{A}}_i^l = \begin{bmatrix} -G_i & A_i^l G_i & \frac{1}{2} B_i^l \overline{K}_i & \frac{1}{2} B_i^l \overline{K}_i & \frac{\mathcal{T}_i}{2} B_i^l \overline{K}_i & B_i^l \overline{K}_i \end{bmatrix} \\ \overline{\mathbb{T}}_i = \underbrace{\begin{bmatrix} \boldsymbol{\mathcal{T}}_{(3)} G_i^T & \cdots & \boldsymbol{\mathcal{T}}_{(3)} G_i^T & \cdots & \boldsymbol{\mathcal{T}}_{(3)} G_i^T \end{bmatrix}}_{N-1}, \mathbb{M}_i = \mathrm{diag}\underbrace{\left\{ M_{1i} \cdots M_{ji, j\neq i} \cdots M_{Ni} \right\}}_{N-1} \end{cases} \tag{83}$$

In that case, a decentralized event-triggered linear controller gains can be obtained as

$$K_i = \overline{K}_i G_i^{-1}. \tag{84}$$

5.3 EXPANDING TO DISCRETE-TIME SYSTEMS

In this section, we will study the problem of the decentralized event-triggered control for discrete-time large-scale fuzzy interconnected systems.

5.3.1 Problem Formulation

Here, the i-th closed-loop fuzzy control system is given by

$$x_i\left(t+1\right) = A_i\left(\mu_i\right)x_i\left(t\right) + B_i\left(\mu_i\right)K_i\left(\mu_i\right)\hat{x}_i\left(t\right) + \sum_{j=1,j\neq i}^{N}\bar{A}_{ij}\left(\mu_i,\mu_j\right)x_j\left(t\right). \qquad (85)$$

We propose an ETM in the sensor, which operates as

$$\text{ETM}: \text{Both } x_i\left(t\right) \text{ and } \varsigma_i\left(t\right)\text{are sent} \Leftrightarrow x_i\left(t\right) - \hat{x}_i\left(t\right) > \sigma_i x_i\left(t\right), \qquad (86)$$

where $\sigma_i \geq 0$ is a suitably chosen design parameter.

Based on the operating condition given in (6), an event-triggered strategy is formulated as follows:

$$\hat{x}_i\left(t\right) = \begin{cases} x_i\left(t\right), & \text{when } x_i\left(t\right) - \hat{x}_i\left(t-1\right) > \sigma_i x_i\left(t\right), \\ \hat{x}_i\left(t+1\right), & \text{when } x_i\left(t\right) - \hat{x}_i\left(t-1\right) \leq \sigma_i x_i\left(t\right), \end{cases} \qquad (87)$$

$$\hat{\varsigma}_i\left(t\right) = \begin{cases} \varsigma_i\left(t\right), & \text{when } x_i\left(t\right)\text{is sent}, \\ \hat{\varsigma}_i\left(t-1\right), & \text{when } x_i\left(t\right)\text{is not sent}, \end{cases} \qquad (88)$$

In that case, we propose an event-triggered fuzzy controller as below

$$u_i\left(t\right) = K_i\left(\hat{\mu}_i\right)\hat{x}_i\left(t\right), t \in \left[t_i^k, t_i^{k+1}\right) \qquad (89)$$

with

$$\begin{cases} K_i\left(\hat{\mu}_i\right) := \sum_{l=1}^{r_i}\hat{\mu}_i^f\left[\hat{\varsigma}_i\left(t\right)\right]K_i^f, \sum_{l=1}^{r_i}\hat{\mu}_i^f\left[\hat{\varsigma}_i\left(t\right)\right] := 1 \\ \hat{\mu}_i^f\left[\hat{\varsigma}_i\left(t\right)\right] := \dfrac{\Pi_{\varnothing=1}^g\hat{\mu}_{i\varnothing}^f\left[\hat{\varsigma}_{i\varnothing}\left(t\right)\right]}{\sum_{\varsigma=1}^{r_i}\Pi_{\varnothing=1}^g\hat{\mu}_{i\varnothing}^\varsigma\left[\hat{\varsigma}_{i\varnothing}\left(t\right)\right]} \geq 0, \end{cases} \qquad (90)$$

where $\hat{\mu}_{i\emptyset}^{f}\left[\hat{\varsigma}_{i\emptyset}\left(t\right)\right]$ is the grade of membership of $\hat{\varsigma}_{i\emptyset}\left(t\right)$ in $F_{i\emptyset}^{f}$; In this chapter we will denote $\hat{\mu}_{i}^{f} = \hat{\mu}_{i}^{f}\left[\hat{\varsigma}_{i}\left(t\right)\right]$ for brevity.

Define

$$e_{i}\left(t\right) = \hat{x}_{i}\left(t\right) - x_{i}\left(t\right) \tag{91}$$

Substituting (91) into (85), one has

$$x_{i}\left(t+1\right) = A_{i}\left(\mu_{i}\right)x_{i}\left(t\right) + B_{i}\left(\mu_{i}\right)K_{i}\left(\mu_{i}\right)x_{i}\left(t\right) + \\ B_{i}\left(\mu_{i}\right)K_{i}\left(\mu_{i}\right)e_{i}\left(t\right) + \sum_{j=1,j\neq i}^{N}\overline{A}_{ij}\left(\mu_{i},\mu_{j}\right)x_{j}\left(t\right). \tag{92}$$

5.3.2 Decentralized Event-Triggered Controller Design

Based on the closed-loop fuzzy control system in (92), we will present the design result on the event-triggered fuzzy controller in terms of a set of LMIs, and it is summarized as follows:

Theorem 5.3.1 Given the large-scale T-S fuzzy interconnected system in (85) and an event-triggered fuzzy controller in the form of (89), then the resulting closed-loop fuzzy control system (92) with the assumption (4-17) is asymptotically stable, if there exist symmetric positive definite matrices $\left\{\overline{P}_{i},\overline{U}_{i},M_{ij}\right\} \in \mathfrak{R}^{n_{zi}\times n_{zi}}$, and $\overline{K}_{i}^{f} \in \mathfrak{R}^{n_{ui}\times n_{zi}}, G_{i} \in \mathfrak{R}^{n_{zi}\times n_{zi}}$, and positive scalar σ_{i}, such that for all $l \in \mathcal{L}_{i}, j \neq i, \left\{i,j\right\} \in \mathcal{N}$, the following LMIs hold:

$$\overline{\rho}_{i}^{l}\sum\nolimits_{i}^{ll} + X_{i}^{ll} < 0, \tag{93}$$

$$\underline{\rho}_{i}^{l}\sum\nolimits_{i}^{ll} + X_{i}^{ll} < 0, \tag{94}$$

$$\overline{\rho}_{i}^{s}\sum\nolimits_{i}^{ls} + \overline{\rho}_{i}^{l}\sum\nolimits_{i}^{sl} + X_{i}^{ls} + X_{i}^{sl} < 0, \tag{95}$$

$$\underline{\rho}_{j}^{s}\sum\nolimits_{i}^{ls} + \underline{\rho}_{j}^{l}\sum\nolimits_{i}^{sl} + X_{i}^{ls} + X_{i}^{sl} < 0, \tag{96}$$

$$\underline{\rho}_i^s \sum_i^{ls} + \bar{\rho}_i^l \sum_i^{sl} + X_i^{ls} + X_i^{sl} < 0, \tag{97}$$

$$\bar{\rho}_i^s \sum_i^{ls} + \underline{\rho}_i^l \sum_i^{sl} + X_i^{ls} + X_i^{sl} < 0, \tag{98}$$

$$\begin{bmatrix} X_i^{11} & \cdots & X_i^{1r_i} \\ \vdots & \ddots & \vdots \\ X_i^{r_i 1} & \cdots & X_i^{r_i r_i} \end{bmatrix} > 0, \tag{99}$$

where

$$\begin{cases} \Sigma_i^{lf} = \begin{bmatrix} \bar{P}_i - G_i - G_i^T + \left\{ \sum_{j=1, j\neq i}^{N} \sum_{s=1}^{r_j} \left[\bar{A}_{ij}^{ls} \right] M_{ij} \left[\bar{A}_{ij}^{ls} \right]^T \right\} & \left(A_i^l G_i^T + B_i^l \bar{K}_i^f \right) & B_i^l \bar{K}_i^f & 0 \\ \star & -\bar{P}_i + \sigma_i^2 \bar{U}_i & 0 & G_i \mathbb{I} \\ \star & \star & -\bar{U}_i & 0 \\ \star & \star & \star & -\mathbb{M}_i \end{bmatrix} \\ \mathbb{I} = \underbrace{\left[I \cdots I \cdots I \right]}_{N-1}, \mathbb{M}_i = \mathrm{diag} \underbrace{\left\{ M_{1i} \cdots M_{ji, j\neq i} \cdots M_{Ni} \right\}}_{N-1} \end{cases} \tag{100}$$

In that case, a decentralized fuzzy controller gains can be obtained as

$$K_i^f = \bar{K}_i^f G_i^{-T}, f \in \mathcal{L}_i. \tag{101}$$

Proof: Consider a discrete-time Lyapunov function as below,

$$\begin{aligned} V(t) &= \sum_{i=1}^{N} V_i(t) \\ &= \sum_{i=1}^{N} x_i^T(t) P_i x_i(t) \end{aligned} \tag{102}$$

where P_i is positive symmetric matrix.

Define $\Delta V(t) = V(t+1) - V(t)$, it yields

$$\Delta V\left(t\right) = \sum_{i=1}^{N} \Delta V_i\left(t\right)$$

$$= \sum_{i=1}^{N} x_i^T\left(t+1\right) P_i x_i\left(t+1\right) - x_i^T\left(t\right) P_i x_i\left(t\right) \tag{103}$$

In addition, we define the matrix $G_i^{-1} \in \Re^{n_{xi} \times n_{xi}}$ and symmetric positive definite matrix $M_{ij} \in \Re^{n_{xi} \times n_{xi}}$, and Lemma 2.3.1, one has

$$
\begin{aligned}
0 \; &= \sum_{i=1}^{N} \left\{ 2x_i^T\left(t+1\right) G_i^{-1} \begin{bmatrix} -x_i\left(t+1\right) + A_i\left(\mu_i\right) x_i\left(t\right) + \\ B_i\left(\mu_i\right) K_i\left(\mu_i\right) x_i\left(t\right) + B_i\left(\mu_i\right) K_i\left(\mu_i\right) e_i\left(t\right) \end{bmatrix} \right\} \\
&+ \sum_{i=1}^{N} \left\{ 2x_i^T\left(t+1\right) G_i^{-1} \left[\sum_{j=1,j\neq i}^{N} \bar{A}_{ij}\left(\mu_i,\mu_j\right) x_j\left(t\right) \right] \right\} \\
&\leq \sum_{i=1}^{N} \left\{ 2x_i^T\left(t+1\right) G_i^{-1} \begin{bmatrix} -x_i\left(t+1\right) + A_i\left(\mu_i\right) x_i\left(t\right) \\ +B_i\left(\mu_i\right) K_i\left(\mu_i\right) x_i\left(t\right) + B_i\left(\mu_i\right) K_i\left(\mu_i\right) e_i\left(t\right) \end{bmatrix} \right\} \\
&+ \sum_{i=1}^{N} \left\{ x_i^T\left(t+1\right) G_i^{-1} \left\{ \sum_{j=1,j\neq i}^{N} \sum_{l=1}^{r_i} \mu_i^l \sum_{s=1}^{r_j} \mu_j^s \left[\bar{A}_{ij}^{ls}\right] M_{ij} \left[\bar{A}_{ij}^{ls}\right]^T \right\} G_i^{-T} x_i\left(t+1\right) \right\} \\
&+ \sum_{i=1}^{N} \sum_{j=1,j\neq i}^{N} x_j^T\left(t\right) M_i^{-1} x_j\left(t\right) \\
&\leq \sum_{i=1}^{N} \left\{ 2x_i^T\left(t+1\right) G_i^{-1} \begin{bmatrix} -x_i\left(t+1\right) + A_i\left(\mu_i\right) x_i\left(t\right) \\ +B_i\left(\mu_i\right) K_i\left(\mu_i\right) x_i\left(t\right) + B_i\left(\mu_i\right) K_i\left(\mu_i\right) e_i\left(t\right) \end{bmatrix} \right\} \\
&+ \sum_{i=1}^{N} \left\{ x_i^T\left(t+1\right) G_i^{-1} \left\{ \sum_{j=1,j\neq i}^{N} \sum_{l=1}^{r_i} \mu_i^l \sum_{s=1}^{r_j} \left[\bar{A}_{ij}^{ls}\right] M_{ij} \left[\bar{A}_{ij}^{ls}\right]^T \right\} G_i^{-T} x_i\left(t+1\right) \right\} \\
&+ \sum_{i=1}^{N} \sum_{j=1,j\neq i}^{N} x_i^T\left(t\right) M_{ji}^{-1} x_i\left(t\right)
\end{aligned}
$$

$$\tag{104}$$

Based on the event-triggered policy in (33), it can be known that

$$e_i\left(t\right) \leq \sigma_i x_i\left(t\right) \tag{105}$$

It follows from (102)-(105) that

$$\Delta V\left(kT\right) \leq \sum_{i=1}^{N} x_i^T\left(t+1\right) P_i x_i\left(t+1\right) - x_i^T\left(kT\right) P_i x_i\left(t\right)$$

$$+\sum_{i=1}^{N}\left\{ 2x_i^T\left(t+1\right)G_i^{-1}\begin{bmatrix} -x_i\left(t+1\right)+A_i\left(\mu_i\right)x_i\left(t\right) \\ +B_i\left(\mu_i\right)K_i\left(\mu_i\right)x_i\left(t\right)+B_i\left(\mu_i\right)K_i\left(\mu_i\right)e_i\left(t\right) \end{bmatrix}\right\}$$

$$+\sum_{i=1}^{N}\left\{ x_i^T\left(t+1\right)G_i^{-1}\left\{ \sum_{j=1,j\neq i}^{N}\sum_{l=1}^{r_i}\mu_i^l\sum_{s=1}^{r_j}\left[\bar{A}_{ij}^{ls}\right]M_{ij}\left[\bar{A}_{ij}^{ls}\right]^T\right\}G_i^{-T}x_i\left(t+1\right)\right\}$$

$$+\sum_{i=1}^{N}\sum_{j=1,j\neq i}^{N} x_i^T\left(t\right)M_{ji}^{-1}x_i\left(t\right)+\sum_{i=1}^{N}\sigma_i^2 x_i^T\left(t\right)U_i x_i\left(t\right)-e_i^T\left(t\right)U_i e_i\left(t\right)$$

$$=\sum_{i=1}^{N}\sum_{l=1}^{r_i}\sum_{f=1}^{r_i}\mu_i^l\hat{\mu}_i^f\chi_i^T\left(T,t\right)\Sigma_i^{lf}\chi_i\left(T,t\right)$$

$$\tag{106}$$

where

$$\Sigma_i^{lf}=\begin{bmatrix} P_i+G_i^{-1}\left\{ \sum\limits_{j=1,j\neq i}^{N}\sum\limits_{s=1}^{r_j}\left[\bar{A}_{ij}^{ls}\right]M_{ij}\left[\bar{A}_{ij}^{ls}\right]^T\right\}G_i^{-T} & 0 & 0 \\ \star & -P_i+\sum\limits_{j=1,j\neq i}^{N}M_{ji}^{-1}+\sigma_i^2 U_i & 0 \\ \star & \star & -U_i \end{bmatrix}$$

$$+\,\mathrm{Sym}\left\{ \begin{bmatrix} G_i^{-1} \\ 0 \\ 0 \end{bmatrix}\begin{bmatrix} -I & A_i^l & B_i^l K_i^f & B_i^l K_i^f \end{bmatrix}\right\}.$$

$$\tag{107}$$

By using Schur complement to $\Sigma_i^{lf} < 0$ in (107), it yields

$$\begin{bmatrix} \varnothing_i & G_i^{-1}\left(A_i^l+B_i^l K_i^f\right) & G_i^{-1}B_i^l K_i^f & 0 \\ \star & -P_i+\sigma_i^2 U_i & 0 & \mathbb{I} \\ \star & \star & -U_i & 0 \\ \star & \star & \star & -\mathbb{M}_i \end{bmatrix} < 0,$$

$$\tag{108}$$

where

$$
\begin{cases}
\mathbb{I} = \underbrace{\left[I \cdots I \cdots I \right]}_{N-1}, \mathbb{M}_i = \mathrm{diag} \underbrace{\left\{ M_{1i} \cdots M_{ji,j\neq i} \cdots M_{Ni} \right\}}_{N-1}, \\
\varnothing_i = P_i - G_i^{-1} - G_i^{-T} + G_i^{-1} \left\{ \sum_{j=1,j\neq i}^{N} \sum_{s=1}^{r_j} \left[\bar{A}_{ij}^{ls} \right] M_{ij} \left[\bar{A}_{ij}^{ls} \right]^T \right\} G_i^{-T}.
\end{cases}
\tag{109}
$$

Define

$$
\Gamma_i := \mathrm{diag} \left\{ G_i G_i G_i \underbrace{I \cdots I \cdots I}_{N-1} \right\}, \bar{P}_i = G_i P_i G_i^T, \bar{U}_i = G_i U_i G_i^T, \bar{K}_i^f = K_i^f G_i^T.
\tag{110}
$$

By performing a congruence transformation to (108) by Γ_i, and taking the relation in (110) and the results in the Appendix E, it is easy to see that the inequalities in (93)-(99) imply $\Delta V\left(x\left(t\right)\right) < 0$. Thus, completing this proof.

It is noted that the when the knowledge between μ_i^l and $\hat{\mu}_i^f$ is unavailable, the result on decentralized event-triggered linear controller can be obtained as below.

Theorem 5.3.2 Given the large-scale T-S fuzzy interconnected system in (85) and an event-triggered linear controller, then the resulting closed-loop fuzzy control system is asymptotically stable, if there exist symmetric positive definite matrices $\left\{ \bar{P}_i, \bar{U}_i, M_{ij} \right\} \in \Re^{n_{zi} \times n_{zi}}$, and $\bar{K}_i \in \Re^{n_{ui} \times n_{zi}}, G_i \in \Re^{n_{zi} \times n_{zi}}$, and positive scalar σ_i, such that for all $l \in \mathcal{L}_i, j \neq i, \left\{ i,j \right\} \in \mathcal{N}$, the following LMIs hold:

$$
\begin{bmatrix}
\bar{P}_i - G_i - G_i^T + \left\{ \sum_{j=1,j\neq i}^{N} \sum_{s=1}^{r_j} \left[\bar{A}_{ij}^{ls} \right] M_{ij} \left[\bar{A}_{ij}^{ls} \right]^T \right\} & \left(A_i^l G_i^T + B_i^l \bar{K}_i \right) & B_i^l \bar{K}_i & 0 \\
\star & -\bar{P}_i + \sigma_i^2 \bar{U}_i & 0 & G_i \mathbb{I} \\
\star & \star & -\bar{U}_i & 0 \\
\star & \star & \star & -\mathbb{M}_i
\end{bmatrix} < 0,
\tag{111}
$$

where $\mathbb{I} = \underbrace{\left[I \cdots I \cdots I \right]}_{N-1}, \mathbb{M}_i = \text{diag} \underbrace{\left\{ M_{1i} \cdots M_{ji, j \neq i} \cdots M_{Ni} \right\}}_{N-1}$

In that case, a decentralized linear controller gains can be obtained as

$$K_i = \bar{K}_i G_i^{-T}. \tag{112}$$

5.4 SELF-TRIGGERED CONTROL

In the following, we will present the decentralized self-triggered control for large-scale T-S fuzzy interconnected systems.

5.4.1 Problem Formulation

Before proposing the main results, assume that

1. t_i^k denotes the instant when the sampler obtains the measured data from the plant;
2. t_i^b presents the instant when the actuator obtains the control data from the controller.

In that case, we introduce the following controller

$$u_i \left(t \right) = K_i \left(\hat{\mu}_i \right) x_i \left(t_i^b \right), s \in \mathcal{L}_i \tag{113}$$

where $K_i \left(\hat{\mu}_i \right) = \sum_{f=1}^{r_i} \hat{\mu}_i^f K_i^f, \hat{\mu}_i^f = \hat{\mu}_i^f \left[\varsigma_i \left(t_i^b \right) \right].$

Then, the closed-loop large-scale fuzzy control system is given by

$$\dot{x}_i \left(t \right) = A_i \left(\mu_i \right) x_i \left(t \right) + B_i \left(\mu_i \right) K_i \left(\hat{\mu}_i \right) x_i \left(t_i^b \right) + \sum_{j=1, j \neq i}^{N} \bar{A}_{ij} \left(\mu_i, \mu_j \right) x_j \left(t \right) \tag{114}$$

where

$$A_i\left(\mu_i\right) := \sum_{l=1}^{r_i}\mu_i^l A_i^l, B_i\left(\mu_i\right) := \sum_{l=1}^{r_i}\mu_i^l B_i^l, K_i\left(\hat{\mu}_i\right) = \sum_{l=1}^{r_i}\hat{\mu}_i^f K_i^f,$$

$$\overline{A}_{ij}\left(\mu_i,\mu_j\right) := \sum_{l=1}^{r_i}\sum_{s=1}^{r_j}\mu_i^l\mu_j^s\overline{A}_{ij}^{ls}. \tag{115}$$

5.4.2 Decentralized Self-Triggered Controller Design

Define $e_i\left(t\right) = x_i\left(t\right) - x_i\left(t_i^b\right)$, the self-triggered criterion for the fuzzy control system in (114) can be established as below.

Theorem 5.4.1 Given the large-scale T-S fuzzy interconnected system in (2) and an event-triggered fuzzy controller in the form of (113), and assume that there exist symmetric positive definite matrices $\left\{\overline{Q}_i,\overline{M}_i,F_i,H_{ij},\overline{W}_i,S_i\right\} \in \mathfrak{R}^{n_{zi}\times n_{zi}}$, such that for all $l \in \mathcal{L}_i, j \neq i, \{i,j\} \in \mathcal{N}$, the following LMIs hold:

$$\Omega_{i(1)}^{ll} < 0, l \in \mathcal{L}_i \tag{116}$$

$$\Omega_{i(2)}^{ll} < 0, l \in \mathcal{L}_i \tag{117}$$

$$\Omega_{i(1)}^{lf} + \Omega_{i(1)}^{fl} < 0, l \leq f \tag{118}$$

$$\Omega_{i(2)}^{lf} + \Omega_{i(2)}^{fl} < 0, l \leq f \tag{119}$$

where

$$\begin{cases} \Omega_{i(1)}^{lf} = \begin{bmatrix} \text{Sym}\left\{A_i^l F_i + B_i^l \overline{K}_i^f\right\} + \sum_{j=1,j\neq i}^{N}\left[\sum_{s=1}^{r_j}\overline{A}_{ij}^{ls} H_{ij}\left[\overline{A}_{ij}^{ls}\right]^T\right] + \overline{Q}_i & F_i \mathbb{I} \\ \star & -\mathbb{H}_i \end{bmatrix} \\ \Omega_{i(1)}^{lf} = \begin{bmatrix} -\overline{Q}_i + \overline{W}_i & B_i^l \overline{K}_i^f \\ \star & -\overline{M}_i \end{bmatrix}, \mathbb{I} = \underbrace{\left[I\cdots I\cdots I\right]}_{N-1}, \mathbb{H}_i = \text{diag}\underbrace{\left\{H_{1i}\cdots H_{ji,j\neq i}\cdots H_{Ni}\right\}}_{N-1} \end{cases} \tag{120}$$

If the self-triggered policy satisfies

$$e_i^T \left(t \right) \mathcal{M}_i e_i \left(t \right) - x_i^T \left(t_i^b \right) \mathcal{W}_i x_i \left(t_i^b \right) < 0 \tag{121}$$

where $\mathcal{M}_i = M_i - W_i + S_i^{-1}, \mathcal{W}_i = W_i - W_i S_i W_i^T$. Then, the closed-loop system in (114) is asymptotically stable, and the event-triggered controller gains can be obtained as

$$K_i^f = \bar{K}_i^f F_i^{-1}, f \in \mathcal{L}_i. \tag{122}$$

Proof. Consider the Lyapunov function

$$
\begin{aligned}
V\left(x\left(t \right) \right) &= \sum_{i=1}^{N} V_i \left(x_i \left(t \right) \right) \\
&= \sum_{i=1}^{N} x_i^T \left(t \right) P_i x_i \left(t \right),
\end{aligned}
\tag{123}
$$

where P_i is positive define symmetrical matrix.

Consider the following inequalities

$$\mathrm{Sym}\left(P_i A_i \left(\mu_i \right) + P_i B_i \left(\mu_i \right) K_i \left(\hat{\mu}_i \right) \right) + \sum_{j=1, j \neq i}^{N} \left[P_i \sum_{s=1}^{r_j} \bar{A}_{ij}^{ls} H_{ij} \left[\bar{A}_{ij}^{ls} \right]^T P_i + H_{ji}^{-1} \right] + Q_i < 0, \tag{124}$$

$$P_i B_i \left(\mu_i \right) K_i \left(\hat{\mu}_i \right) M_i^{-1} \left(\star \right) - Q_i + W_i < 0. \tag{125}$$

By taking the derivative of $V\left(x\left(t \right) \right)$, and along the trajectory of (114), and consider the relation in (124) and (125), it yields

$$\dot{V}\left(x\left(t \right) \right) = \sum_{i=1}^{N} 2 x_i^T \left(t \right) P_i A_i \left(\mu_i \right) x_i \left(t \right) + 2 x_i^T \left(t \right) P_i B_i \left(\mu_i \right) K_i \left(\hat{\mu}_i \right) x_i \left(t_i^b \right)$$

$$+\sum_{i=1}^{N}\sum_{j=1,j\neq i}^{N} 2x_i^T\left(t\right)P_i\bar{A}_{ij}\left(\mu_i,\mu_j\right)x_j\left(t\right)$$

$$\leq \sum_{i=1}^{N}x_i^T\left(t\right)\left[\mathrm{Sym}\left(P_iA_i\left(\mu_i\right)+P_iB_i\left(\mu_i\right)K_i\left(\hat{\mu}_i\right)\right)+P_iB_i\left(\mu_i\right)K_i\left(\hat{\mu}_i\right)M_i^{-1}\left(\star\right)\right]x_i\left(t\right)$$

$$+\sum_{i=1}^{N}\left\{e_i^T\left(t\right)M_ie_i\left(t\right)+\sum_{j=1,j\neq i}^{N}\left[x_i^T\left(t\right)P_i\bar{A}_{ij}\left(\mu_i,\mu_j\right)H_i\left(\star\right)+x_j\left(t\right)H_i^{-1}x_j\left(t\right)\right]\right\}$$

$$\leq \sum_{i=1}^{N}\left\{x_i^T\left(t\right)\left[\mathrm{Sym}\left(P_iA_i\left(\mu_i\right)+P_iB_i\left(\mu_i\right)K_i\left(\hat{\mu}_i\right)\right)+P_iB_i\left(\mu_i\right)K_i\left(\hat{\mu}_i\right)M_i^{-1}\left(\star\right)\right]x_i\left(t\right)\right\}$$

$$+\sum_{i=1}^{N}\left\{e_i^T\left(t\right)M_ie_i\left(t\right)+\sum_{j=1,j\neq i}^{N}\left[x_i^T\left(t\right)P_i\sum_{s=1}^{r_j}\bar{A}_{ij}^{ls}H_{ij}\left[\bar{A}_{ij}^{ls}\right]^T P_ix_i\left(t\right)+x_i^T\left(t\right)H_{ji}^{-1}x_i\left(t\right)\right]\right\}$$

$$\leq \sum_{i=1}^{N}\left\{e_i^T\left(t\right)M_ie_i\left(t\right)-x_i^T\left(t\right)Q_ix_i\left(t\right)+x_i^T\left(t\right)P_iB_i\left(\mu_i\right)K_i\left(\hat{\mu}_i\right)M_i^{-1}\left(\star\right)x_i\left(t\right)\right\}$$

$$\leq \sum_{i=1}^{N}\left\{e_i^T\left(t\right)M_ie_i\left(t\right)-x_i^T\left(t\right)W_ix_i\left(t\right)\right\}$$

$$= \sum_{i=1}^{N}\left\{e_i^T\left(t\right)M_ie_i\left(t\right)-\left[x_i\left(t_i^b\right)+e_i\left(t\right)\right]^T W_i\left[x_i\left(t_i^b\right)+e_i\left(t\right)\right]\right\}$$

$$\leq \sum_{i=1}^{N}\left\{e_i^T\left(t\right)\left(M_i-W_i+S_i^{-1}\right)e_i\left(t\right)-x_i^T\left(t_i^b\right)\left(W_i-W_iS_iW_i^T\right)x_i\left(t_i^b\right)\right\}.$$

$$= \sum_{i=1}^{N}\left\{e_i^T\left(t\right)\mathcal{M}_ie_i\left(t\right)-x_i^T\left(t_i^b\right)\mathcal{W}_ix_i\left(t_i^b\right)\right\} \tag{126}$$

where $\left\{\mathcal{M}_i,\mathcal{W}_i\right\}$ is defined in (121).

By using Schur complement to (124) and (125), it yields

$$
\left[\begin{array}{cc} \mathrm{Sym}\left(P_i A_i\left(\mu_i\right) + P_i B_i\left(\mu_i\right) K_i\left(\hat{\mu}_i\right)\right) + \displaystyle\sum_{j=1, j\neq i}^{N}\left[P_i \sum_{s=1}^{r_j} \overline{A}_{ij}^{ls} H_{ij}\left[\overline{A}_{ij}^{ls}\right]^T P_i\right] + Q_i & \mathbb{I} \\ \star & -\mathbb{H}_i \end{array}\right] < 0,
$$

(127)

$$
\left[\begin{array}{cc} -Q_i + W_i & P_i B_i\left(\mu_i\right) K_i\left(\hat{\mu}_i\right) \\ \star & -M_i \end{array}\right] < 0,
$$

(128)

where $\mathbb{I} = \underbrace{\left[I \cdots I \cdots I\right]}_{N-1}$, $\mathbb{H}_i = \mathrm{diag}\underbrace{\left\{H_{1i} \cdots H_{ji, j\neq i} \cdots H_{Ni}\right\}}_{N-1}$.

Define

$$
\begin{cases} \Gamma_{i1} \doteq \mathrm{diag}\left\{F_i\ \mathbb{I}\right\}, F_i = P_i^{-1}, \overline{Q}_i = F_i Q_i F_i, \overline{K}_i^f = K_i^f F_i, \\ \Gamma_{i2} \doteq \mathrm{diag}\left\{F_i\ F_i\right\}, \overline{W}_i = F_i W_i F_i. \end{cases}
$$

(129)

Now, by performing a congruence transformation to (127) by Γ_{i1}, and to (128) by Γ_{i2}, and considering the relation in (129), and Lemma 2.3.1, the inequalities in (101)-(102) can be obtained. Thus, the proof is completed.

NOTE: It is noted that the proposed self-triggered control strategy in (121) is required to continuously monitor the system state, which is not suitable for practical implementation. To improve the problem, in the following, we present a novel self-triggered control strategy to estimate the next sampling instant based on the current sampled-data. In that case, continuously monitor on the system state can be avoided.

NOTE: It is also noted that the proposed self-triggered control strategy in (121) only requires the information on self-system dynamics. Information on the other subsystem is not required known. Therefore, the design scheme is decentralized control.

Theorem 5.4.2 Given the large-scale T-S fuzzy interconnected system in (2) and an event-triggered linear controller in the form of (121), then the fuzzy control system satisfies the sampling period

$$T\left(t_i^b\right) = \frac{1}{\alpha_i}\ln\left|\frac{\alpha_i\rho_i\left(x_i\left(t_i^b\right)\right)}{\beta_{i1}^* x_i\left(t_i^b\right)_2 + \sum_{j=1,j\neq i}^{N}\beta_{ij2}^* x_{j2}^*} + 1\right|, \tag{130}$$

where

$$\alpha_i = \sqrt{\mathcal{M}_i}A_i\left(\mu_i\right)\left[\sqrt{\mathcal{M}_i}\right]^{-1},$$
$$\beta_{i1} = \sqrt{\mathcal{M}_i}\left[A_i\left(\mu_i\right) + B_i\left(\mu_i\right)K_i\left(\hat{\mu}_i\right)\right], \beta_{ij2} = \sqrt{\mathcal{M}_i}\bar{A}_{ij}\left(\mu_i,\mu_j\right). \tag{131}$$

Then, the closed-loop control is stabilization.

Proof. For simply, we define

$$z_i\left(t\right) = \sqrt{\mathcal{M}_i}e_i\left(t\right), \tag{132}$$

and

$$\rho_i\left(x_i\left(t_i^b\right)\right) = \sqrt{x_i^T\left(t_i^b\right)\mathcal{W}_i x_i\left(t_i^b\right)} \tag{133}$$

Based on the self-triggered policy in (121) and the relations in (132) and (133), one has

$$z_i\left(t\right)_2 < \rho_i\left(x_i\left(t_i^b\right)\right). \tag{134}$$

The time derivative of $z_i\left(t\right)_2$ satisfies

$$\frac{d}{dt} z_i\left(t\right)_2 = \sqrt{\mathcal{M}_i} \dot{e}_i\left(t\right)_2$$

$$= \sqrt{\mathcal{M}_i}\left\{ A_i\left(\mu_i\right) e_i\left(t\right) + \left[A_i\left(\mu_i\right) + B_i\left(\mu_i\right) K_i\left(\hat{\mu}_i\right)\right] x_i\left(t_i^b\right) + \sum_{j=1, j \neq i}^{N} \bar{A}_{ij}\left(\mu_i, \mu_j\right) x_j\left(t\right) \right\}$$

$$\leq \sqrt{\mathcal{M}_i} A_i\left(\mu_i\right)\left[\sqrt{\mathcal{M}_i}\right]^{-1} z_i\left(t\right)_2 + \sqrt{\mathcal{M}_i}\left[A_i\left(\mu_i\right) + B_i\left(\mu_i\right) K_i\left(\hat{\mu}_i\right)\right] x_i\left(t_i^b\right)_2$$

$$+ \sum_{j=1, j \neq i}^{N} \sqrt{\mathcal{M}_i} \bar{A}_{ij}\left(\mu_i, \mu_j\right) x_j\left(t\right)_2$$

$$= \alpha_i z_i\left(t\right)_2 + \beta_{i1}\left(t\right) x_i\left(t_i^b\right)_2 + \sum_{j=1, j \neq i}^{N} \beta_{ij2}\left(t\right) x_j\left(t\right)_2$$

$$\leq \alpha_i z_i\left(t\right)_2 + \beta_{i1}^* x_i\left(t_i^b\right)_2 + \sum_{j=1, j \neq i}^{N} \beta_{ij2}^* x_{j2}^*$$

$$(135)$$

where

$$\alpha_i = \sqrt{\mathcal{M}_i} A_i\left(\mu_i\right)\left[\sqrt{\mathcal{M}_i}\right]^{-1},$$

$$\beta_{i1}\left(t\right) = \sqrt{\mathcal{M}_i}\begin{bmatrix} A_i\left(\mu_i\right) \\ +B_i\left(\mu_i\right) K_i\left(\hat{\mu}_i\right) \end{bmatrix}, \beta_{ij2}\left(t\right) = \sqrt{\mathcal{M}_i} \bar{A}_{ij}\left(\mu_i, \mu_j\right),$$

$$(136)$$

and $\left\{\beta_{i1}^*, \beta_{ij2}^*\left(t\right), x_j^*\right\}$ represent upper bounds for $\beta_{i1}\left(t\right)$, $\beta_{ij2}\left(t\right)$ and $x_j\left(t\right)$, respectively.

The initial condition is $z_i\left(t\right) \equiv 0$. Using this in the differential inequality in (135) yields,

$$z_i\left(t\right)_2 \leq \frac{\beta_{i1}^* x_i\left(t_i^b\right)_2 + \sum_{j=1, j \neq i}^{N} \beta_{ij2}^* x_{j2}^*}{\alpha_i}\left(e^{\alpha_i\left(t - t_i^b\right)} - 1\right)$$

$$(137)$$

for all $t \in \left[t_i^b, t_i^{b+1}\right)$.

It is easy to see from (134) that the fuzzy control is stabilization if $z_i\left(t\right)_2$ satisfies the inequality in (137). It is also noted that the up bounding of $z_i\left(t\right)_2$ is given by (137). Thus, the threshold value satisfies that

$$t_i^{b+1} = \frac{1}{\alpha_i} \ln \left(\frac{\alpha_i \rho_i \left(x_i \left(t_i^b \right) \right)}{\beta_{i1}^* x_i \left(t_i^b \right)_2 + \sum_{j=1, j\neq i}^N \beta_{ij2}^* x_{j2}^*} + 1 \right) + t_i^b. \tag{138}$$

Thus, the proof is completed.

5.5 ILLUSTRATIVE EXAMPLES

This chapter has shown theoretically design results to reduce the data transmission for feedback control of large-scale T-S fuzzy interconnected systems, including both the event-triggered and self-triggered controls. In this section, we use two numerical examples to further verify the derived results. The solver used in the section is the LMI Toolbox in Matlab.

Example 1

Consider a continuous-time large-scale interconnected system with three fuzzy subsystems as below.

Plant Rule R_i^{11}: IF $\varsigma_{i1}(t)$ is F_{i1}^1 and $\varsigma_{j2}(t)$ is F_{j2}^1 and $\varsigma_{k3}(t)$ is F_{k3}^1, THEN

$$\dot{x}_i(t) = A_i^1 x_i(t) + \overline{A}_{ij,j\neq i}^{11} x_j(t) + \overline{A}_{ik,k\neq i,k\neq j}^{11} x_k(t), i \in \{1,2,3\}$$

Plant Rule R_i^{12}: IF $\varsigma_{i1}(t)$ is F_{i1}^1 and $\varsigma_{j2}(t)$ is F_{j2}^2 and $\varsigma_{k3}(t)$ is F_{k3}^1, THEN

$$\dot{x}_i(t) = A_i^1 x_i(t) + \overline{A}_{ij,j\neq i}^{12} x_j(t) + \overline{A}_{ik,k\neq i,k\neq j}^{11} x_k(t), i \in \{1,2,3\}$$

Plant Rule R_i^{13}: IF $\varsigma_{i1}(t)$ is F_{i1}^1 and $\varsigma_{j2}(t)$ is F_{j2}^1 and $\varsigma_{k3}(t)$ is F_{k3}^2, THEN

$$\dot{x}_i(t) = A_i^1 x_i(t) + \overline{A}_{ij,j\neq i}^{11} x_j(t) + \overline{A}_{ik,k\neq i,k\neq j}^{12} x_k(t), i \in \{1,2,3\}$$

Plant Rule R_i^{14}: IF $\varsigma_{i1}(t)$ is F_{i1}^1 and $\varsigma_{j2}(t)$ is F_{j2}^2 and $\varsigma_{k3}(t)$ is F_{k3}^2, THEN

$$\dot{x}_i(t) = A_i^1 x_i(t) + \overline{A}_{ij,j\neq i}^{12} x_j(t) + \overline{A}_{ik,k\neq i,k\neq j}^{12} x_k(t), i \in \{1,2,3\}$$

Plant Rule R_i^{21}: IF $\varsigma_{i1}(t)$ is F_{i1}^2 and $\varsigma_{j2}(t)$ is F_{j2}^1 and $\varsigma_{k3}(t)$ is F_{k3}^1, THEN

$$\dot{x}_i(t) = A_i^2 x_i(t) + \bar{A}_{ij,j\neq i}^{11} x_j(t) + \bar{A}_{ik,k\neq i,k\neq j}^{11} x_k(t), i \in \{1,2,3\}$$

Plant Rule R_i^{22}: IF $\varsigma_{i1}(t)$ is F_{i1}^2 and $\varsigma_{j2}(t)$ is F_{j2}^2 and $\varsigma_{k3}(t)$ is F_{k3}^1, THEN

$$\dot{x}_i(t) = A_i^2 x_i(t) + \bar{A}_{ij,j\neq i}^{12} x_j(t) + \bar{A}_{ik,k\neq i,k\neq j}^{11} x_k(t), i \in \{1,2,3\}$$

Plant Rule R_i^{23}: IF $\varsigma_{i1}(t)$ is F_{i1}^2 and $\varsigma_{j2}(t)$ is F_{j2}^1 and $\varsigma_{k3}(t)$ is F_{k3}^2, THEN

$$\dot{x}_i(t) = A_i^2 x_i(t) + \bar{A}_{ij,j\neq i}^{11} x_j(t) + \bar{A}_{ik,k\neq i,k\neq j}^{12} x_k(t), i \in \{1,2,3\}$$

Plant Rule R_i^{24}: IF $\varsigma_{i1}(t)$ is F_{i1}^2 and $\varsigma_{j2}(t)$ is F_{j2}^2 and $\varsigma_{k3}(t)$ is F_{k3}^2, THEN

$$\dot{x}_i(t) = A_i^2 x_i(t) + \bar{A}_{ij,j\neq i}^{12} x_j(t) + \bar{A}_{ik,k\neq i,k\neq j}^{12} x_k(t), i \in \{1,2,3\}$$

where

$$A_1^1 = \begin{bmatrix} -2.1 & 0.4 \\ 0 & -3.3 \end{bmatrix}, A_1^2 = \begin{bmatrix} -2.5 & 0.2 \\ 0 & -2.8 \end{bmatrix},$$

$$A_{12}^{11} = \begin{bmatrix} 0.7 & 0 \\ 0 & 0.2 \end{bmatrix}, A_{12}^{12} = \begin{bmatrix} 0.6 & 0 \\ 0 & 0.2 \end{bmatrix}, A_{12}^{21} = \begin{bmatrix} 0.7 & 0 \\ 0 & 0.1 \end{bmatrix}, A_{12}^{22} = \begin{bmatrix} 0.6 & 0 \\ 0 & 0.3 \end{bmatrix},$$

$$A_{13}^{11} = \begin{bmatrix} 0.1 & 0 \\ 0 & 0.4 \end{bmatrix}, A_{13}^{12} = \begin{bmatrix} 0.2 & 0 \\ 0 & 0.4 \end{bmatrix}, A_{13}^{21} = \begin{bmatrix} 0.1 & 0 \\ 0 & 0.5 \end{bmatrix}, A_{13}^{22} = \begin{bmatrix} 0.2 & 0 \\ 0 & 0.5 \end{bmatrix},$$

for the subsystem 1, and

$$A_2^1 = \begin{bmatrix} -2.6 & 0.6 \\ 0 & -2.2 \end{bmatrix}, A_2^2 = \begin{bmatrix} -2.8 & 0.3 \\ 0 & -2.2 \end{bmatrix},$$

$$A_{21}^{11} = \begin{bmatrix} 0.4 & 0 \\ 0 & 0.1 \end{bmatrix}, A_{21}^{12} = \begin{bmatrix} 0.6 & 0 \\ 0 & 0.3 \end{bmatrix}, A_{21}^{21} = \begin{bmatrix} 0.5 & 0 \\ 0 & 0.2 \end{bmatrix}, A_{21}^{22} = \begin{bmatrix} 0.6 & 0 \\ 0 & 0.4 \end{bmatrix},$$

$$A_{23}^{11} = \begin{bmatrix} 0.1 & 0 \\ 0 & 0.3 \end{bmatrix}, A_{23}^{12} = \begin{bmatrix} 0.3 & 0 \\ 0 & 0.4 \end{bmatrix}, A_{23}^{21} = \begin{bmatrix} 0.2 & 0 \\ 0 & 0.5 \end{bmatrix}, A_{23}^{22} = \begin{bmatrix} 0.2 & 0 \\ 0 & 0.4 \end{bmatrix},$$

for the subsystem 2, and

$$A_3^1 = \begin{bmatrix} -1.9 & 0.5 \\ 0 & -2.6 \end{bmatrix}, A_3^2 = \begin{bmatrix} -2.1 & 0.1 \\ 0 & -2.3 \end{bmatrix},$$

$$A_{31}^{11} = \begin{bmatrix} 0.4 & 0 \\ 0 & 0.5 \end{bmatrix}, A_{31}^{12} = \begin{bmatrix} 0.2 & 0 \\ 0 & 0.6 \end{bmatrix}, A_{31}^{21} = \begin{bmatrix} 0.3 & 0 \\ 0 & 0.7 \end{bmatrix}, A_{31}^{22} = \begin{bmatrix} 0.2 & 0 \\ 0 & 0.8 \end{bmatrix},$$

$$A_{32}^{11} = \begin{bmatrix} 0.2 & 0 \\ 0 & 0.3 \end{bmatrix}, A_{32}^{12} = \begin{bmatrix} 0.4 & 0 \\ 0 & 0.2 \end{bmatrix}, A_{32}^{21} = \begin{bmatrix} 0.1 & 0 \\ 0 & 0.4 \end{bmatrix}, A_{32}^{22} = \begin{bmatrix} 0.3 & 0 \\ 0 & 0.5 \end{bmatrix},$$

for the subsystem 3.

Here, given $\tau_i = 0.06, h_i = 0.02$, and by using Theorem 5.2.2, we find a maximum event-triggered parameter $\sigma_i = 0.08$ for the considered system, and the obtained controller gains are

$$K_1 = \begin{bmatrix} -7.3897 & -0.7587 \end{bmatrix}, K_2 = \begin{bmatrix} -7.1899 & -0.0891 \end{bmatrix},$$
$$K_3 = \begin{bmatrix} -7.5951 & -0.5528 \end{bmatrix}.$$

However, by using Theorem 5.2.4, the maximum event-triggered parameter can be improved to $\sigma_i = 0.14$, and the corresponding controller gains are

$$K_1 = \begin{bmatrix} -6.2138 & -0.6596 \end{bmatrix}, K_2 = \begin{bmatrix} -6.2102 & -0.1416 \end{bmatrix},$$
$$K_3 = \begin{bmatrix} -6.5893 & -0.6598 \end{bmatrix}.$$

The detail comparison can be shown in Table 1. It is easy to see that the results based on the SSG method are less conservative than the results based on Wirtinger's inequality. Under the initial conditions $x_1(0) = \begin{bmatrix} 1.1 & -0.6 \end{bmatrix}^T$, $x_2(0) = \begin{bmatrix} 1.5 & -0.8 \end{bmatrix}^T$, and $x_3(0) = \begin{bmatrix} 0.4 & -0.9 \end{bmatrix}^T$, and take the above controller

Table 1. Comparison results of event-triggered parameter σ_i for different methods

Methods	Theorem 5.2.2	Theorem 5.2.4
Maximum event-triggered parameter	0.08	0.14

gains, Figures 2-5 show the state responses for the closed-loop large-scale fuzzy interconnected system, respectively. Thus, showing the effectiveness of the design methods of decentralized event-triggered control.

Example 2

Consider a discrete-time large-scale fuzzy interconnected system with the parameters as below,

$$A_1^1 = \begin{bmatrix} 1.5 & 0 \\ 0.05 & 0.7 \end{bmatrix}, A_1^2 = \begin{bmatrix} 1.8 & 0 \\ 0.09 & 0.7 \end{bmatrix}, B_1^1 = B_1^2 = \begin{bmatrix} 1 \\ 0 \end{bmatrix}$$

$$A_{12}^{11} = \begin{bmatrix} 0.04 & 0 \\ 0.02 & 0.07 \end{bmatrix}, A_{12}^{12} = \begin{bmatrix} 0.03 & 0 \\ 0.01 & 0.08 \end{bmatrix}, A_{12}^{21} = \begin{bmatrix} 0.05 & 0 \\ 0.01 & 0.06 \end{bmatrix}, A_{12}^{22} = \begin{bmatrix} 0.07 & 0 \\ 0.03 & 0.05 \end{bmatrix}$$

$$A_{13}^{11} = \begin{bmatrix} 0.04 & 0 \\ 0.04 & 0.03 \end{bmatrix}, A_{13}^{12} = \begin{bmatrix} 0.03 & 0 \\ 0.03 & 0.04 \end{bmatrix}, A_{13}^{21} = \begin{bmatrix} 0.04 & 0 \\ 0.02 & 0.05 \end{bmatrix}, A_{13}^{22} = \begin{bmatrix} 0.05 & 0 \\ 0.03 & 0.02 \end{bmatrix}$$

Figure 2. Response of the closed-loop system 1

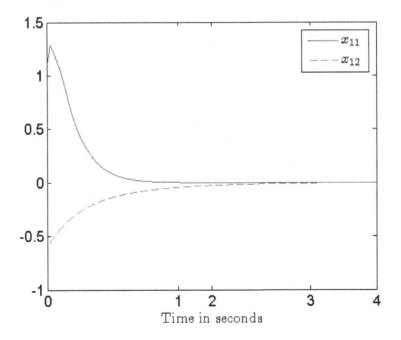

Figure 3. Response of the closed-loop system 2

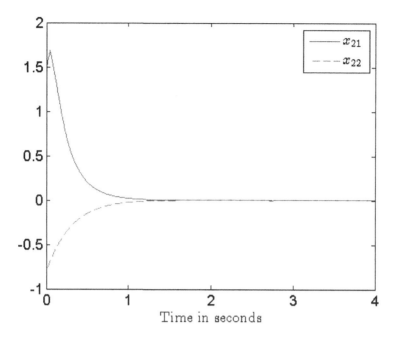

Figure 4. Response of the closed-loop system 3

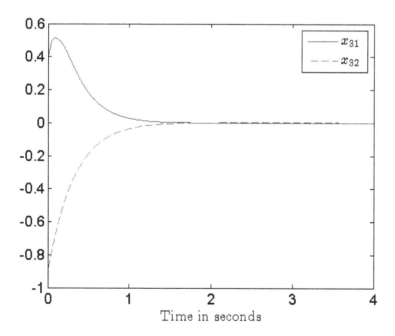

Figure 5. Response of the event-triggered times

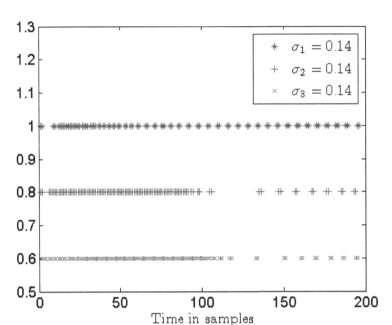

for the subsystem 1, and

$$A_2^1 = \begin{bmatrix} 1.8 & 0 \\ 0.05 & 0.7 \end{bmatrix}, A_2^2 = \begin{bmatrix} 1.2 & 0 \\ 0.09 & 0.7 \end{bmatrix}, B_2^1 = B_2^2 = \begin{bmatrix} 1 \\ 0 \end{bmatrix},$$

$$A_{21}^{11} = \begin{bmatrix} 0.04 & 0 \\ 0.02 & 0.05 \end{bmatrix}, A_{21}^{12} = \begin{bmatrix} 0.05 & 0 \\ 0.01 & 0.06 \end{bmatrix}, A_{21}^{21} = \begin{bmatrix} 0.04 & 0 \\ 0.05 & 0.04 \end{bmatrix}, A_{21}^{22} = \begin{bmatrix} 0.05 & 0 \\ 0.06 & 0.02 \end{bmatrix}$$

$$A_{23}^{11} = \begin{bmatrix} 0.03 & 0 \\ 0.05 & 0.03 \end{bmatrix}, A_{23}^{12} = \begin{bmatrix} 0.05 & 0 \\ 0.04 & 0.05 \end{bmatrix}, A_{23}^{21} = \begin{bmatrix} 0.04 & 0 \\ 0.02 & 0.04 \end{bmatrix}, A_{23}^{22} = \begin{bmatrix} 0.06 & 0 \\ 0.03 & 0.03 \end{bmatrix}$$

for the subsystem 2, and

$$A_3^1 = \begin{bmatrix} 1.7 & 0 \\ 0.05 & 0.6 \end{bmatrix}, A_3^2 = \begin{bmatrix} 1.4 & 0 \\ 0.09 & 0.6 \end{bmatrix}, B_3^1 = B_3^2 = \begin{bmatrix} 1 \\ 0 \end{bmatrix}$$

$$A_{31}^{11} = \begin{bmatrix} 0.02 & 0 \\ 0.02 & 0.04 \end{bmatrix}, A_{31}^{12} = \begin{bmatrix} 0.03 & 0 \\ 0.03 & 0.02 \end{bmatrix}, A_{31}^{21} = \begin{bmatrix} 0.04 & 0 \\ 0.01 & 0.02 \end{bmatrix}, A_{31}^{22} = \begin{bmatrix} 0.03 & 0 \\ 0.02 & 0.03 \end{bmatrix}$$

$$A_{32}^{11} = \begin{bmatrix} 0.03 & 0 \\ 0.02 & 0.04 \end{bmatrix}, A_{32}^{12} = \begin{bmatrix} 0.02 & 0 \\ 0.03 & 0.05 \end{bmatrix}, A_{32}^{21} = \begin{bmatrix} 0.01 & 0 \\ 0.04 & 0.04 \end{bmatrix}, A_{32}^{22} = \begin{bmatrix} 0.04 & 0 \\ 0.01 & 0.03 \end{bmatrix}$$

for the subsystem 3.

The normalized membership functions are shown in Figure 1, Chapter 3, where $r_i = 5$. It is noted that the open-loop system is unstable. Here, the objective is to design a decentralized fuzzy controller such that the resulting closed-loop control system is asymptotically stable. By using Theorem 5.3.2, we find a maximum event-triggered parameter $\sigma_i = 0.4$ for the considered system, and the obtained controller gains are

$$K_1 = \begin{bmatrix} -1.6343 & -0.0507 \end{bmatrix},$$
$$K_2 = \begin{bmatrix} -1.4970 & -0.0277 \end{bmatrix}, K_3 = \begin{bmatrix} -1.5159 & -0.00303 \end{bmatrix}.$$

Under the initial conditions $x_1(0) = \begin{bmatrix} 1.2 & -0.8 \end{bmatrix}^T$, $x_2(0) = \begin{bmatrix} 0.9 & -1.1 \end{bmatrix}^T$, and $x_3(0) = \begin{bmatrix} 0.5 & -1.4 \end{bmatrix}^T$, and take the above controller gains, Figures 6-9 show the state responses for the closed-loop large-scale fuzzy interconnected system, respectively. Thus, showing the effectiveness of the decentralized fuzzy controller design methods.

5.6 CONCLUSION

The event-triggered control problem for large-scale T-S fuzzy interconnected systems has been studied in this chapter. Various LMI-based co-design results on the event-triggered control scheme have been derived. Also, we further present a self-triggered control strategy in terms of LMIs. Several examples have been given to illustrate the effectiveness of the proposed methods.

Figure 6. Response of the closed-loop system 3

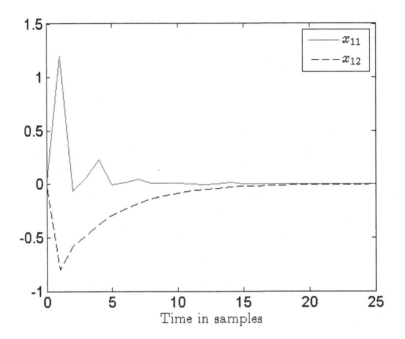

Figure 7. Response of the closed-loop system 3

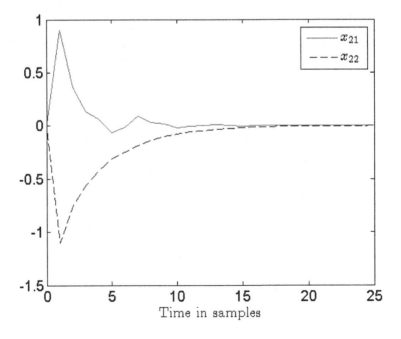

Figure 8. Response of the closed-loop system 3

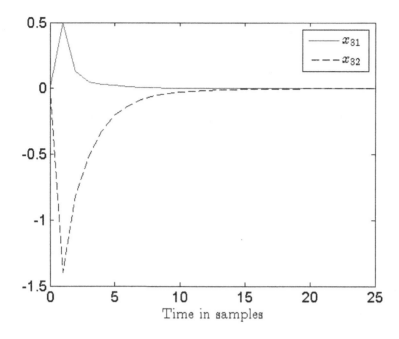

Figure 9. Response of the closed-loop system 3

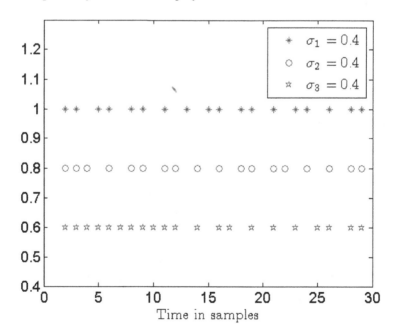

REFERENCES

Ario, C., & Sala, A. (2008). Extensions to "stability analysis of fuzzy control systems subject to uncertain grades of membership." *IEEE Transactions on Systems, Man, and Cybernetics. Part B, Cybernetics, 38*(2), 558–563. doi:10.1109/TSMCB.2007.913596 PMID:18348938

Donkers, M., & Heemels, W. (2012). Output-based event-triggered control with guaranteed L_∞-gain and improved and decentralized event-triggering. *IEEE Transactions on Automatic Control, 57*(6), 1362–1376. doi:10.1109/TAC.2011.2174696

Fridman, E. (2010). A refined input delay approach to sampled-data control. *Automatica, 46*(2), 421–427. doi:10.1016/j.automatica.2009.11.017

Gu, K., Zhang, Y., & Xu, S. (2011). Small gain problem in coupled differential-difference equations, time-varying delays, and direct Lyapunov method. *International Journal of Robust and Nonlinear Control, 21*(4), 429–451. doi:10.1002/rnc.1604

Heemels, W., & Donkers, M. (2013). 2013, Model-based periodic event-triggered control for linear systems,. *Automatica, 49*(3), 698–711. doi:10.1016/j.automatica.2012.11.025

Heemels, W., Donkers, M., Teel, A., Wouw, N., & Nesic, D. (2010). Networked control systems with communication constraints: Tradeoffs between transmission intervals, delays and performance. *IEEE Transactions on Automatic Control, 55*(8), 1781–1796. doi:10.1109/TAC.2010.2042352

Hespanha, J., Naghshtabrizi, P., & Xu, Y. (2007). A survey of recent results in networked control systems. *Proceedings of the 2008 IEEE Conference on American Control* (pp. 138-162). doi:10.1109/JPROC.2006.887288

Hristu, D., & Kumar, P. (2002). Interrupt-based feedback control over a shared communication medium. *Proceedings of the 2002 IEEE Conference on Decision Control* (pp. 3223-3228). doi:10.1109/CDC.2002.1184368

Liu, K., & Fridman, E. (2012). Wirtingers inequality and Lyapunov-based sampled-data stabilization,. *Automatica, 48*(1), 102–108. doi:10.1016/j.automatica.2011.09.029

Tabuada, P., & Wang, X. (2006). Preliminary results on state-triggered scheduling of stabilizing control tasks. *Proceedings of the 2006 IEEE Conference on Decision Control* (pp. 282–287).

Wang, X., & Lemmon, M. (2011). Event-triggering in distributed networked control systems. *IEEE Transactions on Automatic Control*, *56*(3), 586–601. doi:10.1109/TAC.2010.2057951

Xu, S., Lam, J., Zhang, B., & Zou, Y. (2015). New insight into delay-dependent stability of time-delay systems. *International Journal of Robust and Nonlinear Control*, *25*(7), 961–970. doi:10.1002/rnc.3120

Yang, T. (2006). Networked control system: A brief survey. *Proceedings of the 2006 IEEE Conference on Control Theory and Applications* (pp. 403-412).

Yue, D., Tian, E., & Han, Q. (2013). A delay system method for designing event-triggered controllers of networked control systems. *IEEE Transactions on Automatic Control*, *58*(2), 475–481. doi:10.1109/TAC.2012.2206694

Zhang, L., Gao, H., & Kaynak, O. (2013). Network-induced constraints in networked control systems-A survey. *IEEE Transactions on Industrial Informatics*, *9*(1), 403–416. doi:10.1109/TII.2012.2219540

Zhang, X., Han, Q., & Yu, X. (2015). *Survey on recent advances in networked control systems. IEEE Transactions on Industrial Informatics.* Doi: doi:10.1109/TII.2015.2506545

Chapter 6
Sliding–Mode Control of Large–Scale Fuzzy Interconnected Systems

ABSTRACT

This chapter will study the decentralized SMC for large-scale fuzzy interconnected systems. The design result on the decentralized sliding mode control of the continuous-time systems is derived in terms of LMIs. We also extend the result to discrete-time systems. Two simulation examples are provided to validate the advantage of the proposed methods.

6.1 INTRODUCTION

In recent years, many research and engineering societies have focused on the sliding mode control (SMC) design due to its simplicity and robustness against parameter variations and disturbances (Utkin, 1992). The idea of SMC is that for a predesigned switching manifold, the desirable controller drives the state trajectories toward in a vicinity of the switching manifold. Such motion is performed by imposing discontinuous control actions (Bartoszewicz & Żuk, 2010; Yu & Kaynak, 2009). More recently, the SMC technique has been developed for large-scale interconnected systems. In Yan, Edwards, and Spurgeon (2004), a decentralized static output feedback control scheme for nonlinear large-scale systems is proposed using SMC technique. The work in Yan (2003), Shyu, Liu, and Hsu (2005), Chou and

DOI: 10.4018/978-1-5225-2385-7.ch006

Cheng 2003) considered a special large-scale nonlinear system that all the system state variables are available and the interconnection terms are linear, and proposed a decentralized SMC strategy. A decentralized sliding mode control for discrete-time large-scale linear interconnected systems with time delay using only output information is considered in (Mahmoud & Qureshi, 2012).

This chapter will study the decentralized SMC for large-scale T-S fuzzy interconnected systems. The design result on the decentralized SMC is derived in terms of LMIs. We also extend the result to discrete-time systems. Two simulation examples are provided to validate the advantage of the proposed methods.

6.2 DECENTRALIZED SLIDING-MODE CONTROL

In this section, we will study the problem of decentralized SMC for large-scale T-S fuzzy interconnected system.

6.2.1 Problem Formulation

Consider a continuous-time large-scale fuzzy interconnected system, which consists of N subsystems as below,

$$\dot{x}_i(t) = A_i(\mu_i)x_i(t) + B_i u_i(t) + \sum_{j=1, j \neq i}^{N} \bar{A}_{ij}(\mu_i)x_j(t). \tag{1}$$

Here, we make the following assumptions (Yan, Edwards & Spurgeon 2004):

1. $\operatorname{rank}(B_i) = m_i$;
2. All the pairs $\left(A_i^l, B_i\right)$ are completely controllable;
3. There exists a matrix $T_i \in \mathfrak{R}^{n_{zi} \times n_{mi}}$ such that

$$T_i B_i = \begin{bmatrix} 0 \\ \bar{B}_i \end{bmatrix} \tag{2}$$

By using the linear transformation $z_i = T_i x_i$, the fuzzy system in (1) can be rewritten as the regular form as below,

$$\dot{z}_i(t) = T_i A_i(\mu_i) T_i^{-1} z_i(t) + \begin{bmatrix} 0 \\ \overline{B}_i \end{bmatrix} u_i(t) + \sum_{j=1,j\neq i}^{N} T_i \overline{A}_{ij}(\mu_i) T_i^{-1} z_j(t). \tag{3}$$

We further define

$$\begin{bmatrix} z_i(t) = \begin{bmatrix} z_{i1}(t) \\ z_{i2}(t) \end{bmatrix}, T_i A_i(\mu_i) T_i^{-1} = \begin{bmatrix} A_{i1}(\mu_i) & A_{i2}(\mu_i) \\ A_{i3}(\mu_i) & A_{i4}(\mu_i) \end{bmatrix} \\ T_i \overline{A}_{ij}(\mu_i,\mu_j) T_i^{-1} = \begin{bmatrix} \overline{A}_{ij1}(\mu_i) & \overline{A}_{ij2}(\mu_i) \\ \overline{A}_{ij3}(\mu_i) & \overline{A}_{ij4}(\mu_i) \end{bmatrix} \end{bmatrix} \tag{4}$$

Then, it yields

$$\begin{aligned} \dot{z}_{i1}(t) &= A_{i1}(\mu_i) z_{i1}(t) + A_{i2}(\mu_i) z_{i2}(t) + \\ &\sum_{j=1,j\neq i}^{N} \left[\overline{A}_{ij1}(\mu_i) z_{j1}(t) + \overline{A}_{ij2}(\mu_i) z_{j2}(t) \right], \\ \dot{z}_{i2}(t) &= A_{i3}(\mu_i) z_{i1}(t) + A_{i4}(\mu_i) z_{i2}(t) + \\ \overline{B}_i u_i(t) &+ \sum_{j=1,j\neq i}^{N} \left[\overline{A}_{ij3}(\mu_i) z_{j1}(t) + \overline{A}_{ij4}(\mu_i) z_{j2}(t) \right] \end{aligned} \tag{5}$$

Thus, the decentralized fuzzy SMC problem to be addressed in this paper can be expressed as follows. For the system (1), determine the sliding surface and a reaching motion control law $u_i(t)$ such that the sliding motion to be specified in (3) is asymptotically stable.

6.2.2 Sliding Surface Design

It is obvious that the first equation of (5) represents the sliding motion dynamics of the system (1). Hence, the corresponding sliding surface can be chosen as follows (Yu & Kaynak, 2009):

$$s_i(t) = z_{i2}(t) - C_i z_{i1}(t)$$
$$= 0, i \in \mathcal{N} \tag{6}$$

where $C_i \in \mathfrak{R}^{n_{mi} \times (n_{zi} - n_{mi})}$ denotes the sliding surface parameters to be designed. Now, substituting $z_{i2}(t) = C_i z_{i1}(t)$ into the system in (5), it yields

$$\dot{z}_{i1}(t) = A_{i1}(\mu_i) z_{i1}(t) + A_{i2}(\mu_i) C_i z_{i1}(t) +$$
$$\sum_{j=1, j \neq i}^{N} \left[\bar{A}_{ij1}(\mu_i) z_{j1}(t) + \bar{A}_{ij2}(\mu_i) C_j z_{j1}(t) \right]. \tag{7}$$

Theorem 6.2.1 The sliding motion (5) is asymptotically stable, if there exist symmetrical positive definite matrices $\{Q_i, M_{ij}\} \in \mathfrak{R}^{(n_{zi} - n_{mi}) \times (n_{zi} - n_{mi})}$, and $\bar{C}_i \in \mathfrak{R}^{n_{mi} \times (n_{zi} - n_{mi})}$, such that the following LMIs hold:

$$\begin{bmatrix} \mathrm{Sym}\left(A_{i1}^l Q_i + A_{i2} \bar{C}_i\right) & \mathbb{A}_i^l & Q_i \mathbb{I} \\ \star & \mathbb{Q}_i - \mathrm{Sym}\{\mathbb{M}_i\} & 0 \\ \star & \star & -\bar{\mathbb{M}}_i \end{bmatrix} < 0 \tag{8}$$

where

$$\begin{cases} \mathbb{M}_i = \mathrm{diag}\underbrace{\left\{M_{i1} \cdots M_{ij, j \neq i} \cdots M_{iN}\right\}}_{N-1}, \bar{\mathbb{M}}_i = \mathrm{diag}\underbrace{\left\{M_{1i} \cdots M_{ji, j \neq i} \cdots M_{Ni}\right\}}_{N-1} \\ \mathbb{Q}_i = \mathrm{diag}\underbrace{\left\{Q_1 \cdots Q_{j, j \neq i} \cdots Q_N\right\}}_{N-1}, \mathbb{I} = \underbrace{\left[I \cdots I \cdots I\right]}_{N-1}, \\ \mathbb{A}_i^l = \underbrace{\left[\mathcal{A}_{i1}^l \cdots \mathcal{A}_{ij, j \neq i}^l \cdots \mathcal{A}_{iN}^l\right]}_{N-1}, \mathcal{A}_{ij}^l = \left[\bar{A}_{ij1}^l Q_j + \bar{A}_{ij2}^l \bar{C}_j\right] \end{cases} \tag{9}$$

In that case, the parameter C_i can be obtained by computing

$$C_i = \bar{C}_i Q_i^{-1} \tag{10}$$

Proof: Firstly, we introduce the following Lyapunov functions:

$$V(t) = \sum_{i=1}^{N} V_i(t)$$

$$= \sum_{i=1}^{N} z_{i1}^T(t) P_i z_{i1}(t). \tag{11}$$

By taking the time derivative of $\dot{V}(x(t))$ along the trajectory of the system in (5), one has

$$\dot{V}(x(t)) = \sum_{i=1}^{N} 2z_{i1}^T(t) P_i \dot{z}_{i1}(t)$$

$$= \sum_{i=1}^{N} 2z_{i1}^T(t) P_i \begin{bmatrix} A_{i1}(\mu_i) z_{i1}(t) \\ +A_{i2}(\mu_i) C_i z_{i1}(t) \end{bmatrix} +$$

$$\sum_{i=1}^{N} 2z_{i1}^T(t) P_i \left\{ \sum_{j=1,j\neq i}^{N} \begin{bmatrix} \overline{A}_{ij1}(\mu_i) z_{j1}(t) \\ +\overline{A}_{ij2}(\mu_i) C_j z_{j1}(t) \end{bmatrix} \right\} \tag{12}$$

Note that

$$2\overline{x}^T \overline{y} \leq \overline{x}^T M^{-1} \overline{x} + \overline{y}^T M \overline{y}, \tag{13}$$

where $\overline{x}, \overline{y} \in \mathfrak{R}^n$ and $M \in \mathfrak{R}^{n \times n}$ is positive definite symmetric matrix.

Define positive definite symmetric matrices $M_{ij} \in \mathfrak{R}^{(n_{zi}-n_{mi}) \times (n_{zi}-n_{mi})}$, it yields

$$\sum_{i=1}^{N} 2z_{i1}^T(t) P_i \left\{ \sum_{j=1,j\neq i}^{N} \left[\overline{A}_{ij1}(\mu_i) + \overline{A}_{ij2}(\mu_i) C_j \right] z_{j1}(t) \right\}$$

$$\leq \sum_{i=1}^{N} \sum_{j=1,j\neq i}^{N} \left\{ z_{i1}^T(t) P_i \left[\overline{A}_{ij1}(\mu_i) + \overline{A}_{ij2}(\mu_i) C_j \right] M_{ij} \left[\overline{A}_{ij1}(\mu_i) + \overline{A}_{ij2}(\mu_i) C_j \right]^T P_i z_{i1}(t) \right\}$$

$$+ \sum_{i=1}^{N} \sum_{j=1,j\neq i}^{N} z_{j1}^T(t) M_{ij}^{-1} z_{j1}(t)$$

$$\leq \sum_{i=1}^{N} \sum_{j=1,j\neq i}^{N} \left\{ z_{i1}^T(t) P_i \left[\overline{A}_{ij1}(\mu_i) + \overline{A}_{ij2}(\mu_i) C_j \right] M_{ij} \left[\overline{A}_{ij1}(\mu_i) + \overline{A}_{ij2}(\mu_i) C_j \right]^T P_i^T z_{i1}(t) \right\}$$

$$+ \sum_{i=1}^{N} \sum_{j=1,j\neq i}^{N} z_{i1}^T(t) M_{ji}^{-1} z_{i1}(t) \tag{14}$$

Based on the relationship in (13), we have

$$
\begin{aligned}
\dot{V}\left(x\left(t\right)\right) & \\
\leq & \sum_{i=1}^{N} 2 z_{i1}^{T}\left(t\right) P_{i}\left\{A_{i1}\left(\mu_{i}\right) z_{i1}\left(t\right) + A_{i2}\left(\mu_{i}\right) C_{i} z_{i1}\left(t\right)\right\} \\
& + \sum_{i=1}^{N} \sum_{j=1, j\neq i}^{N} \left\{ z_{i1}^{T}\left(t\right) P_{i}\left[\bar{A}_{ij1}\left(\mu_{i}\right) + \bar{A}_{ij2}\left(\mu_{i}\right) C_{j}\right] M_{ij}\left[\bar{A}_{ij1}\left(\mu_{i}\right) + \bar{A}_{ij2}\left(\mu_{i}\right) C_{j}\right]^{T} P_{i} z_{i1}\left(t\right)\right\} \\
& + \sum_{i=1}^{N} \sum_{j=1, j\neq i}^{N} z_{i1}^{T}\left(t\right) M_{ji}^{-1} z_{i1}\left(t\right) \\
= & \sum_{i=1}^{N} z_{i1}^{T}\left(t\right) \Phi_{i}\left(\mu_{i}\right) z_{i1}\left(t\right),
\end{aligned}
$$

$$(15)$$

where

$$
\begin{aligned}
\Phi_{i}\left(\mu_{i}\right) = & \operatorname{Sym}\left(P_{i} A_{i1}\left(\mu_{i}\right) z_{i1}\left(t\right) + P_{i} A_{i2}\left(\mu_{i}\right) C_{i} z_{i1}\left(t\right)\right) \\
& + \sum_{j=1, j\neq i}^{N} \left\{ P_{i}\left[\bar{A}_{ij1}\left(\mu_{i}\right) + \bar{A}_{ij2}\left(\mu_{i}\right) C_{j}\right] M_{ij}\left[\bar{A}_{ij1}\left(\mu_{i}\right) + \bar{A}_{ij2}\left(\mu_{i}\right) C_{j}\right]^{T} P_{i}\right\} \\
& + \sum_{j=1, j\neq i}^{N} M_{ji}^{-1}
\end{aligned}
$$

$$(16)$$

By using Schur complement lemma to $\Phi_{i}\left(\mu_{i}\right) < 0$, it yields,

$$
\begin{bmatrix}
\operatorname{Sym}\left(P_{i} A_{i1}\left(\mu_{i}\right) + P_{i} A_{i2}\left(\mu_{i}\right) C_{i}\right) & P_{i}\mathbb{A}_{i}\left(\mu_{i}\right) & \mathbb{I} \\
\star & -\mathbb{M}_{i}^{-1} & 0 \\
\star & \star & -\bar{\mathbb{M}}_{i}
\end{bmatrix} < 0
$$

$$(17)$$

Where

$$\begin{cases} \mathbb{I} = \underbrace{\left[I \cdots I \cdots I \right]}_{N-1}, c_i = \underbrace{\left[C_i^T \cdots C_i^T \cdots C_i^T \right]}_{N-1}, \\ \mathbb{M}_i = \mathrm{diag} \underbrace{\left\{ M_{i1} \cdots M_{ij, j \neq i} \cdots M_{iN} \right\}}_{N-1} \\ \overline{\mathbb{M}}_i = \mathrm{diag} \underbrace{\left\{ M_{1i} \cdots M_{ji, j \neq i} \cdots M_{Ni} \right\}}_{N-1} \\ \mathbb{A}_i \left(\mu_i \right) = \underbrace{\left[\mathcal{A}_{i1} \left(\mu_i \right) \cdots \mathcal{A}_{ij, j \neq i} \left(\mu_i \right) \cdots \mathcal{A}_{iN} \left(\mu_i \right) \right]}_{N-1} \\ \mathcal{A}_{ij} \left(\mu_i \right) = \left[\overline{A}_{ij1} \left(\mu_i \right) + \overline{A}_{ij2} \left(\mu_i \right) C_j \right] \end{cases} \tag{18}$$

Define

$$\Gamma_i = \mathrm{diag} \left\{ Q_i \quad \mathbb{Q}_i \quad \overline{\mathbb{I}} \right\} \tag{19}$$

where $Q_i = P_i^{-1}, \overline{\mathbb{I}} = \mathrm{diag} \underbrace{\left\{ I \cdots I \cdots I \right\}}_{N-1}, \mathbb{Q}_i = \mathrm{diag} \underbrace{\left\{ Q_1 \cdots Q_{j, j \neq i} \cdots Q_N \right\}}_{N-1}$.

Now, by performing a congruence transformation to (17) by Γ_i, it is easy to obtain the inequality in (8). Thus, completing this proof.

6.2.3 Decentralized Sliding-Mode Controller Design

In this subsection, our objective is to design a fuzzy sliding-mode controller such that the specified sliding surface can be reached.

Recalling the relationship in (6) that

$$\begin{aligned} s_i(t) \quad &= z_{i2}(t) - C_i z_{i1}(t) \\ &= \left[-C_i \quad I \right] z_i(t), i \in \mathcal{N}. \end{aligned} \tag{20}$$

Consider the following controller

$$u_i\left(t\right) = -\overline{B}_i^{-1}\left\{\left[C_iA_{i1}\left(\mu_i\right) - A_{i3}\left(\mu_i\right)\right]z_{i1}\left(t\right) + \left[C_iA_{i2}\left(\mu_i\right) - A_{i4}\left(\mu_i\right)\right]z_{i2}\left(t\right)\right\}\operatorname{sign}s_i\left(t\right)$$

$$-\overline{B}_i^{-1}\sum_{i=1}^{N}\sum_{j=1,j\neq i}^{N}C_j\left[\overline{A}_{ji1}\left(\mu_j\right)\quad \overline{A}_{ji2}\left(\mu_j\right)\right]z_i\left(t\right)$$

$$-\overline{B}_i^{-1}\sum_{i=1}^{N}\sum_{j=1,j\neq i}^{N}\left[\overline{A}_{ji3}\left(\mu_j\right)\quad \overline{A}_{ji4}\left(\mu_j\right)\right]z_i\left(t\right)$$

$$(21)$$

The objective in this section is to design a decentralized state-feedback sliding mode control such that the system states are driven to the sliding surface (20). Based on the controller in (21), we obtained the main result as below.

Theorem 6.2.2 Consider the large-scale fuzzy interconnected system in (1). Under the assumptions a)-c), the decentralized sliding mode control (21) drives the system (1) to the composite sliding surface (20) and maintains a sliding motion.

Proof: For the interconnected system (1), a possible reachability condition is described by (Yu & Kaynak 2009)

$$\sum_{i=1}^{N}\frac{s_i^T\left(t\right)S_i\left(t\right)}{S_i\left(t\right)} < 0.\qquad(22)$$

Based on the relationships in (5), (20) and (21), it yields

$$\sum_{i=1}^{N}\frac{s_i^T\left(t\right)S_i\left(t\right)}{S_i\left(t\right)} = \sum_{i=1}^{N}\frac{s_i^T\left(t\right)}{S_i\left(t\right)}\left[-C_i\dot{z}_{i1}\left(t\right) + \dot{z}_{i2}\left(t\right)\right]$$

$$= \sum_{i=1}^{N}\frac{s_i^T\left(t\right)}{S_i\left(t\right)}\left[\begin{array}{l}-C_iA_{i1}\left(\mu_i\right)z_{i1}\left(t\right) - C_iA_{i2}\left(\mu_i\right)z_{i2}\left(t\right)\\ +A_{i3}\left(\mu_i\right)z_{i1}\left(t\right) + A_{i4}\left(\mu_i\right)z_{i2}\left(t\right)\end{array}\right]$$

$$-\sum_{i=1}^{N}\frac{s_i^T\left(t\right)}{S_i\left(t\right)}\sum_{j=1,j\neq i}^{N}C_i\left[\overline{A}_{ij1}\left(\mu_i\right)\quad \overline{A}_{ij2}\left(\mu_i\right)\right]z_j\left(t\right)$$

$$+\sum_{i=1}^{N}\frac{s_i^T\left(t\right)}{S_i\left(t\right)}\sum_{j=1,j\neq i}^{N}\left[\overline{A}_{ij3}\left(\mu_i\right)\quad \overline{A}_{ij4}\left(\mu_i\right)\right]z_j\left(t\right) + \sum_{i=1}^{N}\frac{s_i^T\left(t\right)}{S_i\left(t\right)}\overline{B}_iu_i\left(t\right)$$

$$(23)$$

Note that

$$\sum_{i=1}^{N} \frac{s_i^T(t)}{S_i(t)} \sum_{j=1,j\neq i}^{N} C_i \left[\overline{A}_{ij1}(\mu_i) \quad \overline{A}_{ij2}(\mu_i) \right] z_j(t) =$$

$$\sum_{i=1}^{N} \sum_{j=1,j\neq i}^{N} \frac{s_j^T(t)}{s_j(t)} C_j \left[\overline{A}_{ji1}(\mu_j) \quad \overline{A}_{ji2}(\mu_j) \right] z_i(t) \tag{24}$$

$$\leq \sum_{i=1}^{N} \sum_{j=1,j\neq i}^{N} C_j \left[\overline{A}_{ji1}(\mu_j) \quad \overline{A}_{ji2}(\mu_j) \right] z_i(t)$$

and

$$\sum_{i=1}^{N} \frac{s_i^T(t)}{S_i(t)} \sum_{j=1,j\neq i}^{N} \left[\overline{A}_{ij3}(\mu_i) \quad \overline{A}_{ij4}(\mu_i) \right] z_j(t) =$$

$$\sum_{i=1}^{N} \sum_{j=1,j\neq i}^{N} \frac{s_j^T(t)}{s_j(t)} \left[\overline{A}_{ji3}(\mu_j) \quad \overline{A}_{ji4}(\mu_j) \right] z_i(t) \tag{25}$$

$$\leq \sum_{i=1}^{N} \sum_{j=1,j\neq i}^{N} \left[\overline{A}_{ji3}(\mu_j) \quad \overline{A}_{ji4}(\mu_j) \right] z_i(t)$$

Hence, the decentralized control law proposed in (21), satisfies the reaching condition (22). Thus, the proof is completed.

6.3 EXTENSION TO DISCRETE-TIME SYSTEM

Now, the sliding control results on the continuous-time system will be developed to the discrete-time case.

6.3.1 Problem Formulation

Consider the discrete-time large-scale fuzzy interconnected system as below,

$$x_i(t+1) = A_i(\mu_i) x_i(t) + B_i u_i(t) + \sum_{j=1,j\neq i}^{N} \overline{A}_{ij}(\mu_i) x_j(t) \tag{26}$$

Similarly, by the linear transformation $z_i = T_i x_i$, the system in (26) can be rewritten as

$$
\begin{aligned}
z_{i1}\left(t+1\right) &= A_{i1}\left(\mu_i\right)z_{i1}\left(t\right) + A_{i2}\left(\mu_i\right)z_{i2}\left(t\right) + \\
&\sum_{j=1, j\neq i}^{N}\left[\bar{A}_{ij1}\left(\mu_i\right)z_{j1}\left(t\right) + \bar{A}_{ij2}\left(\mu_i\right)z_{j2}\left(t\right)\right], \\
z_{i2}\left(t+1\right) &= A_{i3}\left(\mu_i\right)z_{i1}\left(t\right) + A_{i4}\left(\mu_i\right)z_{i2}\left(t\right) + \\
&\bar{B}_i u_i\left(t\right) + \sum_{j=1, j\neq i}^{N}\left[\bar{A}_{ij3}\left(\mu_i\right)z_{j1}\left(t\right) + \bar{A}_{ij4}\left(\mu_i\right)z_{j2}\left(t\right)\right]
\end{aligned}
\tag{27}
$$

where

$$
z_i\left(t\right) = \begin{bmatrix} z_{i1}\left(t\right) \\ z_{i2}\left(t\right) \end{bmatrix}, T_i A_i\left(\frac{1}{4}\right)T_i^{-1} = \begin{bmatrix} A_{i1}\left(\mu_i\right) & A_{i2}\left(\mu_i\right) \\ A_{i3}\left(\mu_i\right) & A_{i4}\left(\mu_i\right) \end{bmatrix}
$$

$$
T_i \bar{A}_{ij}\left(\mu_i\right)T_i^{-1} = \begin{bmatrix} \bar{A}_{ij1}\left(\mu_i\right) & \bar{A}_{ij2}\left(\mu_i\right) \\ \bar{A}_{ij3}\left(\mu_i\right) & \bar{A}_{ij4}\left(\mu_i\right) \end{bmatrix}
\tag{28}
$$

Then, the decentralized fuzzy SMC problem to be addressed in this paper can be expressed as follows.

For the system (26), determine the sliding surface and a reaching motion control law $u_i\left(t\right)$ such that the sliding motion to be specified in (27) is asymptotically stable.

6.3.2 Sliding Surface Design

It is obvious that the first equation of system (27) represents the sliding motion dynamics of system (26), thus the corresponding sliding surface can be chosen as follows (Yu & Kaynak, 2009):

$$
\begin{aligned}
s_i\left(t\right) &= z_{i2}\left(t\right) - C_i z_{i1}\left(t\right) \\
&= 0, i \in \mathcal{N}
\end{aligned}
\tag{29}
$$

where $C_i \in \mathfrak{R}^{n_{mi} \times \left(n_{xi}-n_{mi}\right)}$ denotes the sliding surface parameters to be designed.

Now, substituting $z_{i2}(t) = C_i z_{i1}(t)$ into the system in (27), it yields

$$
\begin{aligned}
z_{i1}(t+1) = &A_{i1}(\mu_i) z_{i1}(t) + A_{i2}(\mu_i) C_i z_{i1}(t) + \\
&\sum_{j=1,j\neq i}^{N} \left[\overline{A}_{ij1}(\mu_i) z_{j1}(t) + \overline{A}_{ij2}(\mu_i) C_j z_{j1}(t) \right].
\end{aligned}
\tag{30}
$$

Theorem 6.3.2 The sliding motion (27) is asymptotically stable, if there exist symmetrical positive definite matrices $\{\overline{P}_i, M_{ij}\} \in \mathfrak{R}^{(n_{zi}-n_{mi})\times(n_{zi}-n_{mi})}$, and matrix $Q_i \in \mathfrak{R}^{(n_{zi}-n_{mi})\times(n_{zi}-n_{mi})}$, and $\overline{C}_i \in \mathfrak{R}^{n_{mi}\times(n_{zi}-n_{mi})}$, such that the following LMIs hold:

$$
\begin{bmatrix}
\overline{P}_i - \text{Sym}\{Q_i\} & A_{i1}^l Q_i^T + A_{i2}^l \overline{C}_i & \mathbb{A}_i^l & Q_i \mathbb{I} \\
\star & -P_i & 0 & 0 \\
\star & \star & \mathbb{M}_i - \text{Sym}\{\mathbb{Q}_i\} & 0 \\
\star & \star & \star & -\overline{\mathbb{M}}_i
\end{bmatrix} < 0
\tag{31}
$$

where

$$
\begin{cases}
\mathbb{M}_i = \text{diag}\underbrace{\{M_{i1} \cdots M_{ij,j\neq i} \cdots M_{iN}\}}_{N-1}, \mathbb{I} = \underbrace{[I \cdots I \cdots I]}_{N-1} \\
\overline{\mathbb{M}}_i = \text{diag}\underbrace{\{M_{1i} \cdots M_{ji,j\neq i} \cdots M_{Ni}\}}_{N-1} \\
\mathbb{A}_i^l = \underbrace{[\mathcal{A}_{i1}^l \cdots \mathcal{A}_{ij,j\neq i}^l \cdots \mathcal{A}_{iN}^l]}_{N-1}, \mathcal{A}_{ij}^l = [\overline{A}_{ij1}^l Q_j^T + \overline{A}_{ij2}^l \overline{C}_j]
\end{cases}
\tag{32}
$$

In that case, the parameter C_i can be obtained by computing

$$
C_i = \overline{C}_i Q_i^{-T}
\tag{33}
$$

Proof: Firstly, we introduce the following Lyapunov functions:

$$
\begin{aligned}
V(t) &= \sum_{i=1}^{N} V_i(t) \\
&= \sum_{i=1}^{N} z_{i1}^T(t) P_i z_{i1}(t)
\end{aligned}
$$

(34)

where $P_i \in \mathfrak{R}^{(n_{zi}-n_{mi}) \times (n_{zi}-n_{mi})}$ is the positive definite matrix.

Define

$$
\Delta V_i(t) = V_i(t+1) - V_i(t),
$$

and define the matrix $G_i \in \mathfrak{R}^{(n_{zi}-n_{mi}) \times (n_{zi}-n_{mi})}$, and the positive definite matrix $M_{ij} \in \mathfrak{R}^{(n_{zi}-n_{mi}) \times (n_{zi}-n_{mi})}$, and taking the Young's inequality, one has

$$
\begin{aligned}
\Delta V(t) &= \sum_{i=1}^{N} \left\{ V_i(t+1) - V_i(t) + 2 z_{i1}^T(t) G_i \begin{bmatrix} -z_{i1}(t+1) + A_{i1}(\mu_i) z_{i1}(t) \\ + A_{i2}(\mu_i) C_i z_{i1}(t) \end{bmatrix} \right\} \\
&\quad + 2 G_i \sum_{i=1}^{N} \sum_{j=1,j\neq i}^{N} \left[\bar{A}_{ij1}(\mu_i) + \bar{A}_{ij2}(\mu_i) C_j \right] z_{j1}(t) \\
&\leq \sum_{i=1}^{N} \left\{ z_{i1}^T(t+1) P_i z_{i1}(t+1) - z_{i1}^T(t) P_i z_{i1}(t) \right\} \\
&\quad + \sum_{i=1}^{N} \left\{ 2 z_{i1}^T(t+1) G_i \left[-z_{i1}(t+1) + A_{i1}(\mu_i) z_{i1}(t) + A_{i2}(\mu_i) C_i z_{i1}(t) \right] \right\} \\
&\quad + \sum_{i=1}^{N} \sum_{j=1,j\neq i}^{N} z_{i1}^T(t+1) G_i \begin{bmatrix} \bar{A}_{ij1}(\mu_i) \\ + \bar{A}_{ij2}(\mu_i) C_j \end{bmatrix} M_{ij} \begin{bmatrix} \bar{A}_{ij1}(\mu_i) \\ + \bar{A}_{ij2}(\mu_i) C_j \end{bmatrix} G_i^T z_{i1}(t+1) \\
&\quad + \sum_{i=1}^{N} \sum_{j=1,j\neq i}^{N} z_{i1}(t) M_{ji}^{-1} z_{i1}(t) \\
&= \sum_{i=1}^{N} \left\{ \begin{bmatrix} z_{i1}(t+1) \\ z_{i1}(t) \end{bmatrix}^T \Phi_i(\mu_i) \begin{bmatrix} z_{i1}(t+1) \\ z_{i1}(t) \end{bmatrix} \right\}
\end{aligned}
$$

(35)

where

$$\Phi_i\left(\mu_i\right) = \begin{bmatrix} \Phi_{i(1)}\left(\mu_i\right) & G_i\left(A_{i1}\left(\mu_i\right) + A_{i2}\left(\mu_i\right)C_i\right) \\ \star & -P_i + \sum\limits_{j=1,j\neq i}^{N} M_{ji}^{-1} \end{bmatrix}, \tag{36}$$

with
$$\Phi_{i(1)}\left(\mu_i\right) = P_i - \mathrm{Sym}\left\{G_i\right\} + \sum\limits_{j=1,j\neq i}^{N} G_i\left[\bar{A}_{ij1}\left(\mu_i\right) + \bar{A}_{ij2}\left(\mu_i\right)C_j\right]M_{ij}\left[\bar{A}_{ij1}\left(\mu_i\right) + \bar{A}_{ij2}\left(\mu_i\right)C_j\right]G_i^T.$$

By using Schur complement lemma to $\Phi_i\left(\mu_i\right) < 0$, it yields

$$\begin{bmatrix} P_i - \mathrm{Sym}\left\{G_i\right\} & G_i\left(A_{i1}\left(\mu_i\right) + A_{i2}\left(\mu_i\right)C_i\right) & \mathbb{A}_i\left(\mu_i\right) & \mathbb{I} \\ \star & -P_i & 0 & 0 \\ \star & \star & -\mathbb{M}_i^{-1} & 0 \\ \star & \star & \star & -\bar{\mathbb{M}}_i \end{bmatrix} < 0 \tag{37}$$

where

$$\begin{cases} \mathbb{I} = \underbrace{\begin{bmatrix} I \cdots I \cdots I \end{bmatrix}}_{N-1}, \mathbb{M}_i = \mathrm{diag}\underbrace{\left\{M_{i1} \cdots M_{ij,j\neq i} \cdots M_{iN}\right\}}_{N-1} \\ \bar{\mathbb{M}}_i = \mathrm{diag}\underbrace{\left\{M_{1i} \cdots M_{ji,j\neq i} \cdots M_{Ni}\right\}}_{N-1} \\ \mathbb{A}_i\left(\mu_i\right) = \underbrace{\begin{bmatrix} \mathcal{A}_{i1}\left(\mu_i\right) \cdots \mathcal{A}_{ij,j\neq i}\left(\mu_i\right) \cdots \mathcal{A}_{iN}\left(\mu_i\right) \end{bmatrix}}_{N-1} \\ \mathcal{A}_{ij}\left(\mu_i\right) = \begin{bmatrix} \bar{A}_{ij1}\left(\mu_i\right) + \bar{A}_{ij2}\left(\mu_i\right)C_j \end{bmatrix} \end{cases} \tag{38}$$

Define

$$\Gamma_i = \mathrm{diag}\left\{G_i^{-1} \quad G_i^{-1} \quad \mathbb{Q}_i \quad \bar{\mathbb{I}}\right\}, \bar{P}_i = G_i^{-1}P_iG_i^{-T}, \bar{C}_i = C_iG_i^{-T}, Q_i = G_i^{-1} \tag{39}$$

where $\bar{\mathbb{I}} = \mathrm{diag}\underbrace{\left\{I \cdots I \cdots I\right\}}_{N-1}, \mathbb{Q}_i = \mathrm{diag}\underbrace{\left\{Q_1 \cdots Q_{j,j\neq i} \cdots Q_N\right\}}_{N-1}.$

Now, by performing a congruence transformation to (37) by Γ_i, it is easy to obtain the inequality in (31). Thus, completing this proof.

6.3.3 Decentralized Sliding-Mode Controller Design

In this subsection, we will synthesize a fuzzy sliding-mode controller such that the specified sliding surface can be reached.

Recalling the relationship in (29) that

$$
\begin{aligned}
s_i\left(t\right) &= z_{i2}\left(t\right) - C_i z_{i1}\left(t\right) \\
&= \begin{bmatrix} -C_i & I \end{bmatrix} z_i\left(t\right), i \in \mathcal{N}
\end{aligned}
\tag{40}
$$

Consider the following controller

$$
\begin{aligned}
u_i\left(t\right) &= \bar{B}_i^{-1}\left\{\left[C_i A_{i1}\left(\mu_i\right) - A_{i3}\left(\mu_i\right)\right] z_{i1}\left(t\right) + \left[C_i A_{i2}\left(\mu_i\right) - A_{i4}\left(\mu_i\right)\right] z_{i2}\left(t\right)\right\} \\
&\quad - \bar{B}_i^{-1} \sum_{j=1, j \neq i}^{N} \bar{A}_{ji1}\left(\mu_j\right) + \bar{A}_{ij3}\left(\mu_j\right) z_{i1}\left(t\right) \\
&\quad - \bar{B}_i^{-1} \sum_{j=1, j \neq i}^{N} \bar{A}_{ji2}\left(\mu_j\right) + \bar{A}_{ij4}\left(\mu_j\right) z_{i2}\left(t\right)
\end{aligned}
\tag{41}
$$

Theorem 6.3.2 Consider the large-scale fuzzy interconnected system (27). Under the assumptions 1–3, the decentralized sliding mode control (41) drives the system (27) to the composite sliding surface (30) and maintains a sliding motion.

Proof: The objective in this section is to design a decentralized static output feedback sliding mode control such that the system states are driven to the sliding surface (40). For the interconnected system (26), a possible reachability condition is described by (Yu & Kaynak, 2009)

$$
\sum_{i=1}^{N} \left\{ s_i^2\left(t+1\right) - s_i^2\left(t\right) \right\} < 0.
\tag{42}
$$

Based on the relationships in (40) and (41), it yields

$$
\begin{aligned}
s_i(t+1) &= z_{i2}(t+1) - C_i z_{i1}(t+1) \\
&= A_{i3}(\mu_i) z_{i1}(t) + A_{i4}(\mu_i) z_{i2}(t) + \bar{B}_i u_i(t) \\
&\quad + \sum_{j=1, j\neq i}^{N} \left[\bar{A}_{ij3}(\mu_i,\mu_j) z_{j1}(t) + \bar{A}_{ij4}(\mu_i,\mu_j) z_{j2}(t) \right] \\
&\quad - C_i \left\{ A_{i1}(\mu_i) z_{i1}(t) + A_{i2}(\mu_i) z_{i2}(t) + \sum_{j=1, j\neq i}^{N} \begin{bmatrix} \bar{A}_{ij1}(\mu_i,\mu_j) z_{j1}(t) \\ +\bar{A}_{ij2}(\mu_i,\mu_j) z_{j2}(t) \end{bmatrix} \right\} \\
&\leq \sum_{j=1, j\neq i}^{N} - C_i \bar{A}_{ij1}(\mu_i) + \bar{A}_{ij3}(\mu_i) z_{j1}(t) \\
&\quad + \sum_{j=1, j\neq i}^{N} - C_i \bar{A}_{ij2}(\mu_i,\mu_j) + \bar{A}_{ij4}(\mu_i) z_{j2}(t) \\
&\quad - \sum_{j=1, j\neq i}^{N} - C_j \bar{A}_{ji1}(\mu_j) + \bar{A}_{ji3}(\mu_j) z_{i1}(t) \\
&\quad - \sum_{j=1, j\neq i}^{N} - C_j \bar{A}_{ji2}(\mu_j) + \bar{A}_{ij4}(\mu_j) z_{i2}(t)
\end{aligned}
\tag{43}
$$

It follows from (43) that

$$
\begin{aligned}
\sum_{i=1}^{N} \left\{ s_i^2(t+1) - s_i^2(t) \right\} &= \sum_{i=1}^{N} 2 \left\{ \sum_{j=1, j\neq i}^{N} - C_i \bar{A}_{ij1}(\mu_i) + \bar{A}_{ij3}(\mu_i) z_{j1}(t) \right. \\
&\quad \left. \times \left[\sum_{j=1, j\neq i}^{N} - C_i \bar{A}_{ij2}(\mu_i) + \bar{A}_{ij4}(\mu_i) z_{j2}(t) \right] \right\} \\
&\quad - \sum_{i=1}^{N} 2 \left\{ \sum_{j=1, j\neq i}^{N} - C_i \bar{A}_{ij1}(\mu_i) + \bar{A}_{ij3}(\mu_i) z_{j1}(t) \right. \\
&\quad \left. \times \sum_{j=1, j\neq i}^{N} - C_j \bar{A}_{ji2}(\mu_j) + \bar{A}_{ji4}(\mu_j) z_{i2}(t) \right\} \\
&\quad - \left[z_{i2}(t) - C_i z_{i1}(t) \right]^2 \\
&< 0
\end{aligned}
\tag{44}
$$

Thus, the proof is completed.

6.4 ILLUSTRATIVE EXAMPLES

This chapter has shown theoretically the SMC scheme on large-scale fuzzy interconnected systems, including both the continuous-time and discrete-time cases. In this section, we use several examples to further verify the derived results. The solver used in the section is the LMI Toolbox in Matlab.

Example 1

Consider a continuous-time large-scale interconnected system with three fuzzy subsystems as below.

Plant Rule R_i^1: IF $\varsigma_{i1}(t)$ is F_{i1}^1, THEN

$$\dot{x}_i(t) = A_i^1 x_i(t) + B_i^1 u_i(t) + \bar{A}_{ij,j\neq i}^1 x_j(t), i \in \{1,2,3\}$$

Plant Rule R_i^2: IF $\varsigma_{i1}(t)$ is F_{i1}^2, THEN

$$\dot{x}_i(t) = A_i^2 x_i(t) + B_i^2 u_i(t) + \bar{A}_{ij,j\neq i}^2 x_j(t), i \in \{1,2,3\}$$

where

$$A_1^1 = \begin{bmatrix} -2.1 & 0.4 \\ 0 & -3.3 \end{bmatrix}, A_1^2 = \begin{bmatrix} -2.5 & 0.2 \\ 0 & -2.8 \end{bmatrix}, B_1^1 = B_1^2 = \begin{bmatrix} 0 \\ 1 \end{bmatrix},$$

$$A_{12}^1 = \begin{bmatrix} 0.7 & 0 \\ 0 & 0.2 \end{bmatrix}, A_{12}^2 = \begin{bmatrix} 0.6 & 0 \\ 0 & 0.2 \end{bmatrix}, A_{13}^1 = \begin{bmatrix} 0.7 & 0 \\ 0 & 0.2 \end{bmatrix}, A_{13}^2 = \begin{bmatrix} 0.6 & 0 \\ 0 & 0.2 \end{bmatrix}$$

for the subsystem 1, and

$$A_2^1 = \begin{bmatrix} -2.1 & 0.4 \\ 0 & -3.3 \end{bmatrix}, A_2^2 = \begin{bmatrix} -2.5 & 0.2 \\ 0 & -2.8 \end{bmatrix}, B_2^1 = B_2^2 = \begin{bmatrix} 0 \\ 1 \end{bmatrix},$$

$$A_{21}^1 = \begin{bmatrix} 0.7 & 0 \\ 0 & 0.2 \end{bmatrix}, A_{21}^2 = \begin{bmatrix} 0.6 & 0 \\ 0 & 0.2 \end{bmatrix}, A_{23}^1 = \begin{bmatrix} 0.7 & 0 \\ 0 & 0.2 \end{bmatrix}, A_{23}^2 = \begin{bmatrix} 0.6 & 0 \\ 0 & 0.2 \end{bmatrix}$$

for the subsystem 2, and

$$A_3^1 = \begin{bmatrix} -2.1 & 0.4 \\ 0 & -3.3 \end{bmatrix}, A_3^2 = \begin{bmatrix} -2.5 & 0.2 \\ 0 & -2.8 \end{bmatrix}, B_3^1 = B_3^2 = \begin{bmatrix} 0 \\ 1 \end{bmatrix},$$

$$A_{31}^1 = \begin{bmatrix} 0.7 & 0 \\ 0 & 0.2 \end{bmatrix}, A_{31}^2 = \begin{bmatrix} 0.6 & 0 \\ 0 & 0.2 \end{bmatrix}, A_{32}^1 = \begin{bmatrix} 0.7 & 0 \\ 0 & 0.2 \end{bmatrix}, A_{32}^2 = \begin{bmatrix} 0.6 & 0 \\ 0 & 0.2 \end{bmatrix}$$

for the subsystem 3.

Here, by using Theorem 6.2.2, we find a feasible solution to the SMC problem for the considered system, and the sliding surface parameters are

$$C_1 = -9.8028, C_2 = -9.3658, C_3 = -9.8077.$$

Example 2

Consider a discrete-time large-scale fuzzy interconnected system with the parameters as below,

$$A_1^1 = \begin{bmatrix} 0.8 & 0 \\ 0.05 & 0.7 \end{bmatrix}, A_1^2 = \begin{bmatrix} 0.8 & 0 \\ 0.09 & 0.7 \end{bmatrix}, B_1^1 = B_1^2 = \begin{bmatrix} 0 \\ 1 \end{bmatrix},$$

$$A_{12}^1 = \begin{bmatrix} 0.04 & 0 \\ 0.02 & 0.07 \end{bmatrix}, A_{12}^2 = \begin{bmatrix} 0.03 & 0 \\ 0.01 & 0.08 \end{bmatrix}, A_{13}^1 = \begin{bmatrix} 0.04 & 0 \\ 0.02 & 0.07 \end{bmatrix}, A_{13}^2 = \begin{bmatrix} 0.03 & 0 \\ 0.01 & 0.08 \end{bmatrix}$$

for the subsystem 1, and

$$A_2^1 = \begin{bmatrix} 0.8 & 0 \\ 0.05 & 0.7 \end{bmatrix}, A_2^2 = \begin{bmatrix} 0.6 & 0 \\ 0.09 & 0.7 \end{bmatrix}, B_2^1 = B_2^2 = \begin{bmatrix} 0 \\ 1 \end{bmatrix},$$

$$A_{21}^1 = \begin{bmatrix} 0.04 & 0 \\ 0.02 & 0.05 \end{bmatrix}, A_{21}^2 = \begin{bmatrix} 0.05 & 0 \\ 0.01 & 0.06 \end{bmatrix}, A_{23}^1 = \begin{bmatrix} 0.04 & 0 \\ 0.02 & 0.05 \end{bmatrix}, A_{23}^2 = \begin{bmatrix} 0.05 & 0 \\ 0.01 & 0.06 \end{bmatrix}$$

for the subsystem 2, and

$$A_3^1 = \begin{bmatrix} 0.7 & 0 \\ 0.05 & 0.6 \end{bmatrix}, A_3^2 = \begin{bmatrix} 0.8 & 0 \\ 0.09 & 0.6 \end{bmatrix}, B_3^1 = B_3^2 = \begin{bmatrix} 0 \\ 1 \end{bmatrix},$$

$$A_{31}^1 = \begin{bmatrix} 0.02 & 0 \\ 0.02 & 0.04 \end{bmatrix}, A_{31}^2 = \begin{bmatrix} 0.03 & 0 \\ 0.03 & 0.02 \end{bmatrix}, A_{32}^1 = \begin{bmatrix} 0.02 & 0 \\ 0.02 & 0.04 \end{bmatrix}, A_{32}^2 = \begin{bmatrix} 0.03 & 0 \\ 0.03 & 0.02 \end{bmatrix}$$

for the subsystem 3.

Here, by using Theorem 6.3.2, we find a feasible solution to the SMC problem for the considered system, and the sliding surface parameters are

$$C_1 = -1.5092, C_2 = -1.4482, C_3 = -1.5165.$$

6.5 CONCLUSION

The decentralized SMC problem for large-scale fuzzy interconnected systems has been studied in this chapter. The design results on the decentralized SMC control for continuous-time systems and for discrete-time ones have been derived, respectively. Several examples have been given to illustrate the proposed methods.

REFERENCES

Bartoszewicz, A., & Żuk, J. (2010). Sliding mode control—Basic concepts and current trends. *Proceedings of the IEEE International Symposium on Industrial Electronics* (pp. 3772-3777). doi:10.1109/ISIE.2010.5637990

Chou, C., & Cheng, C. (2003). A decentralized model reference adaptive variable structure controller for large-scale time-varying delay systems. *IEEE Transactions on Automatic Control*, 48(7), 1213–1217. doi:10.1109/TAC.2003.814263

Mahmoud, M., & Qureshi, A. (2012). Decentralized sliding-mode output-feedback control of interconnected discrete-delay systems. *Automatica*, 48(5), 808–814. doi:10.1016/j.automatica.2012.02.008

Shyu, K., Liu, W., & Hsu, K. (2005). Design of large-scale time-delayed systems with dead-zone input via variable structure control. *Automatica*, *41*(7), 1239–1246. doi:10.1016/j.automatica.2005.03.004

Utkin, V. (1992). *Sliding Modes in Control and Optimization* (1st ed.). Berlin, Germany: Springer-Verlag. doi:10.1007/978-3-642-84379-2

Yan, J. (2003). Memoryless adaptive decentralized sliding mode control for uncertain large-scale systems with time-varying delays. *Journal of Dynamic Systems, Measurement, and Control*, *125*(2), 172–176. doi:10.1115/1.1567315

Yan, X., Edwards, C., & Spurgeon, S. (2004). Decentralised robust sliding mode control for a class of nonlinear interconnected systems by static output feedback. *Automatica*, *40*(4), 613–620. doi:10.1016/j.automatica.2003.10.025

Yu, X., & Kaynak, O. (2009). Sliding-mode control with soft computing: A survey. *IEEE Transactions on Industrial Electronics*, *56*(9), 3275–3285. doi:10.1109/TIE.2009.2027531

Chapter 7
Practical Application

ABSTRACT

In this chapter, we pay our attention to the two practical applications (Microgrid and Multi-Motors driven) for the proposed methods.

7.1 APPLICATION TO MICROGRID

Motivated by environmental deterioration and energy security, there is a global trend toward the use of renewable energy sources (RES). Power network with large-scale renewable energy such as solar and wind energy has become the trend of modern power industry, and the trend impacting on power systems is more and more prominent (Ding, Xu, Wang, Wang, Song, & Chen, 2016). Recently, a great deal of attention has been devoted to the control of micro-grid systems using the recent developed nonlinear control theory, particularly the decentralized control (Etemadi, Davison, & Iravani, 2012; Mohamed & El-Saadany, 2008) and the distributed control (Anand, Fernandes, & Guerrero, 2013; Sun, Zhang, Xing, & Guerrero, 2011) to distributed energy resource units.

Here, consider a solar photovoltaic (PV) power systems using DC/DC converter as shown in Figure 1, which dynamic model can be given by

DOI: 10.4018/978-1-5225-2385-7.ch007

Figure 1. PV power system

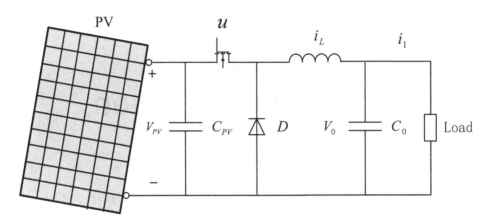

$$\begin{cases} \dot{V}_{pv} = \dfrac{1}{C_{pv}}\left(i_{pv} - i_L u\right) \\[2mm] \overset{\cdot}{i}_L = \dfrac{1}{L}\left(R_0\left(i_1 - i_L\right) - R_L i_L - V_0 + \left(V_D + V_{pv} - R_M i_L\right)u\right) - \dfrac{V_D}{L} \\[2mm] \dot{V}_0 = \dfrac{1}{C_0}\left(i_L - i_1\right) \end{cases} \qquad (1)$$

where V_{pv}, i_L, and V_0 are the **PV** array voltage, the current on the inductance L, and the voltage of the capacitance C_0, respectively; R_0, R_L, and R_M are the internal resistance on the capacitance C_0, the inductance L, and the power MOSFET, respectively; V_D is the forward voltage of the power diode; i_1 is the measurable load current.

Then, consider a permanent magnetic synchronous generator (PMSG) as shown in Figure 2, where it's dynamic model in rotor reference frame can be given by

Figure 2. PMSG system

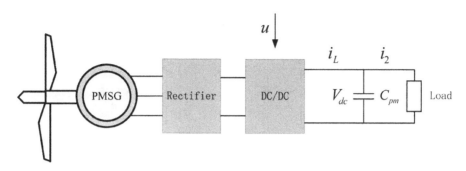

$$\begin{cases} L_q \dfrac{di_q}{dt} = -R_s i_q - \omega_e L_q i_d + \omega_e \psi_m - \dfrac{\pi V_{dc} i_q u}{3\sqrt{3}\sqrt{i_d^2 + i_q^2}} \\[4mm] L_d \dfrac{di_d}{dt} = -R_s i_d - \omega_e L_d i_q - \dfrac{\pi V_{dc} i_d u}{3\sqrt{3}\sqrt{i_d^2 + i_q^2}} \\[4mm] \dot{\omega}_e = \dfrac{P}{2J}\left[\dfrac{1}{2} C_p \rho P A v^4 / \left(2r\omega_e\right) - 3P\psi_m i_q / 4 \right] \\[4mm] \dfrac{dV_{dc}}{dt} = \dfrac{1}{C_{pm}}\left(\dfrac{\pi}{2\sqrt{3}} \sqrt{i_d^2 + i_q^2}\, u - i_2 \right) \end{cases} \tag{2}$$

where L_q and L_d. are the stator inductances in the $d-q$ axes; i_q and i_d are the stator inductances in the $d-q$ axes; i_2 is the measurable load current; ψ_m is the flux linkage by the stator windings; R_s is the stator resistance; P is the number of poles; ρ is the air density; v is the cube of the wind speed; C_p is the power coefficient; A is the swept area; ω_e is the electrical angular speed; J is the inertia of the rotating system.

Now, consider a DC micro-grid with PV and PMSG as shown in Figure 3, where V_0 and V_{DC} are the output voltages for PV and for PMSG, respectively; R_1 and R_2. are the line resistances for PV and for PMSG, respectively.

By using the Thèvenin theorem, it has

$$\left(\dfrac{R_1 R_2}{R_1 + R_2} + R_0 \right) I_0 = \dfrac{V_0 R_1 + V_{dc} R_2}{R_1 + R_2}, I_0 = I_1 + I_2. \tag{3}$$

Figure 3. DC micro-grid with PV and PMSG

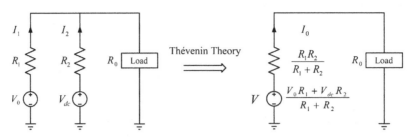

For simply, we assume that $i_{pv} = 1.1 i_L, 0.8 i_L = i_1$ $0.8 i_q = i_2, v = \omega_e$, and follows from (1)-(3) that the DC micro-grid model can be given by

$$\dot{x}_i(t) = A_i(t) x_i(t) + \sum_{j=1, j \neq i}^{N} A_{ij}(t) x_j(t), i \in \{1, 2\} \tag{4}$$

Where

$$
\left\{
A_1(t) =
\begin{bmatrix}
0 & \dfrac{1.1}{C_{pv}} & 0 \\[3mm]
0 & -\dfrac{(R_0 + R_L)}{L} & \dfrac{R_0 R_1}{L(R_1 + R_2)\left(\dfrac{R_1 R_2}{R_1 + R_2} + R_0\right)} - \dfrac{1}{L} \\[6mm]
0 & \dfrac{1}{C_0} & -\dfrac{R_1}{C_0(R_1 + R_2)\left(\dfrac{R_1 R_2}{R_1 + R_2} + R_0\right)}
\end{bmatrix},
B_1(t) =
\begin{bmatrix}
\dfrac{1}{C_{pv}} i_L \\[3mm]
\dfrac{(V_D + V_{pv} - R_M i_L)}{L} \\[3mm]
0
\end{bmatrix}
\right.
$$

$$
A_{12}(t) = -
\begin{bmatrix}
0 & 0 & 0 \\[3mm]
\dfrac{0.8 R_0}{L} & 0 & \dfrac{R_2 R_0}{L(R_1 + R_2)\left(\dfrac{R_1 R_2}{R_1 + R_2} + R_0\right)} \\[6mm]
\dfrac{0.8}{C_0} & 0 & -\dfrac{R_2}{C_0(R_1 + R_2)\left(\dfrac{R_1 R_2}{R_1 + R_2} + R_0\right)}
\end{bmatrix},
x_1(t) =
\begin{bmatrix}
V_{pv} \\ i_L \\ V_0
\end{bmatrix}
$$

$$\tag{5}$$

and

$$\left\{ \begin{matrix} A_2\left(t\right) = \begin{bmatrix} -\dfrac{R_s}{L_q} & \dfrac{\psi_m}{L_q} - i_d & 0 \\[2mm] -\dfrac{3P^2\psi_m}{8J} & \dfrac{C_p\rho P^2 A\omega_e^3}{8Jr} & 0 \\[2mm] 0 & 0 & -\dfrac{R_2}{\left(R_1 + R_2\right)\left[\dfrac{R_1 R_2}{R_1 + R_2} + R_0\right]C_{pm}} \end{bmatrix}, \ x_2\left(t\right) = \begin{bmatrix} i_q \\ \omega_e \\ V_{dc} \end{bmatrix} \right.$$

$$\left. B_2\left(t\right) = \begin{bmatrix} -\dfrac{\pi V_{dc}i_q}{3\sqrt{3}L_q\sqrt{i_d^2 + i_q^2}} \\[2mm] 0 \\[2mm] \dfrac{\pi}{2\sqrt{3}C_{pm}}\sqrt{i_d^2 + i_q^2} \end{bmatrix}, \ A_{21}\left(t\right) = \begin{bmatrix} 0 & 0 & 0 \\[2mm] 0 & 0 & 0 \\[2mm] 0 & \dfrac{0.8}{C_{pm}} & -\dfrac{R_1}{\left(R_1 + R_2\right)\left[\dfrac{R_1 R_2}{R_1 + R_2} + R_0\right]C_{pm}} \end{bmatrix} \right\}$$

$$\tag{6}$$

In this simulation, the parameter values are given by Table 1. Now, by linearizing the nonlinear interconnected system around $i_L = \left(1.1\text{A}, 1.5\text{A}\right)$, $V_{pv} = \left(10.3\text{V}, 9.2\text{V}\right)$, $i_q = \left(1.3\text{A}, 1.0\text{A}\right), i_d = \left(0.4\text{A}, 0.1\text{A}\right)$, $\omega_e = \left(300\text{r}\,/\,\min, 250\text{r}\,/\,\min\right), V_{dc} = \left(13.3\text{V}, 9.8\text{V}\right)$, the T-S fuzzy model can be obtained as

Plant Rule R_1^1: IF $\left(i_L, V_{pv}\right)$ is $\left(1.1\text{A}, 10.3\text{V}\right)$, THEN

$$\dot{x}_1\left(t\right) = A_1^1 x_1\left(t\right) + B_1^1 u_1\left(t\right) + \bar{A}_{12}^1 x_2\left(t\right),$$

Plant Rule R_1^2: IF $\left(i_L, V_{pv}\right)$ is $\left(1.1\text{A}, 9.2\text{V}\right)$, THEN

$$\dot{x}_1\left(t\right) = A_1^2 x_1\left(t\right) + B_1^2 u_1\left(t\right) + \bar{A}_{12}^2 x_2\left(t\right),$$

Table 1. Parameter values for micro-grid model

PV		PMSG	
Parameters	**Values**	**Parameters**	**Values**
C_{pv}	0.0517	R_s	1.9
L	0.0602	ψ_m	0.2876
V_D	5.2	L_q	0.0602
R_0	0.4	L_d	0.0602
R_L	1.9	P	12
R_M	0.9	J	2.61×10^2
C_0	0.0672	C_p	0.0672
R_1	0.23	ρ	1.225
		A	10.6362
		r	1.84
		C_{pm}	0.0564
		R_2	0.32

Plant Rule R_1^3 : IF $\left(i_L, V_{pv} \right)$ is $\left(1.5\text{A}, 10.3\text{V} \right)$, THEN

$$\dot{x}_1 \left(t \right) = A_1^3 x_1 \left(t \right) + B_1^3 u_1 \left(t \right) + \bar{A}_{12}^3 x_2 \left(t \right),$$

Plant Rule R_1^4 : IF $\left(i_L, V_{pv} \right)$ is $\left(1.5\text{A}, 9.2\text{V} \right)$, THEN

$$\dot{x}_1 \left(t \right) = A_1^4 x_1 \left(t \right) + B_1^4 u_1 \left(t \right) + \bar{A}_{12}^4 x_2 \left(t \right),$$

Plant Rule R_2^1: IF $\left(i_q, i_d, \omega_e, V_{dc}\right)$ is $\left(1.3\mathrm{A}, 0.4\mathrm{A}, 300\,\dfrac{\mathrm{r}}{\min}, 13.3\mathrm{V}\right)$, THEN

$$\dot{x}_2\left(t\right) = A_2^1 x_2\left(t\right) + B_2^1 u_2\left(t\right) + \bar{A}_{21}^1 x_1\left(t\right),$$

Plant Rule R_2^2: IF $\left(i_q, i_d, \omega_e, V_{dc}\right)$ is $\left(1.3\mathrm{A}, 0.4\mathrm{A}, 300\,\dfrac{\mathrm{r}}{\min}, 9.8\mathrm{V}\right)$, THEN

$$\dot{x}_2\left(t\right) = A_2^2 x_2\left(t\right) + B_2^2 u_2\left(t\right) + \bar{A}_{21}^2 x_1\left(t\right),$$

Plant Rule R_2^3: IF $\left(i_q, i_d, \omega_e, V_{dc}\right)$ is $\left(1.3\mathrm{A}, 0.4\mathrm{A}, 250\,\dfrac{\mathrm{r}}{\min}, 13.3\mathrm{V}\right)$, THEN

$$\dot{x}_2\left(t\right) = A_2^3 x_2\left(t\right) + B_2^3 u_2\left(t\right) + \bar{A}_{21}^3 x_1\left(t\right),$$

Plant Rule R_2^4: IF $\left(i_q, i_d, \omega_e, V_{dc}\right)$ is $\left(1.3\mathrm{A}, 0.4\mathrm{A}, 250\,\dfrac{\mathrm{r}}{\min}, 9.8\mathrm{V}\right)$, THEN

$$\dot{x}_2\left(t\right) = A_2^4 x_2\left(t\right) + B_2^4 u_2\left(t\right) + \bar{A}_{21}^4 x_1\left(t\right),$$

Plant Rule R_2^5: IF $\left(i_q, i_d, \omega_e, V_{dc}\right)$ is $\left(1.3\mathrm{A}, 0.1\mathrm{A}, 300\,\dfrac{\mathrm{r}}{\min}, 13.3\mathrm{V}\right)$, THEN

$$\dot{x}_2\left(t\right) = A_2^5 x_2\left(t\right) + B_2^5 u_2\left(t\right) + \bar{A}_{21}^5 x_1\left(t\right),$$

Plant Rule R_2^6: IF $\left(i_q, i_d, \omega_e, V_{dc}\right)$ is $\left(1.3\mathrm{A}, 0.1\mathrm{A}, 300\,\dfrac{\mathrm{r}}{\min}, 9.8\mathrm{V}\right)$, THEN

$$\dot{x}_2\left(t\right) = A_2^6 x_2\left(t\right) + B_2^6 u_2\left(t\right) + \bar{A}_{21}^6 x_1\left(t\right),$$

Plant Rule R_2^7: IF $\left(i_q, i_d, \omega_e, V_{dc}\right)$ is $\left(1.3\mathrm{A}, 0.1\mathrm{A}, 250\,\dfrac{\mathrm{r}}{\min}, 13.3\mathrm{V}\right)$, THEN

$$\dot{x}_2\left(t\right) = A_2^7 x_2\left(t\right) + B_2^7 u_2\left(t\right) + \bar{A}_{21}^7 x_1\left(t\right),$$

Plant Rule R_2^8: IF $\left(i_q, i_d, \omega_e, V_{dc}\right)$ is $\left[1.3\text{A}, 0.1\text{A}, 250\,\dfrac{\text{r}}{\text{min}}, 9.8\text{V}\right]$, THEN

$$\dot{x}_2(t) = A_2^8 x_2(t) + B_2^8 u_2(t) + \overline{A}_{21}^8 x_1(t),$$

Plant Rule R_2^9: IF $\left(i_q, i_d, \omega_e, V_{dc}\right)$ is $\left[1.0\text{A}, 0.4\text{A}, 300\,\dfrac{\text{r}}{\text{min}}, 13.3\text{V}\right]$, THEN

$$\dot{x}_2(t) = A_2^9 x_2(t) + B_2^9 u_2(t) + \overline{A}_{21}^9 x_1(t),$$

Plant Rule R_2^{10}: IF $\left(i_q, i_d, \omega_e, V_{dc}\right)$ is $\left[1.0\text{A}, 0.4\text{A}, 300\,\dfrac{\text{r}}{\text{min}}, 9.8\text{V}\right]$, THEN

$$\dot{x}_2(t) = A_2^{10} x_2(t) + B_2^{10} u_2(t) + \overline{A}_{21}^{10} x_1(t),$$

Plant Rule R_2^{11}: IF $\left(i_q, i_d, \omega_e, V_{dc}\right)$ is $\left[1.0\text{A}, 0.4\text{A}, 250\,\dfrac{\text{r}}{\text{min}}, 13.3\text{V}\right]$, THEN

$$\dot{x}_2(t) = A_2^{11} x_2(t) + B_2^{11} u_2(t) + \overline{A}_{21}^{11} x_1(t),$$

Plant Rule R_2^{12}: IF $\left(i_q, i_d, \omega_e, V_{dc}\right)$ is $\left[1.0\text{A}, 0.4\text{A}, 250\,\dfrac{\text{r}}{\text{min}}, 9.8\text{V}\right]$, THEN

$$\dot{x}_2(t) = A_2^{12} x_2(t) + B_2^{12} u_2(t) + \overline{A}_{21}^{12} x_1(t),$$

Plant Rule R_2^{13}: IF $\left(i_q, i_d, \omega_e, V_{dc}\right)$ is $\left[1.0\text{A}, 0.1\text{A}, 300\,\dfrac{\text{r}}{\text{min}}, 13.3\text{V}\right]$, THEN

$$\dot{x}_2(t) = A_2^{13} x_2(t) + B_2^{13} u_2(t) + \overline{A}_{21}^{13} x_1(t),$$

Plant Rule R_2^{14}: IF $\left(i_q, i_d, \omega_e, V_{dc}\right)$ is $\left[1.0\text{A}, 0.1\text{A}, 300\,\dfrac{\text{r}}{\text{min}}, 9.8\text{V}\right]$, THEN

$$\dot{x}_2(t) = A_2^{14} x_2(t) + B_2^{14} u_2(t) + \overline{A}_{21}^{14} x_1(t),$$

Plant Rule R_2^{15} : IF $\left(i_q, i_d, \omega_e, V_{dc} \right)$ is $\left[1.0\text{A}, 0.1\text{A}, 250\,\dfrac{\text{r}}{\text{min}}, 13.3\text{V} \right]$, THEN

$$\dot{x}_2\left(t \right) = A_2^{15} x_2\left(t \right) + B_2^{15} u_2\left(t \right) + \bar{A}_{21}^{15} x_1\left(t \right),$$

Plant Rule R_2^{16} : IF $\left(i_q, i_d, \omega_e, V_{dc} \right)$ is $\left[1.0\text{A}, 0.1\text{A}, 250\,\dfrac{\text{r}}{\text{min}}, 9.8\text{V} \right]$, THEN

$$\dot{x}_2\left(t \right) = A_2^{16} x_2\left(t \right) + B_2^{16} u_2\left(t \right) + \bar{A}_{21}^{16} x_1\left(t \right),$$

Now, by using Theorem 3.2.1, we find a feasible solution to the stabilization design problem for the micro-grid system. Under the initial conditions $x_1\left(0 \right) = \begin{bmatrix} 5 & 1.1 & 4.1 \end{bmatrix}^T$, $x_2\left(0 \right) = \begin{bmatrix} 1.3 & 20 & 8 \end{bmatrix}^T$, and take the above solution, Figures 4 and 5 show the state responses for the closed-loop large-scale fuzzy interconnected system, respectively. Thus, showing the effectiveness of the decentralized fuzzy controller design methods.

Figure 4. Response of PV system

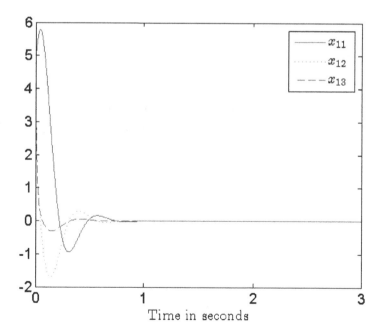

Figure 5. Response of PMSG system

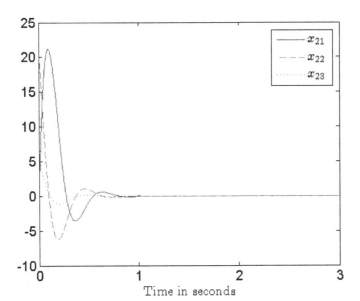

7.2 APPLICATION TO MULTI-MOTORS

With the increasing demands of requiring synchronously high productivity and high accuracy for mechanical systems, The use of timing belts in drive trains is characterized by attractive features such as high-speed, high-efficiency, long-travel distance, and low cost. However, they bring uncertain dynamics and higher transmission error since they are subject to elastic system which induces vibrations, compliance, and higher friction. Consequently, belt-drives suffer from lower repeatability and accuracy (Hace, Jezernik, & Sabanovic, 2005).

Here, consider a surface-mounted permanent magnet synchronous motor (PMSM), which can be represented by the following differential equation (Choi, Vu, & Jung, 2012):

$$\begin{cases} \dfrac{di_{qs}}{dt} = -\dfrac{R}{L}i_{qs} - \dfrac{\lambda}{L}\omega - i_{ds}\omega + \dfrac{1}{L}V_{qs} \\[2mm] \dfrac{di_{ds}}{dt} = -\dfrac{R}{L}i_{ds} + i_{qs}\omega + \dfrac{1}{L}V_{ds} \\[2mm] \dot{\omega} = \dfrac{3P^2\lambda}{8J}i_{qs} - \dfrac{B}{J}\omega - \dfrac{P}{2J}T_L \\[2mm] T_e = \dfrac{3}{4}P\lambda i_{qs} \end{cases} \tag{7}$$

where T_L denotes the load torque, ω is the electrical-rotor angular speed, i_{qs} and i_{ds} are the q-axis and d-axis currents, V_{qs} and V_{ds} are the q-axis and d-axis voltage, and $\{k_1 \cdots k_6\}$ are the parameter values depending on the stator resistance, the stator inductance, the rotor inertia, the viscous friction coefficient, and the magnetic flux.

Then, the mathematical model of the belt-driven servomechanism can be given by (Sabanovic, Sozbilir, Goktug, & Sabanovic, 2003; Quan, Shen, Li, & Zhu, 2011)

$$
\begin{cases}
\left(G^2 J_m + J_G + J_{w1}\right)\ddot{\omega}_{w1} = G T_e + k_1\left(s\right)\left(s - r\omega_{w1}\right) - k_3 r^2 \left(\omega_{w1} - \omega_{w2}\right) \\
\quad -\left(B_{w1} + G B_m\right)\dot{\omega}_{w1} - T_{w1} \\
J_{w2}\ddot{\omega}_{w2} = k_3 r^2 \left(\omega_{w1} - \omega_{w2}\right) - k_2\left(s\right)\left(r\omega_{w2} - s\right)r - B_{w2}\dot{\omega}_{w2} - T_{w2} \\
\dfrac{M}{2}\ddot{s} = k_2\left(s\right)\left(r\omega_{w2} - s\right) - k_1\left(s\right)\left(s - r\omega_{w1}\right) - B_l\dot{s} - F_f
\end{cases}
\tag{8}
$$

where J_m, J_G, J_{w1} and J_{w2} are moment inertia of the driving motor, reducer, deriving wheel and the driven pulley respectively; G denotes the reduction ratio; M denotes the load mass, r is the radius of the pulleys; ω_{w1} and ω_{w2} angular speed of driving wheel and the driven pulley, respectively; B_m, B_{w1}, B_{w1} are the viscous friction coefficient of driving motor and wheel, and the driven pulley, respectively; s is the moving distance ; r is the radius of wheel; F_f is the friction force.

Now, assume that $\omega_{w1} = G\omega_{w1}$, and consider a double-motors system with S_1 and S_2 as shown in Figure 6,

The condition that the motion between S_1 and S_2 is asynchronous, which can be considered as the mass-spring-damper system as show in Figure 7. Its dynamics are

$$
\begin{cases}
M_\theta = J_\theta \ddot{\theta} + B_l \dot{\theta} + k_l \theta \\
F_{M1} = \cos\theta \dfrac{M_\theta}{l}
\end{cases}
\tag{9}
$$

where θ is the asynchronous angle between $\mathbb{S}_1$ and $\mathbb{S}_2$; B_l is the viscous friction coefficient of sliding guide; k_l is the stiffness coefficient; M_θ is the torque; F_{M1} is the asynchronous force.

Figure 6. A double-motors system

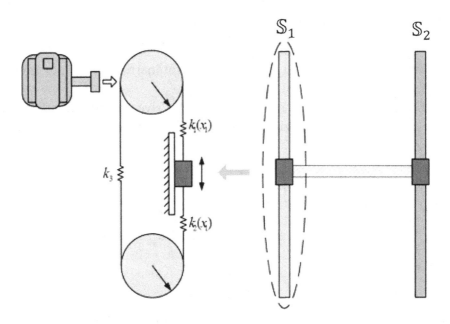

Figure 7. A double-motors system

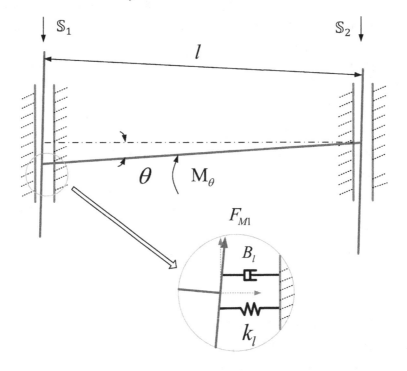

Practical Application

Table 2. Comparison Parameter values for micro-grid model

$\mathbb{S}_1$		$\mathbb{S}_2$	
Parameters	Values	Parameters	Values
R	0.92 Ω	R	0.97 Ω
L	0.00551 H	L	0.00562 H
λ	0.079234 V·s/rad	λ	0.079153 V·s/rad
P	12	P	12
G	12	G	12
J	2.44×10⁻⁵ kg·m²	J	2.61×10⁻⁵ kg·m²
J_m	2.44×10⁻⁵ kg·m²	J_m	2.61×10⁻⁵ kg·m²
J_G	2.44×10⁻⁵ kg·m²	J_G	2.61×10⁻⁵ kg·m²
J_{w1}	1.54×10⁻⁵ kg·m²	J_{w1}	1.75×10⁻⁵ kg·m²
J_{w2}	1.54×10⁻⁵ kg·m²	J_{w2}	1.75×10⁻⁵ kg·m²
$J_\blacklozenge$	12.44 kg·m²	$J_\blacklozenge$	12.98 kg·m²
k_3	133.213 N/rad	k_3	135.7939 N/rad
k_l	2.5×10³ kg·m²	k_l	2.5×10³ kg·m²
B_{w1}	0.0003 N·m·s/rad	B_{w1}	0.0003 N·m·s/rad
B_{w2}	0.0003 N·m·s/rad	B_{w2}	0.0003 N·m·s/rad
B_l	20 N·m·s/rad	B_l	20 N·m·s/rad
l	1.2 m	l	1.2 m

In this simulation, we choose the parameters as shown in Table 2,

Based on the parameter values in Table 1 (Chapter 3), and by linearizing the nonlinear function in (2), it yields

207

$$F_{M1} \approx 2166.7 \left(\frac{S_1 - S_2}{l} \right),$$ (7)

where S_1 and S_2 are the moving distance for $\mathbb{S}_1$ and $\mathbb{S}_2$, respectively.

Here, for simply we assume that $S_2 = S_1 - \theta S_2$, where θ denotes an unsynchronized scalar between S_1 and S_2. The double-motors system can be given by

$$\dot{x}_i(t) = A_i(t)x_i(t) + \sum_{j=1, j \neq i}^{N} A_{ij}(t)x_j(t), i \in \{1,2\}$$ (8)

where

$$A_i(t) = \begin{vmatrix} -\dfrac{R_{(i)}}{L_{(i)}} & 0 & -G_{(i)}\dfrac{\lambda_{(i)}}{L_{(i)}} - G_{(i)}i_{d(i)} & 0 & 0 & 0 & 0 & 0 \\ 0 & -\dfrac{R_{(i)}}{L_{(i)}} & G_{(i)}i_{q(i)} & 0 & 0 & 0 & 0 & 0 \\ 0 & 0 & 0 & 0 & 0 & 1 & 0 & 0 \\ 0 & 0 & 0 & 1 & 0 & 0 & 0 & 1 \\ 0 & 0 & 0 & 0 & 0 & 0 & 1 & 0 \\ 0 & 0 & 0 & 0 & 0 & 0 & 0 & 1 \\ -\dfrac{\frac{3}{4J_{w2}}G_{(i)}P_{(i)}\lambda_{(i)}}{G_{(i)}^2 J_{m(i)} + J_{G(i)} + J_{w(i)}} & 0 & \dfrac{k_{1(i)}r^2 + k_{3(i)}r^2}{G_{(i)}^2 J_{m(i)} + J_{G(i)} + J_{w(i)}} & \dfrac{k_{(i)}^1 r}{G_{(i)}^2 J_{m(i)} + J_{G(i)} + J_{w(i)}} & \dfrac{k_{3(i)}r^2}{G_{(i)}^2 J_{m(i)} + J_{G(i)} + J_{w(i)}} & \dfrac{-B_{(i)}^{w1} - G(i)B_{m(i)}}{G_{(i)}^2 J_{m(i)} + J_{G(i)} + J_{w(i)}} & 0 & 0 \\ 0 & 0 & \dfrac{k_{3(i)}r^2}{J_{w2(i)}} & \dfrac{k_{2(i)}r}{J_{w2(i)}} & \dfrac{k_{3(i)}r^2}{J_{w2(i)}} - \dfrac{k_{2(i)}r^2}{J_{w2(i)}} & 0 & -\dfrac{B_{w2(i)}}{J_{w2(i)}} & 0 \\ 0 & 0 & \dfrac{2k_{3(i)}r}{M} & -\dfrac{2k_{2(i)}}{M} - \dfrac{2k_{1(i)}}{M} & \dfrac{2k_{3(i)}r}{M} & 0 & 0 & -\dfrac{2B_{i(i)}}{M} \end{vmatrix}$$

$$A_{12}(t) = \begin{bmatrix} 0 & 0 & 0 & 0 & 0 & 0 & 0 & 0 & 0 \\ 0 & 0 & 0 & 0 & 0 & 0 & 0 & 0 & 0 \\ 0 & 0 & 0 & 0 & 0 & 0 & 0 & 0 & 0 \\ 0 & 0 & 0 & 0 & 0 & 0 & 0 & 0 & 0 \\ 0 & 0 & 0 & 0 & 0 & 0 & 0 & 0 & 0 \\ 0 & 0 & 0 & 0 & 0 & 0 & 0 & 0 & 0 \\ 0 & 0 & 0 & 0 & 0 & 0 & 0 & 0 & 0 \\ 0 & 0 & 0 & 0 & 0 & -\dfrac{4333.4\theta}{Ml} & 0 & 0 & 0 \end{bmatrix}, \quad B_1(t) = \begin{bmatrix} \dfrac{1}{L_{(i)}} & 0 \\ 0 & \dfrac{1}{L_{(i)}} \\ 0 & 0 \\ 0 & 0 \\ 0 & 0 \\ 0 & 0 \\ 0 & 0 \\ 0 & 0 \\ 0 & 0 \end{bmatrix},$$

$$x_1(t) = \begin{bmatrix} i_{qs(i)} \\ i_{ds(i)} \\ \omega_{w1(i)} \\ S_{(i)} \\ \omega_{w2(i)} \\ a_{w1(i)} \\ a_{w2(i)} \\ v_{(i)} \end{bmatrix}$$

By linearizing the nonlinear interconnected system around $i_{ds} = (4\text{A}, -4\text{A}), S = (0.2\text{m}, 0.8\text{m})$, the T-S fuzzy model can be obtained as

Plant Rule R_i^1: IF $\left(i_{ds(i)}, S_{(i)}\right)$ is $(4\text{A}, 0.2\text{m})$, THEN

$$\dot{x}_i(t) = A_i^1 x_i(t) + B_i^1 u_i(t) + \bar{A}_{ij,j\neq i}^1 x_j(t), i = \{1,2\}$$

Plant Rule R_i^2: IF $\left(i_{ds(i)}, S_{(i)}\right)$ is $(4\text{A}, 0.8\text{m})$, THEN

$$\dot{x}_i(t) = A_i^2 x_i(t) + B_i^2 u_i(t) + \bar{A}_{ij,j\neq i}^2 x_j(t), i = \{1,2\}$$

Plant Rule R_i^3: IF $\left(i_{ds(i)}, S_{(i)}\right)$ is $(-4\text{A}, 0.2\text{m})$, THEN

$$\dot{x}_i(t) = A_i^3 x_i(t) + B_i^3 u_i(t) + \bar{A}_{ij,j\neq i}^3 x_j(t), i = \{1,2\}$$

Plant Rule R_i^4: IF $\left(i_{ds(i)}, S_{(i)}\right)$ is $(-4\text{A}, 0.8\text{m})$, THEN

$$\dot{x}_i(t) = A_i^4 x_i(t) + B_i^4 u_i(t) + \bar{A}_{ij,j\neq i}^4 x_j(t), i = \{1,2\}$$

Now, by using Theorem 3.2.5, we find a feasible solution to the stabilization design problem for the double-motors model. Under the initial conditions $x_1(0) = \begin{bmatrix} 1 & -0.8 & 0 & 0.24 & 0 & 10 & 0 & 0.8 \end{bmatrix}^T$, $x_2(0) = \begin{bmatrix} 1 & -1.1 & 0 & 0.27 & 0 & 10 & 0 & 1.2 \end{bmatrix}^T$, and take the above solution, Figures 8 and 9 show the state responses for the closed-loop large-scale fuzzy interconnected system, respectively. Thus, showing the effectiveness of the decentralized fuzzy controller design methods.

Figure 8. Response of motor system 1

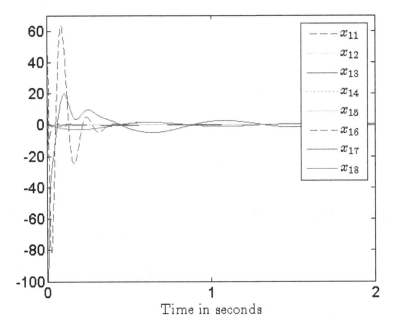

Figure 9. Response of motor system 2

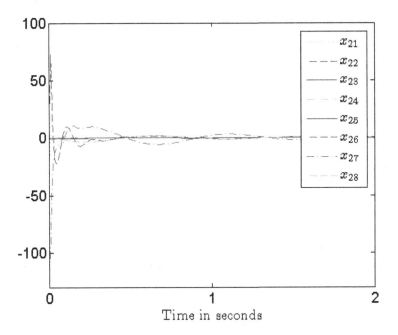

7.3 CONCLUSION

This chapter has considered practical applications in the power system and in multi-motors system. They are subject to nonlinear interconnected systems, which are presented by T-S fuzzy model. By using the theoretical results to obtain fuzzy controller gains, simulation studies have validated the effectiveness of the proposed methods.

REFERENCES

Anand, S., Fernandes, B., & Guerrero, J. (2013). Distributed control to ensure proportional load sharing and improve voltage regulation in low-voltage DC microgrids. *IEEE Transactions on Power Electronics*, 28(4), 1900–1913. doi:10.1109/TPEL.2012.2215055

Chiu, C., & Ouyang, Y. (2011). Robust maximum power tracking control of uncertain photovoltaic systems: A unified T-S fuzzy model-based approach. *IEEE Transactions on Control Systems Technology*, 19(6), 1516–1526. doi:10.1109/TCST.2010.2093900

Choi, H., Vu, N., & Jung, J. (2012). Design and Implementation of a Takagi–Sugeno Fuzzy Speed Regulator for a Permanent Magnet Synchronous Motor. *IEEE Transactions on Industrial Electronics*, 59(8), 3069–3077. doi:10.1109/TIE.2011.2141091

Ding, M., Xu, Z., Wang, W., Wang, X., Song, W., & Chen, D. (2016). A review on China s large-scale PV integration: Progress, challenges and recommendations,'. *Renewable & Sustainable Energy Reviews*, 53, 639–652. doi:10.1016/j.rser.2015.09.009

Etemadi, A., Davison, E., & Iravani, R. (2012). A decentralized robust control strategy for multi-DER microgrids—Part I: Fundamental concepts. *IEEE Transactions on Power Delivery*, 27(4), 1843–1853. doi:10.1109/TPWRD.2012.2202920

Hace, A., Jezernik, K., & Sabanovic, A. (2005). Improved design of VSS controller for a linear belt-driven servomechanism. *IEEE/ASME Transactions on Mechatronics*, 10(4), 385–390. doi:10.1109/TMECH.2005.852448

Hosseinzadeh, M., & Salmasi, F. (2014). Power management of an isolated hybrid AC/DC micro-grid with fuzzy control of battery banks. *IET Renewable Power Generation*, *9*(5), 484–493. doi:10.1049/iet-rpg.2014.0271

Mohamed, Y., & El-Saadany, E. (2008). Adaptive decentralized droop controller to preserve power sharing stability of paralleled inverters in distributed generation microgrids. *IEEE Transactions on Power Electronics*, *23*(6), 2806–2816. doi:10.1109/TPEL.2008.2005100

Quan, J., Shen, C., Li, C., & Zhu, X. (2011). Research on positioning control strategy for linear belt driven. *Proceedings of the 2011 2nd International Conference on Artificial Intelligence, Management Science and Electronic Commerce* (pp. 4256-4259). doi:10.1109/AIMSEC.2011.6010105

Sabanovic, A., Sozbilir, O., Goktug, G., & Sabanovic, N. (2003). Sliding mode control of timing-belt servosystem. *Proceedings of the IEEE International Symposium Industrial Electronics* (V*ol.* 2, pp. 684-689).

Sun, K., Zhang, L., Xing, Y., & Guerrero, G. (2011). A distributed control strategy based on DC bus signaling for modular photovoltaic generation systems with battery energy storage. *IEEE Transactions on Power Electronics*, *26*(10), 3032–3045. doi:10.1109/TPEL.2011.2127488

Valenciaga, F., Puleston, P., Battaiotto, P., & Mantz, R. (2000). Passivity/ sliding mode control of a stand-alone hybrid generation system. *IEE Proceedings. Control Theory and Applications*, *147*(6), 680–686. doi:10.1049/ip-cta:20000803

Chapter 8

Conclusions and Recommendations for Further Research of Large–Scale Fuzzy Interconnected Control Systems

ABSTRACT

In this chapter, our purpose hereafter is to shed more light on some prevailing aspects and potential remarks in the fuzzy control of large-scale fuzzy interconnected systems from fuzzy modeling and analysis aspects, control aspects, application aspects, and future research.

8.1 FUZZY MODELING AND ANALYSIS ASPECTS

A predominant characteristic of large-scale nonlinear interconnected systems is the interconnections with different interacting subsystems. How to process the interconnections is one of the most difficult problems, especially when nonlinear dynamics appears in the interconnections.

8.1.1 Explosive Fuzzy Rules

A large-scale system consists of several subsystems with interconnections connected to the other subsystems. Thus, it is quite natural to seek nonlinear dynamics on the interconnections, when considering large-scale nonlinear

DOI: 10.4018/978-1-5225-2385-7.ch008

interconnected systems. In general, the nonlinear interconnection $\overline{A}_{ij}^{ls}$ includes the fuzzy index term l of the i-th subsystem and the fuzzy index term s of the j-th subsystem, when using fuzzy-model-based presentation. It must be emphasized that this condition will lead to a large number of fuzzy rules, when the number of subsystems increases. It is also noted that a large increase of the number of fuzzy rules will generally cause a large increase in the number of LMI-based results if using the traditional control methods. Consequently, it is worth studying a new way to reduce the number of LMIs for the proposed solutions to large-scale fuzzy interconnected systems.

In this book, we have proposed some bounding inequalities approaches to eliminate the fuzzy index term s of the j-th subsystem (Chapter 2). Based on the techniques, we proposed some design results on the decentralized control for large-scale fuzzy interconnected systems. It is noted that using bounding inequalities induces design conservatism to some extent. The developed results lead a tradeoff between the number of LMIs and the design conservatism.

8.1.2 Asynchronous Premise Variables

The concept of parallel distributed compensation (PDC) is widely proposed in the sense that the fuzzy system and the fuzzy controller share the same premise membership functions. Although the PDC design concept can relax the results on stabilization conditions when compared with the proposed linear controller. However, when considering these cases that the premise variables of the fuzzy controller undergo sampled-data measurement (Chapter 4), and/or event-triggered control (Chapter 5), and/or network-induced delay (Chapter 4), the asynchronous variables are more realistic. It is noted that when the asynchronous knowledge on the premise membership functions of the fuzzy controllers and the fuzzy systems is unavailable, it generally leads to a linear controller instead of a fuzzy one. In Chapters 4 and 5, we assumed the asynchronous bounding and designed the fuzzy controller. It is also noted an asynchronous increase on the premise membership functions of the fuzzy controllers and the fuzzy systems will induce more conservative on stabilization conditions. The developed results lead a tradeoff between the asynchronous condition and the design conservatism.

8.1.3 No Coupling Large-Scale Systems

Multiple vehicles, such as unmanned aerial vehicles, unmanned ground vehicles, and unmanned underwater vehicles, have been a very active research subject studied extensively by the research and engineering societies. Such systems can be regarded as a class of large-scale systems without interconnections, and their structures might dictate a technique for the underlying analysis and design problems including coordinated control. In this way, the analysis and design subproblems are directly associated with the subsystems in addition to a coordinator that supervises the overall job.

8.1.4 Weakly Coupling Large-Scale Systems

As stated throughout the book, we mean here that large-scale interconnected system is comprised of several interacting subsystems with weakly interconnections. Analytical and design problems of such large-scale systems with weakly coupled subsystems can be decomposed according to the subsystem structure of the overall system, but the resulting subproblems are still dependent upon each other. In that case, the decentralized control was used and the interconnections was processed as disturbances as shown in Chapters 3-5.

8.1.5 Strongly Coupling Large-Scale Systems

This is evidently the general case. Due to the strong interdependence among subsystems, the decentralized control approach is no longer applicable to the large-scale systems with strong interconnections. Rather, analytical and design problems cannot be effectively divided along the boundaries of the subsystems. With regards to the distributed control method, some interconnections can be provided in the feedback signs to compensate its effects as shown in Chapters 3-5. However, the information communication among subsystems should be considered when using the distributed subsystems in the sense that the subsystems locate at different places.

8.2 CONTROL ASPECTS

In general, three main control approaches: centralized control, decentralized control, and distributed control, have been widely proposed to large-scale interconnected systems.

8.2.1 Centralized Control Method

The idea of centralized control is to require a central controller when implementing schedule tasks, making control decisions, and realizing optimization algorithms. However, a central controller suffers from the excessive information processing and heavy computational burdens, and failures, thus it may degrade systems' performance, even stability. Thus, the extent of applicability of the centralized control principle to large-scale interconnected systems seems unpractical.

Strictly speaking, the centralized control is, therefore, applicable only for relatively small-scale systems in the sense that the subsystems locate at a small district, and the dimensionality and information processing of the plant does not pose severe difficulties in the analytical and design problems.

8.2.2 Decentralized Control Method

After the large-scale system has been separated into several subsystems with weakly coupling, the corresponding design problem can be decomposed accordingly, and a number of independent controllers can be implemented in large-scale systems instead of a single controller. The idea named decentralized control, and has been realized in the form of several subsystems without communications. In fact, the subproblems resulting on a decomposition procedure of the overall problem happen usually that case with weakly coupling.

8.2.3 Distributed Control Method

For the large-scale systems with strongly coupling, the decentralized control strategy appears weaker stability margins and performance. It is worth noting that the supplemental feedbacks containing the interconnected information are provided in the distributed control for the local controllers to ensure the requirements of stability and performance. As a result, the distributed control avoids those deficiencies appearing in the cases of centralized control and decentralized control.

8.3 APPLICATION ASPECTS

As repeatedly emphasized through the book, the distinctive features on the complexity of large-scale systems are information interconnections and high dimensionality. Their utilizations depend on the practical application under consideration, one aspect or another dominates. The methods described in this book take account of these two aspects from their specific fields of application. In conclusion, the theory of decentralized control contributes to the application of large-scale system with weak interconnections. In distributed dynamical processes, distributed control provides the supplemental feedbacks containing the interconnected information for the local controllers to ensure the requirements of stability and performance, which makes it suitable for large-scale system with strong interconnections. Moreover, the decentralized control only requires information from local subsystem, thus no communication network is needed. The distributed control needs the information communication among subsystems, and subsystems generally local in different areas. Thus, besides the uncertainties, the complexity and high cost are needed for the existence of communication network.

8.4 FUTURE RESEARCH

After decomposition of the control problem into several subproblems, each subproblem has the independent characteristic. The control law implementation then separates with the help of that assumption. Such approach is referred to as the decentralized control. Recently, research results are available on the decentralized control issue of large-scale fuzzy interconnected systems but little prior work on the distributed control is reported. In this book, research efforts have been devoted to stability analysis and decentralized/distributed controller design of large-scale fuzzy interconnected systems. It should be clear that the investigation of distributed control is incomplete. Research issues to be investigated further include:

- By using asynchronous method in Appendix E, a fuzzy controller can be designed when the asynchronous premise variables happen in the fuzzy controller and the fuzzy system. However, this approach increases computational burden. It is much more challenge to derive the design results on fuzzy controller without bringing conservativeness, and increasing computational complexity in solving corresponding LMIs;

- By using some bounding techniques, the fuzzy rules generated by the interconnections to the j-th fuzzy subsystem will be eliminated. In that case, the derived results lead to a significant reduction in the number of LMIs. However, this approach induces design conservatism to some extent. How to reduce the number of LMIs but without bringing conservativeness;

- Consider a singular large-scale nonlinear interconnected system contains N subsystems as follows:

$$E_i \dot{x}_i(t) = A_i(t) x_i(t) + \sum_{j=1, j \neq i}^{N} \overline{A}_{ij}(t) x_j(t) + B_i(t) u_i(t).$$

The existing results on linear singular systems can't be directly developed for the stability analysis and controller design of singular large-scale fuzzy interconnected systems because of the singular matrix E_i, interconnection term $\overline{A}_{ij}(t)$, and the fuzzy premise variables. This scheme is rarely considered and will be left as further research;

- For large-scale networked system, at each transmission instant only a single node is open access through the network according to the so-called scheduling protocol. One interesting future research topic is the extension of the proposed methods to the filtering and control designs for large-scale networked nonlinear systems with integrated communication delays and multiple packet dropouts;

- In practical applications, it is difficult to design the filtering and controller for large-scale networked nonlinear systems based on synchronous communication due to geographical scalability. Thus, asynchronous communication is more realistic. One interesting future research topic is the extension of the proposed methods for large-scale networked nonlinear systems based on asynchronous communication.

Appendix

A. Schur Complement

Let A, B and D be appropriately matrices, and the matrices A, D are symmetric. Then

$$\begin{bmatrix} A & B \\ B^T & D \end{bmatrix} > 0 . \tag{A-1}$$

If and only if any of the following inequality holds:

$(\text{i}) \quad A > 0 \, \text{and} \, D - B^T A^{-1} B > 0; \tag{A-2}$

$(\text{ii}) \quad D > 0 \, \text{and} \, A - B D^{-1} B^T > 0. \tag{A-3}$

B. Jensen's Inequality

For any constant symmetric positive definite matrix $M \in \mathfrak{R}^{n_z \times n_z}$ and scalars $d_2 > d_1 \geq 0$, the following inequality holds

$$\left[\int_{d_1}^{d_2} x(\alpha) \, d\alpha \right]^T M \left[\int_{d_1}^{d_2} x(\alpha) \, d\alpha \right] \leq (d_2 - d_1) \int_{d_1}^{d_2} x^T(\alpha) M x(\alpha) \, d\alpha . \tag{B-1}$$

C. Wirtinger's Inequality

Let $z(t) \in W[a,b]$ and $z(a) = 0$. Then the following inequality holds for any $n \times n$-matrix $R > 0$,

$$\int_a^b z^T(\alpha) R z(\alpha) d\alpha \leq \frac{4(b-a)^2}{\pi^2} \int_a^b \dot{z}^T(\alpha) R \dot{z}(\alpha) d\alpha.$$ (C-1)

D. SSG Method

Consider an interconnected system consisting of two subsystems: the forward subsystem $\mathcal{S}_{i1} : x(t) = \mathbf{G}y(t)$ and the feedback subsystem $\mathcal{S}_{i2} : y(t) = \Delta x(t)$. The interconnected system is asymptotically stable for all Δ if $\|\mathbf{G}\| < 1$ holds.

E. Asynchronous Premise Variables

Assume that the membership functions satisfy $\underline{\rho}_l \leq \frac{\hat{\mu}_l}{\mu_l} \leq \overline{\rho}_l, l \in \mathcal{L}$. Then,

$\sum_{l=1}^{r}\sum_{s=1}^{r} \mu_l \hat{\mu}_s \sum_{ls} < 0$ holds if there exist matrices $X_{ls} = X_{ls}^T$, such that for all $\{l,s\} \in \mathcal{L}$, the following inequalities hold

$$\overline{p}_l \sum\nolimits_{ll} + X_{ll} < 0,$$

$$\underline{p}_l \sum\nolimits_{ll} + X_{ll} < 0,$$

$$\overline{p}_s \sum\nolimits_{ls} + \overline{p}_l \sum\nolimits_{sl} + X_{ls} + X_{sl} < 0,$$

$$\underline{p}_s \sum\nolimits_{ls} + \underline{p}_l \sum\nolimits_{sl} + X_{ls} + X_{sl} < 0,$$

Appendix

$$\underline{p}_s \sum {}_{ls} + \overline{p}_l \sum {}_{sl} + X_{ls} + X_{sl} < 0,$$

$$\overline{p}_s \sum {}_{ls} + \underline{p}_l \sum {}_{sl} + X_{ls} + X_{sl} < 0,$$

$$\begin{bmatrix} X_{11} & \cdots & X_{1r} \\ \vdots & \ddots & \vdots \\ X_{r1} & \cdots & X_{rr} \end{bmatrix} > 0 \qquad\qquad\qquad (E\text{-}1)$$

Index

Recommended Reference Books

ISBN: 978-1-4666-5888-2
© 2015; 10,384 pp.
List Price: $3,160

ISBN: 978-1-4666-6359-6
© 2015; 745 pp.
List Price: $412

ISBN: 978-1-4666-6485-2
© 2015; 354 pp.
List Price: $156

ISBN: 978-1-4666-7304-5
© 2015; 313 pp.
List Price: $156

ISBN: 978-1-4666-6639-9
© 2015; 309 pp.
List Price: $160

ISBN: 978-1-4666-7278-9
© 2015; 469 pp.
List Price: $196

Publishing Information Science and Technology Research Since 1988

www.igi-global.com   ✉ Sign up at www.igi-global.com/newsletters   f facebook.com/igiglobal   t twitter.com/igiglobal

Stay Current on the Latest Emerging Research Developments

Become an IGI Global Reviewer for Authored Book Projects

The overall success of an authored book project is dependent on quality and timely reviews.

In this competitive age of scholarly publishing, constructive and timely feedback significantly decreases the turnaround time of manuscripts from submission to acceptance, allowing the publication and discovery of progressive research at a much more expeditious rate. Several IGI Global authored book projects are currently seeking highly qualified experts in the field to fill vacancies on their respective editorial review boards:

Applications may be sent to:
development@igi-global.com

Applicants must have a doctorate (or an equivalent degree) as well as publishing and reviewing experience. Reviewers are asked to write reviews in a timely, collegial, and constructive manner. All reviewers will begin their role on an ad-hoc basis for a period of one year, and upon successful completion of this term can be considered for full editorial review board status, with the potential for a subsequent promotion to Associate Editor.

If you have a colleague that may be interested in this opportunity, we encourage you to share this information with them.

Printed in the United States
By Bookmasters